Jenny Rose is Associate Professor of Religion at Claremont Graduate University and Visiting Associate Professor of Religion at Stanford University. She is the author of *The Image of Zoroaster: The Persian Mage Through European Eyes* (2000).

'It is a tall order to explain and summarize well such a polyglot scriptural and religious tradition as Zoroastrianism, with its 3,000 years of history extending across so much of Asia and on into the global diaspora. But Jenny Rose's excellent and highly informative book is a most impressive response to the challenge. Rose adopts a refreshingly new approach that is both matter of fact in style and thoughtfully conceived, as well as being derived from the best new scholarly work of recent decades.' – *Alan Williams, Professor of Iranian Studies & Comparative Religions, University of Manchester*

'Jenny Rose's lively and engaging account comprises a very readable, well informed survey of Zoroastrianism and its history. The book is a pleasure to read throughout, and the author's writing style is markedly beautiful, placing her very much within Mary Boyce's literary tradition. Rose has read widely round the subject, engaging with important primary and secondary sources and rendering her thorough treatment of Zoroastrianism fully up-to-date. I particularly welcomed her valuable discussion of Zoroastrianism in Central Asia. All in all, the book is a fine example of considered synthesis and compression. This is a book one wants to read from beginning to end without putting it down. It will find a warm welcome from students of the subject and their teachers.' – *Almut Hintze, Zartoshty Professor of Zoroastrianism, SOAS, University of London*

I.B.TAURIS INTRODUCTIONS TO RELIGION

In recent years there has been a surge of interest in religion and in the motivations behind religious belief and commitment. Avoiding oversimplification, jargon or unhelpful stereotypes, I.B.Tauris Introductions to Religion embraces the opportunity to explore religious tradition in a sensitive, objective and nuanced manner. A specially commissioned series for undergraduate students, it offers concise, clearly written overviews, by leading experts in the field, of the world's major religious faiths, and of the challenges posed to all the religions by progress, globalization and diaspora. Covering the fundamentals of history, theology, ritual and worship, these books place an emphasis above all on the modern world, and on the lived faiths of contemporary believers. They explore, in a way that will engage followers and non-believers alike, the fascinating and sometimes difficult contradictions or reconciling ancient tradition with headlong cultural and technological change.

'I.B.Tauris Introductions to Religion offers students of religion something fresh, intelligent and accessible. Without dumbing down the issues, or making complex matters seem more simple than they need to be, the series manages to be both conceptually challenging while also providing beginning undergraduates with the complete portfolio of books that they need to grasp the fundamentals of each tradition. To be religious is in the end to be human. The I.B.Tauris series looks to be an ideal starting point for anyone interested in this vital and often elusive component of all our societies and cultures.' – *John M. Hull, Emeritus Professor of Religious Education, University of Birmingham*

'The I.B.Tauris Introductions to Religion series promises to be just what busy teachers and students need: a batch of high-quality, highly accessible books by leading scholars that are thoroughly geared towards pedagogical needs and student course use. Achieving a proper understanding of the role of religion in the world is, more than ever, an urgent necessity. This attractive-looking series will contribute towards that vital task.' – *Christopher Partridge, Professor of Religious Studies, Lancaster University*

'The I.B.Tauris series promises to offer more than the usual kind of humdrum introduction. The volumes will seek to explain and not merely to describe religions, will consider religions as ways of life and not merely as sets of beliefs and practices, and will explore differences as well as similarities among specific communities of adherents worldwide. Strongly recommended.' – *Robert A. Segal, Professor of Religious Studies, University of Aberdeen*

Please see here for the full series list

Zoroastrianism

An Introduction

by

Jenny Rose

BLOOMSBURY ACADEMIC

LONDON · NEW YORK · OXFORD · NEW DELHI · SYDNEY

BLOOMSBURY ACADEMIC
Bloomsbury Publishing Plc
50 Bedford Square, London, WC1B 3DP, UK
1385 Broadway, New York, NY 10018, USA

BLOOMSBURY, BLOOMSBURY ACADEMIC and the Diana logo are
trademarks of Bloomsbury Publishing Plc

First published in Great Britain 2012
Reprinted 2019, 2020 (twice)

A catalogue record for this book is available from the British Library.

ISBN: PB: 978-1-35012-871-2
HB: 978-1-84885-088-0
eISBN: 978-0-85773-548-5

I.B. Tauris Introductions to Religion

Typesetting by Tetragon, London
Printed and bound in Great Britain

To find out more about our authors and books visit www.bloomsbury.
com and sign up for our newsletters.

To the memory of my grandmother, Shereen Khorshid Boga, and of Dr Katy Dalal, keeper of the Frenchman family history

Contents

Acknowledgements

The study of the Zoroastrian religion involves more areas of specialization than any one person is capable of mastering in a lifetime. These fields include art history, archeology, anthropology, numismatics, philology, sociology, Classical studies, and Central Asian and Chinese studies. I have, therefore, called extensively – and shamelessly – upon the expertise of colleagues from various academic disciplines, and of Zoroastrians from around the world, to help fill the gaps in my knowledge.

I would, therefore, like to offer my grateful thanks to the following (listed alphabetically), who either read and commented upon draft chapters, or who answered my onslaught of questions, and some brave souls who did both: Poras Balsara, Carlo Cereti, Jamsheed Choksy, Vesta Curtis, Touraj Daryaee, Malcolm Deboo, Albert Dien, Shorena Kurtsikidze, Christian Luczanits, Jesse Palsetia, Martin Schwartz, Nicholas Sims-Williams, Oktor Skjaervø, Michael Stausberg, Matt Stolper, David Stronach, Jamshid Varza, Phiroze Vasunia and Yuhan Vevaina. Almut Hintze deserves a medal for reading the final text with her keen-but-kindly eye for detail. Special thanks go to Poras and Burzin Balsara, Manijeh and Behram Deboo, Neekaan Oshidary, Dr. Mobed Rostam Vahidi, Parviz and Susan Varjavand, Jamshid Varza and Anahita Sidhwa for sharing their personal experiences and reflections, and to the hospitable Zardoshtis of Taft and Mazra-ye Kalantar in Iran for welcoming me into their homes and their *Darb-i Mihrs* in the spring of 2009.

My thanks to Poras Balsara, Frantz Grenet, Hajime Inagaki, Barbara Kaim, Judith Lerner and Keyvan Safdari for providing some great images, and to CGU graduate student, Lucas Schulte, for some sterling editing. I am also indebted to my husband, Bruce Benedict, for applying his journalistic skills to the final text, his photo-editing talents to the illustrations and for always asking questions that pierce at the heart of the matter.

John Hinnells, who valiantly read through the whole manuscript as it evolved, merits a special mention and much appreciation. When I was writing my Masters thesis, I spent many hours studying the books in John's personal library in Manchester. He is owed a particular debt of gratitude for his enduring encouragement of those wanting to know more about the Zoroastrian religion.

Any mistakes in the content of this text are mine alone.

Jenny Rose

Mission Viejo, California

List of Abbreviations

A2S	Artaxerxes II inscription, Susa
Av.	Avestan
AZ	*Ayadgar-i Zareran*
Bd.	(Greater) *Bundahishn*
BEIC	British East India Company
BPP	Bombay Parsi Punchayat
Chron.	*Chronicles*
CK	*Chim-i Kustig*
Dan.	*Daniel*
DB	Darius' inscription, Bisutun
Dd	*Dadestan-i Denig*
DE	Darius' inscription, Elvend
Dk	*Denkard*
DN	Darius' inscription, Naqsh-e Rostam
DP	Darius' inscription, Persepolis
DS	Darius' inscription, Susa

Ezek.   *Ezekiel*

FEZANA   Federation of Zoroastrian Associations of North America

HN   *Hadokht Nask*

KAP   *Karnamag-i Ardashir-i Papagan*

KKZ   Kerdir's inscription on Ka'ba-ye Zardosht

Macc.   *Maccabees*

MHD   *Madayan-i Hazar Dadestan*

MMP   Manichaean Middle Persian

MP   Middle Persian

MX   *Menog-i Xrad*

Neh.   *Nehemiah*

Ner.   *Nerangestan*

NP   New Persian

OAv.   Old Avestan

OI   Old Indic

OIr.   Old Iranian

OP   Old Persian

PFT   Persepolis Fortification Tablets

PGuj.   Parsi Gujarati

PRDd   *Pahlavi Rivayat accompanying Dadestan-i Denig*

Qesse	*Qesse-ye Sanjan*
Riv.	*Rivayats*
RV	*Rig Veda*
SGW	*Shkand Gumanig Wizar*
ShE	*Shahrestaniha-i Eranshahr*
SKZ	Shapur's inscription on Ka'ba-ye Zardosht
Sogd.	Sogdian
Vd	*Videvdad*
Visp.	*Visperad*
WAPIZ	World Alliance of Parsi (and) Irani Zarthoshtis
WZO	World Zoroastrian Organization
XP	Xerxes' inscription, Persepolis
Y	*Yasna*
YAv.	Young Avestan
YH	*Yasna Haptanhaiti*
Yt	Yasht

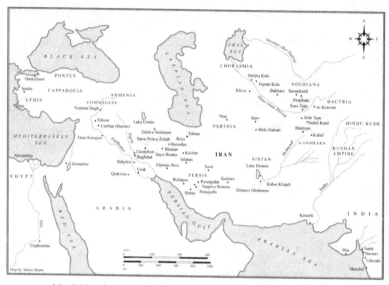

Map 1. Map showing the main places mentioned from different historical eras.

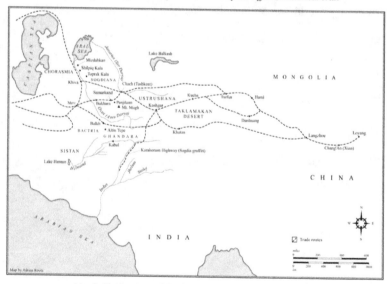

Map 2. Chorasmian and Sogdian sites, fourth–ninth centuries CE.

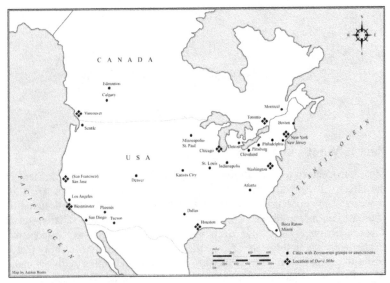

Map 3. Map showing cities in North America with Zoroastrian groups or associations, and Dar-i Mihrs. *Based on information from FEZANA Journal (Winter 2004), 55–59.*

Zoroastrianism: An Introduction

Part 1: What's in an 'ism'?

Most introductory texts to Zoroastrianism begin with a leading statement to the effect that it is one of the world's oldest religions, which it is. There is, however, no consensus as to the interpretation of the designation 'Zoroastrianism', whether applied at the inception of the religion or at subsequent stages. The use of a singular label – such as 'Buddhism', 'Christianity' or, in this case, 'Zoroastrianism' – suggests a static entity that is easier to grasp, but which is reduced to a monolith, reflecting neither breadth of belief and practice, nor historical development. This tunnel-vision approach to any religion that has evolved over centuries, and has been sustained in different cultural settings, is no longer sustainable in any academic study of religion.

Religions are born and grow within fluid and ever-changing socio-political and cultural contexts. Any scholarly analysis must therefore consider the interplay between such prevailing conditions and the ideologies that emerge. Due to the long history of the religion, it is difficult to define succinctly what 'Zoroastrianism' was in the past. The manner in which an author writing today defines the religion will, of necessity, bias the presentation of material. Such is my dilemma: how to reflect the culturally varied and historically evolving range of interpretations of 'Zoroastrianism', while also discerning whether a continuity of certain emblematic themes exists from the earliest time to the present.

The task of determining what constitutes 'Zoroastrianism' at any given point in time is both stimulated and stymied by continuing archeological and linguistic discoveries, which provide new perspectives prompting a constant re-evaluation of the term. For instance, until recently it was assumed that the 'Zoroastrianism' of the Sasanian period (c. 224 to mid-seventh century CE) was most clearly expressed in the self-proclaimed 'orthodoxy' of Middle Persian priestly writings. This assumption was held partly because there was no real conception of other forms of expression of the religion, either within or beyond the borders of Iran. But in the last few decades concrete examples of a Zoroastrian remnant of both hieratic and domestic ritual have been elucidated in Armenian, Georgian and Central Asian settings, as well as within Iran itself. Closer scrutiny of individual Middle Persian texts has also revealed them to be more diverse and contradictory than previously understood.

It is, then, more accurate to refer to 'Zoroastrian beliefs and practices' and 'Zoroastrian communities' in the plural – or even to 'Zoroastrianisms' – rather than to apply a single label of 'Zoroastrianism' at any given time. To speak in such plural terms is also to acknowledge the narration and appropriation of the religion and its eponymous founder, Zarathushtra, by both Zoroastrians and 'outsiders'. Herodotus first wrote of the beliefs and practices of the Ancient Persians in the late fifth century BCE. This pattern of appropriation and reinterpretation, augmented by Islamic historiographers and poets between the ninth and thirteenth centuries CE, has continued to the present day. Such confusion of sources leads to a plurality of approaches, and divergence of opinions both in the scholarly literature and within the Zoroastrian communities. This divergence is most clearly exemplified in the realm of philology, a field of study crucial to any understanding of the textual history of religion, but one which often creates distortions because of the tendency of some translators to be driven by theological or anthropological presuppositions, rather than by purely scientific literary analysis. It is an understatement, then, to say that the term 'Zoroastrianism' is somewhat elusive, since it resonates differently depending on the person using it. Recent attempts to analyze and categorize the various types of approach to the religion are on the whole unsatisfactory, in that such classification precludes all others, whereas, in fact, each approach incorporates overlapping elements.[1]

In recent years, the use of 'Zoroastrianism' to describe the religion has been challenged from within by faith practitioners as being of Greek (therefore 'outsider') etymology, rather than Iranian ('insider'). This approach recognizes that to talk about 'Zoroastrianism' is to use a construct that has been imposed on the religion by outsiders. The Greek form *Zoroastres* was first used by Xanthos of Lydia in the mid-fifth century CE, and was the base for subsequent European versions of the name until Nietzsche popularized the Iranian form *Zarathushtra*. Some adherents choose to refer to their religion by the ancient Iranian terms *Mazdayasna* ('worship of Ahura Mazda'), *daena Mazdayasni* ('the religion of Mazda worship') or *daena vanguhi*. This latter term, usually translated as 'the good religion', occurs in the *Gathas*, the oldest texts of the religion (*Gathas* 5.53.4). The word *daena* comes from a root 'to see', and therefore means something like '[religious] insight'. The phrase becomes inverted as *weh den* in Middle Persian, and *behdin* in New Persian.

In one Middle Persian text, the *den* ('religion') is said to be the 'sea of the sacred word (*manthra*)'.[2] Zoroastrians now use a variant of this concept when they refer to their religion as *Zarathushti Din* (the 'religion of Zarathushtra' or 'the Zoroastrian religion'). Although the use of 'Mazdayasna' or 'Mazdaism' is closer to ancient terms of self-definition, it is less accessible to a current reading audience. So the terms 'Zoroastrian' and 'Zoroastrianism' appear throughout this book, but should be read with the above caveats in mind, particularly that Zarathushtra does not have to be invoked, or even mentioned, for the religion to be defined as belonging to the evolution of Zoroastrianism.

Many Zoroastrians from India continue to use the ethno-religious term 'Parsi' denoting their original 1,000-year-old, 'Persian' roots. Later Zoroastrian immigrants from Iran to India are known as 'Iranis'. This diversity of self-definition operates alongside ongoing discussion among Zoroastrians concerning what constitutes the fundamental doctrines, rituals and practices of the religion. It is doubtful that a general consensus concerning these crucial issues will be found among the various groups, even though some core elements may be agreed upon.

Zoroastrians regard the *Gathas* as the authoritative, original teachings of Zarathushtra. For some, anything that is perceived as differing from Gathic teaching is not considered to be authentically 'Zoroastrian', although may be recognized as part of a general continuum. The question as to what extent later, non-Gathic materials reflect either a continuity or divergence of belief and practice was raised in the mid-nineteenth century, but still resonates with Zoroastrians and non-Zoroastrian scholars today, some of whom maintain that anything extraneous to the *Gathas* must be defined as 'post-Gathic Zoroastrianism' or 'post-Gathic Mazdaism'.

This book aims to present the paths, both literal and literary, upon which the religion has been transported through history, and thereby to offer some new perspectives to an understanding of Zoroastrianism. Those paths often lead into uneven or dicey terrain, reflecting the complexities involved in deciphering the various trail markers along the way.

Part 2: Setting the Scene

The exploration of 'Zoroastrianism' presented in this book begins with a consideration of the religion as it is expressed in various forms today, by a small number of adherents from many different backgrounds. It begins and ends with the question, 'Who is a Zoroastrian?' This question is best approached through being alert to the range of self-definitions that provide the current voice of the religion. Although Zoroastrians are divided on this question (as also in their divergent understanding of such correlated issues of theology as conversion and interfaith marriage), they are generally united in maintaining the celebration of seasonal festivals, the rite of initiation, and certain domestic practices including daily prayer. This common core of religion-in-action is explored through several case studies. The emphasis of this initial section focuses on who is, rather than who is not, a Zoroastrian.

Mapping Zoroastrianism

Any effort to recreate an original, 'pristine' form of the religion is, I feel, one that belongs to the domain of the faith community, rather than to an academic approach. An appropriate method for an introductory text such as this is to trace the development of the religion from its earliest oral compositions through later written texts, both sacred and secular, alongside both private and public observance. I recognize, however, that this is an exercise that relies on the fluctuating accessibility and nature of source materials, and contains its own bias of narrative in terms of the interpretation of those sources.

There is also the danger of taking too essentialist an approach. To avoid that, I have tried to focus on recurrent themes that relate to those ultimate questions about the origins, purpose and end events of life. A chronological mapping that charts the religion from prehistoric times through the Iranian migration to the plateau, the three Iranian Empires, and then into diaspora,[3] helps to track the evolution of the beliefs, rituals and emblematic motifs of 'Zoroastrianism' through given points in time. Such mapping also involves a consideration of the prevalent ideologies pertaining in each historical setting, and the deciphering of archeological, geographical and linguistic clues which indicate points of interaction with other religions and cultures in the Ancient Near East, Greece, India, Central Asia and China. This scheme precludes a review of the entire socio-political history of the Iranian peoples, which is supplemented through the Resources suggested at the end of the book.

The map begins with the emergence of the Iranians and Indo-Aryans as separate but related peoples who once shared a common language and mythology. An exploration of both the commonalities and divergences between the worldview of the Sanskrit *Rig Veda* and that of the Old Avesta is one way of determining what is original to the 'Zoroastrian vision', as presented in the *Gathas* and other Old Iranian oral literary texts. This approach helps to highlight the themes and emblems that recur throughout the history of the religion.

The earliest tangible evidence of Iranian ideological expression appears in the monumental art, architecture and inscriptions of the Ancient Persian or Achaemenid Empire (c. 550–330 BCE), alongside smaller finds of personal seals and clay accounting tablets. Such materials provide insight into some of the religious emblems and practices of the Ancient Persians, and, along with contemporary Greek accounts and Avestan texts, help to address questions concerning the application of the term 'Zoroastrian' at this period. Just as the Persians themselves became more established, so their religion grew more institutionalized, marked by the development of temple worship and an accompanying hieratic organization.

Following the invasion of Alexander of Macedon, Greek culture exercised a considerable influence throughout greater Iran, particularly in terms of language, iconography and social custom. Until recently, the lack of internal material from Seleucid and Parthian Iran contributed to the view that the Zoroastrian religion had been neglected until it was 'restored' by the Sasanians. But written data on ostraca, rock reliefs, parchment and coins deciphered in the past few decades contradict this view, pointing instead to both continuity and development within the religion during this period. References by contemporary Greek, Roman, Chinese and Jewish authors, and later Armenian Christian apologists, provide external substantiation for Parthian Zoroastrianism (c. 250 BCE–224 CE). The diversity of these sources denotes a significant interaction between Iranians and the surrounding cultures, and it is during this period that some Zoroastrian themes seem to filter into the apocalyptic ideologies of the Near East, including Jewish apocryphal writing, Gnostic myth and some early Christian texts, as well as into early Buddhist iconography.

The ensuing Sasanian period (224–651 CE) is well documented in both internal and external sources. Middle Persian texts include rock and numismatic inscriptions, as well as several important religious writings from the ninth and tenth centuries CE, which reflect Sasanian theology, mores, civil and religious laws, and mythical history. These, along with Syriac and later Islamic texts, tell us that as the dynasty progressed, the Zoroastrian priesthood increased in authority, and endowed fire temples became powerful centers. This consolidation occurred at the same time that the primacy of the Zoroastrian faith in Iran was being challenged by the missionary activities of Christianity to the west, Buddhism to the east and Manichaeism from within. This last religion incorporated familiar elements from Zoroastrian cosmology and eschatology into its vocabulary.

In recent years, a variant form of Zoroastrianism contemporary to that in Sasanian Iran has emerged from Central Asia, particularly ancient Sogdiana. This adds a valuable new dimension to the study of the religion. Both Sasanians and Sogdians established fire temples in China under the Tang dynasty, marking the beginning of a settled Zoroastrian diaspora outside greater Iran.

The death of the last Sasanian king, Yazdegird III, in 651 CE and the capitulation of Merv to the Arab Muslims marked the end of Zoroastrian rule in Iran. Zoroastrians continued to hold key bureaucratic positions for several generations, however, and their Iranian cultural and religious heritage had a lasting impact on the development of Islam in the region and beyond. Arabic histories provide much information about Zoroastrians in Iran during the early period of Islam. Later, letters sent from Iran to the Parsis in India tell us much about the religious life of both communities between the fifteenth and eighteenth centuries. During this period, we also learn of life in Zoroastrian towns and villages in both countries through Gujarati sources and European travel accounts.

The end of the tenth century saw a period of increased immigration of Zoroastrians to the west of India by sea and overland. The Parsis appear on the whole to have lived peacefully with their Hindu, and then Muslim, neighbors. They adopted Indian dress, spoke Gujarati, and stopped eating beef and pork, but maintained Zoroastrian practices, including disposal of their dead in *dakhmas*, worship at fire temples, and many domestic rituals that also continue in Iran. In the early nineteenth century the Parsis were challenged by Christian missionaries, many of whom were well read in terms of recent translations of Avestan and Pahlavi texts. This galvanized both Parsi priests and lay leaders to become better educated in their own religion, some traveling as far as Europe and America to do so. By this time, Parsis had established themselves in trade and its related industries, and many moved abroad to pursue commercial enterprise in such locations as Hong Kong, East Africa and Britain.

The chronological survey of the history of the religion ends with a consideration of the range of responses of Zoroastrians under Muslim, Hindu and British rule to the religiously 'Other'. How did – and does – such an encounter, particularly with the European 'Other', affect Zoroastrian self-perception? European scholars have created their own vision of the Zoroastrian religion, which has then been fed back into Zoroastrian lore. This dialectic continues to impact Zoroastrian self-definition today, but Western scholarship is increasingly being treated with caution by adherents, who maintain that the divergence of academic translations of the *Gathas* represents a sterile approach to the religion. The wealth of material available through the Internet places information (and misinformation) at everyone's fingertips, and discussions concerning Zoroastrian 'hot topics' are now conducted in a public forum.

Zarathushtra

The conclusion of the book focuses on the person of Zarathushtra, beginning with the significance of the purported author of the *Gathas* to Zoroastrians today. Although, from an early period, supporters of the religion are known as *zarathushtri*, the focus of both internal and external texts – and, one assumes, practices – until the late Sasanian period is firmly on Mazda worship. Zarathushtra, who is present in religious texts from the beginning, is not mentioned in any official inscription from the three Iranian dynasties.

The Zoroastrian conception of Zarathushtra incorporates multiple identifications, and debate continues not only as to his persona, but also the meaning of his name. To paraphrase Nietzsche: Who is Zarathushtra? A priest? A revolutionary prophet? An enlightened philosopher? A ritualist? A thaumaturge? An historical figure, or a figment of faith? Throughout history, many have tried to reconstruct Zarathushtra, from the scant biographical details in the Young Avesta to the full-blown hagiographies of the Middle Persian and New Persian texts. External appropriations of Zoroaster endure from classical Greece to present-day novelists, travel-writers, and even some bold artists and film-makers.

Postscript

I am aware that I, too, am a participant in the process of re-narrating Zarathushtra and the Zoroastrian religion. My own studies of the history of religions and Iranian languages and culture(s) have shaped the ideological and narrative biases in this book. Perhaps the main determinant in my bias is, however, the fact that my grandmother was a Parsi. My genealogical attachment to the Zoroastrian story and history brings with it a certain psychological affinity that has been a significant impetus in my research and writing. My attempt to balance personal narrative and academic detail (which, at times, may seem uneven) reflects my own approach to both the study and teaching of the religion.

Chapter I

Zoroastrians Present and Past

This I ask you, tell me truly, O Ahura
Who was the first father of Order and gave it birth?

Gathas 2.44.3–4[1]

'There is lately published in Paris, a Work intitled Zend-Avesta, or the Writings of Zoroaster, containing the Theological, Philosophical and Moral Ideas of that Legislator, and the ceremonies of Religious Worship that he established.... I have cast my Eye over the Religious Part; it seems to contain a nice Morality, mix'd with abundance of Prayers, Ceremonies and Observations.'

A letter from Benjamin Franklin, London, 1772[2]

Zoroastrians Now: A Living Faith

Our exploration of Zoroastrianism begins with the question, 'Who is a Zoroastrian?' This is a question that in recent years has divided Zoroastrians to the extent that some consider there to be at least two, if not more, forms of the religion today, each one considering itself to be authentic. Opinions diverge on correlated issues of theology, including textual translation and interpretation, conversion, interfaith marriage and disposal of the dead. The range of attendant selfdefinitions will be considered in more detail later, but for the purposes of introducing Zoroastrianism as a lived and living faith, the immediate focus will be on normative praxis. I have chosen this approach because it spotlights an area of the religion that remains vital to its adherents and that addresses in a pragmatic way those ultimate, existentialist questions to do with the purpose and meaning of life: Where do we come from? Why are we here? What happens when we die? What powers do we have to shape our own existence and ending? The answers to such questions enable humans to make sense of the world in which they find themselves.

Such answers as religion provides tend to be couched within a cosmology that establishes an order to existence. Although a clear moral philosophy underpins all Zoroastrian 'faith in action', it is the *pattern* of daily prayers, seasonal rituals, social celebrations and acts of philanthropy that gives a concrete sense of cohesion and continuity for most Zoroastrians, and is their main form of public religious expression. Such concrete expression is an example of the concept that moral understanding has a social reference extending beyond individual rights to the wider community. The notion of a 'connectedness in prayer' among co-religionists is articulated in the Parsi-Gujarati term *hambandagi* (literally, 'bondedness together'),[3] which embodies the sense that the pursuit of goodness is not just a means but an end, leading to cooperation and harmony.

I experienced this 'community unity' for myself when, in the late spring of 2009, I spent a few days in the central Iranian province of Yazd. A Zoroastrian colleague from California was also in the area at the time, and together we visited some of the small villages on the outskirts of the city of Yazd. As we wandered past the adobe-covered buildings of one village, we encountered a couple of elderly women wearing colorful headscarves. My colleague, Jamshid, used the Dari greeting '*Rujkoryak*', a variant on Persian '*Ruzgar-e nik*' meaning 'Good Day', rather than the pan-Islamic '*Salaam aleikum*'. This brought an instant recognition that Jamshid was of the same faith, and an invitation to follow the women down the road to the village hall, where a community seasonal celebration – a *gahanbar* – was taking place.

In a plain, whitewashed room, a *mobedyar*[4] sat on the floor, his knee nudging a folded cloth filled with seven kinds of dried fruits, dates, chickpeas and nuts, which constitute the *lork* – the festival food shared among the community at the end of the recitation of the *gahanbar* prayers (Fig. 1). Members of the community either sat in the hall or chatted quietly together in a reception room just outside, counting off the prayers as they were recited.

This was the second *gahanbar* we had been invited to in as many days, and we encountered another in a neighboring village on the following evening. These successive *gahanbars* celebrated the midspring season traditionally called *Maidhyoi-zaremaya*, a (Young) Avestan word meaning 'mid-greening', in allusion to the growth of crops sown in late winter or early spring. That such pastoral references have endured for over 2,500 years is attested in the farmers' calendar of Old Persian (OP) inscriptions. A sixth century CE Middle Persian (MP) text advocates the importance of observing *gahanbars* as an integral part of 'the ordered existence',[5] and they are recommended in a later New Persian (NP) text as being among the duties prescribed for all Zoroastrians.[6] Participation in such community festivals provides a sense of being part of an unbroken chain of practice that is constantly acting to revitalize the elements of the created world, including the humans who participate. This holistic conception of humans as agents of healing in the world is an ancient notion that is expressed in the *Gathas*, the earliest texts of the religion, and it remains integral to the Zoroastrian ethos.

Fig. 1. Gahanbar celebration in the community prayer hall, Mazra-ye Kalantar, Yazd province, Iran.

Most Zoroastrian praxis can be viewed in this way – as activity intended to strengthen both adherents and the cosmos. A Middle Persian text proposes the idea that each person's thoughts, words and actions have profound repercussions in the wider world.[7] The individual is formally recognized as a participant in the work of reenergizing the world when he or she chooses to adopt the ethical outworking of the code of 'Good Thoughts, Good Words, Good Deeds' at an initiation ceremony. For many Parsi (Indian) Zoroastrians, the post-initiation practice of wearing the *sudreh* (white cotton shirt worn under clothing) and *kusti* (cord worn around the waist over the shirt) acts as a constant reminder of this ethical imperative. The *sudreh* has a small pocket at the front to encourage the accumulation of good deeds, and the *kusti* is wrapped around the waist three times to remind the wearer to generate good thoughts, good words and good deeds at all times. In a passage from the *Chimi Kustig* ('Reasons for the *kusti*'), a father explains to his 'knowledgedesiring' son that the reason for tying the cord around the waist is that the body of a human is 'a world in miniature'.[8] In other words, humans are a microcosmic representation of the macrocosm. The three tassels on each end of the *kusti* are said to remind the wearer of the six *gahanbars*, the seasonal festivals celebrating the cycle of growth and the order of the year. So, the person who wears the *kusti* affirms his or her part in sustaining that growth and order.

Traditionally, the age of religious maturity for Zoroastrians is 15 years old (Vd 18.54), but initiations can take place from the age of seven. A Parsi initiate is referred to as *Navjote*, usually translated as 'new person who offers prayers', but sometimes as 'new birth'. The Persian term for the initiation ceremony of Iranian Zoroastrians is *Sedreh-Pushi*, 'the putting on of the sacred shirt'. The format and symbolism of the initiation ceremony is the same for boys and girls, and are said to date back to ancient times (Fig. 2). The *kusti* may be linked to the same ancient tradition as the sacred thread of Hindu initiation.

One young Parsi acquaintance of mine, Burzin, who comes from a priestly family, had his *navjote* ceremony performed by his father a couple of years ago. Burzin says that he has been asked many times about his religion and the *sudreh-kusti* he wears: 'Once I explain it to my friends at school most of them understand. I wear these garments regularly, except when I am in the gym or go swimming, I remove my *kusti* because I am afraid somebody might pull it by mistake and break it.' Some younger Zoroastrians in diaspora communities may decide not to wear the sacred garments for fear of taunts or teasing by their peers, while others claim that the practice has no material value, being more of a psychological prop or a symbolic gesture. On the other hand, some choose to put on the *sudreh* and *kusti* and to say the accompanying prayers as a means of focusing their intentionality, and to further their spiritual development and that sense of *hambandagi*.

Since his *navjote*, Burzin has taken the further step of being ordained as a priest in the *navar* ceremony, the first initiation into priesthood. Both he and his father, Poras, speak of the encouragement they receive from the community, and the sense of reward they feel through serving their Zoroastrian community in the USA. Although the Zoroastrian priesthood remains exclusively male, and the texts have been composed, transmitted and interpreted by males, women have also contributed significantly to the perpetuation of the religion throughout history. Until the mid-twentieth century, this contribution was largely within the sphere of domestic praxis, including the education of children in their daily prayers, the preparation of the home and community meeting-place for rituals, and social welfare, such as making soup for the needy. This lay activity, sustained for centuries, forms the bedrock on which much popular religious expression is founded.

Fig. 2. Navjote *(initiation) ceremony attended during the author's first visit to Bombay in 1987.*

One such activity is the ritual of perfuming the house with sweetsmelling herbs or incense, which is still regularly performed by Zoroastrians in Iran and India and, to a lesser extent, in diaspora. Iranian Zoroastrians use rue or marjoram, Parsis use sandalwood and *loban*, a tree-resin. My friend Anahita grew up in a Zoroastrian household in Karachi, Pakistan, where, no matter how hectic things were, her mother would do this ritual after saying her *kusti* prayers in the morning. Anahita remembers her grandmother and aunts performing the same ritual each day. In her husband's family, it was the father who walked through the house with the incense. In some homes, this ritual is performed at sunset as well. When Anahita arrived in America, although she lit an oil lamp on special occasions, such as birthdays or *Nav Ruz* (New Year: literally 'New Day'), she did not perform the morning incense ritual until one of her aunts gave her a small fire-holder. Now, on Sundays, or before she sits to pray with the prayer book (*Khordeh Avesta*), she will walk around the house with the *loban* and chant a prayer for the health and well-being of its inhabitants. This allows the smoke and aroma of the incense to waft through her home.

Anahita comments, 'Friends who visit us within an hour of the *loban* will often comment how pleasant it feels.' The *loban* spreads fragrance both literally and figuratively: 'Just as the fire burns brightly, but the sweet aroma of sandalwood and *loban* leaves behind a fragrance, similarly I promise to lead a useful life filled with good deeds that will leave a memorable mark on the world.' The pungent smell of the incense is intended to imbue the house and its occupants with good thoughts, and also to keep bugs away. The maintenance of the home as a physical stronghold against harm is also sustained in both India and Iran through an early morning sweeping of the house and scouring of the front porch.

Such practices incorporate the ancient understanding that both the conceptual (*menog*) and corporeal (*getig*) worlds are to be cared for and sustained by the faithful. The 'dualism' that is often attributed to the Zoroastrian religion is not so much a division between mind and matter, but rather a vertical split between good and evil (see Fig. 3). The dialectical process that engages each Zoroastrian is based on the premise that the actualities of life are intrinsically good, but that the harmony and growth of both the individual and the collective whole are threatened by chaos, confusion and destruction.

The rise of a materialist worldview that poses new challenges concerning the efficacy of any ritual has been accompanied by a correlate decline in status and numbers in the priesthood, and a trend towards laicization of the religion. Such public observance as wearing the *sudreh* and *kusti* has become an issue of normative practice for individual Zoroastrians. Parsis in general tend to be more punctilious about wearing the garments at all times, untying and tying the *kusti* with the recital of certain prayers several times a day: after getting out of bed in the morning; before eating; before and after using the bathroom; and prior to beginning any prayer and going to bed. By comparison, many Iranian Zoroastrians put on the *sudreh* and *kusti* only when they visit the *atashkadeh* ('fire temple') or attend special ceremonies at which the fire will be present. This difference is largely due to the socio-political situations of each group. Iranian Zoroastrians have occasionally been excluded from some Parsi *agiaries* ('fire temples') in India, because they do not wear the *sudreh-kusti* at all times. The spouses and children of intermarried Parsi women have also been barred, since a 1908 'collateral opinion' (*obiter dicta*) defined a Parsi in terms of patrilineality for the purposes of access to Parsi funds and institutions.[9] In practice this has meant that the children of Parsi fathers could be initiated and attend an *agiary*, but not those of Parsi mothers who had married out.

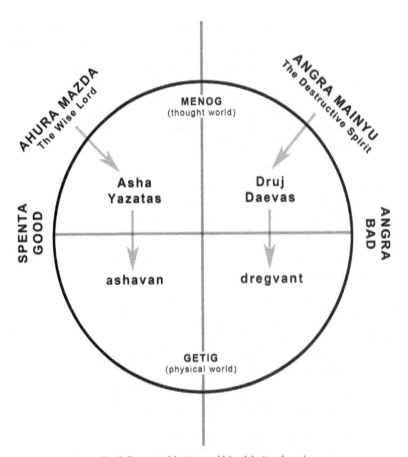

Fig. 3. Diagram of the 'two worlds' and the 'two forces'.

The Parsi community is still struggling with the tensions that the century-old distinction between the terms 'Zoroastrian' and 'Parsi' have brought, alongside the thorny issue of conversion, which besets the entire Zoroastrian world. The debate centers on who is a 'real' Zoroastrian: one who is born into the faith; one who returns to his or her ancestral faith (this is the position taken by some Iranians and Tajiks); or one who believes the teachings of the religion and chooses to follow them. Some look to the priests for guidance in these matters, some look to the sacred texts and others take the view that it is belief, not birth, that determines one's religious adherence, and therefore acknowledge no human hieratic authority.

One of my students, Neekaan, takes a pragmatic perspective when he states that the greatest value he derives from Zoroastrian teachings is 'a devotion to the truth, which is more than simply speaking the truth'. He stated, 'To me, it is the courage to seek truth by being willing to break from the realms of comfort and to see reality as it is, much like a scientist does. The more I study this, the more I learn that the truth may be uncomfortable, and may make the process of seeking truth difficult'. 'But', Neekaan concludes, 'what I love about the Zoroastrian vision is the faith that this devotion to truth, despite its challenges, proves to be wonderful in the end'.

'Zoroastrianism' Then

An anthropologist, who spent a considerable time in Yazd between 1969 and 1977, wrote that to understand religion in today's world 'depends increasingly on an attitude of recovery: of unraveling ancient and half-forgotten meanings; of piecing together clues embodied in language, ritual and customs that are now more emotionally than intellectually compelling; of (re)constructing an intellectual persuasiveness, informed in large part by appreciation for the historical growth of tradition.'[10]

This approach is particularly applicable to Zoroastrianism. Its development over several thousand years means that the language, ritual and customs relating to those patterns of praxis described above provide valid clues to understanding the religion, but not the complete picture. The following section aims to unravel some of the 'ancient meanings' in the earliest Zoroastrian texts, in order to lay the intellectual groundwork for an appreciation of the historical development and application of those concepts. You may find that it is useful to keep a copy of both the glossary and list of abbreviations to hand as I attempt this (re)construction.

The mid-spring *gahanbar* mentioned earlier takes place during the month named *Ordibehesht*, a term derived from the Old Avestan (OAv.) phrase *Asha Vahishta*, meaning 'Best *Asha*'. *Asha* can be translated as 'order' or 'arranged in cosmic cohesion', and thus 'right' in the sense of 'as it should be': it is also often translated as 'truth'. *Asha* is a concept that occurs in the earliest sacral poetry of the Iranians, thought to have been composed at about the same time as the *Rig Veda* (RV), the oldest text in the Hindu tradition, dated around the mid-second millennium BCE. These Iranian poems, known as *Gathas* or 'songs', are still recited in the Old Avestan language in which they were memorized orally for centuries, until they were committed to writing in a specially-invented alphabet around the sixth or seventh century CE. Our earliest extant Avestan manuscripts date from the thirteenth century CE.

The transmission of the *Gathas* from Ahura Mazda to humanity is attributed to an Iranian precursor named Zarathushtra. This view is expressed formally at an early stage in the corpus of Avestan texts in references to 'the *Gathas* of Zarathushtra' (Y 57.8). The *Gathas*, two prayers (known as *Yatha ahu vairyo* or *Ahuna Vairya*, and *Airyema Ishyo*), and a short Old Avestan liturgy, are the primary and oldest sources for our understanding of 'Zoroastrianism' in its earliest form. The *Sitz im Leben* of these texts, and their linguistic comparison with the Sanskrit of the *Rig Veda*, suggests a similar date of around mid-second millennium BCE. There are, however, widely variant opinions concerning this dating, and no consensus likely unless new data is found.[11]

An Ur-homeland

The Iranian and Indo-Aryan language groups diverged sometime during the late third millennium BCE. Gradually, the Indo-Aryans migrated to what is now the Indian subcontinent, and the Iranians moved through western Central Asia towards the Iranian plateau. Later (Young) Avestan texts, particularly the *Videvdad* and some of the *Yashts* (hymns of praise), provide geographical reference for an Iranian migration via a route to the north-east of Iran. These later texts are thought to have become fixed in their present form around the mid-first millennium BCE (see Appendix 1). Avestan is an eastern Iranian language, as are the later Middle Iranian languages of Sogdian and Bactrian, and, more recently, Pashto. Place names in Avestan texts that can be identified with certainty are all to the east or north-east of modern Iran.[12]

In Zoroastrian textual tradition an 'Aryan expanse' (*Airyana Vaejah*) is regarded as the center of the world, a paradisal *axis mundi*, where all great events of the past had taken place. Zarathushtra is said to have been 'renowned in *Airyana Vaejah*' (Yt 9.14) and to have made offerings there (Yt 5.104). *Videvdad* refers to *Airyana Vaejah* as an original homeland of the Iranians. It is described as 'the best of places' created by Ahura Mazda, but then assaulted with harsh winters, lasting ten cold months, with two months of summer (Vd 1.2–3). This depiction is consistent with a location in the south of the Central Asian Steppe. *Videvdad* mentions another 15 Iranian-inhabited lands, including an area settled by Sogdians (corresponding roughly to eastern Uzbekistan/western Tajikistan), one called Marghu (Merv in Turkmenistan) and another Baxdhi (Bactria in northern Afghanistan: see Map 1). Some of these regions are also named in a Young Avestan hymn, which records that from far above 'high Mt. Hara' could be seen the whole domain inhabited by the Iranians, which was replete with wide, fertile river valleys and grass pastures (Yt 10.13–14).

Tour companies in the individual Central Asian Republics lay claim to their country as the birthplace of Zoroastrianism. A Middle Persian account of ancient cities preserves the legend that Zarathushtra brought the religion to Samarkand in Sogdia, where the ruler Vishtaspa ordered the teachings to be written down and deposited in the fire temple.[13] Some archeologists associate the early Iranians with fortified settlements belonging to the so-called 'Bactria-Margiana Archaeological Complex (BMAC)', such as Gonur Tepe in Merv, which dates to the early second millennium BCE. Artifacts found at such BMAC sites point to an Indo-Iranian populace, but linguistic development – particularly regarding the naming of rivers in the region – indicates that the original inhabitants were proto-Indo-Aryans, who were followed by Iranians at a later date.[14] These Iranians can be identified with the 'Yaz 1' complex, dated between 1500 and 1000 BCE, a period marked by the absence of any burial finds in the area.[15]

A western Iranian origin, promoted first by some classical authors, and later by medieval Muslim historiographers, is philologically and archeologically problematic, and appeals mostly to those who maintain that the Iranians arrived on the plateau via the Caucasus and south-western Caspian.[16] Some also adhere to a much later chronological date, placing the Old Avestan texts (and also therefore Zarathushtra, who is connected to the *Gathas*) in the mid-first millennium BCE. This presents linguistic problems and the debate continues, with the majority of Avestan scholars in favor of the earlier date.[17]

To determine a definitive geographical location for *Airyana Vaejah* in an 'X marks the spot' manner would not only remove its semi-mythical status, but would also feed into a prevalent sense of ethno-ideological superiority. As the Iranians progress geographically towards the Iranian plateau, so the Aryan expanse moves with them. It is the place where they are presently located, rather like the *Hawai'iki* of Polynesian myth, until it becomes the name of an identifiable country – the *Eranvej* of Middle Persian texts and the Iran of today.

The Birth of Order

The setting for the *Gathas* is presented as that of mobile pastoralism. This lifestyle is reflected in the hippophoric names of some of the characters mentioned in the *Gathas*, including Jamaspa, Vishtaspa, and Haechataspa: OAv. *aspa* means 'horse'. There are frequent references to the cow, the bull, pasturage and herders, and pastoral metaphor is dominant in both the literal sense, referring to the care of livestock, and also as a literary device to describe the relationship between humanity and the cosmos at large. The struggle for sustenance and growth is expressed in poetic idiom, so that the beleaguered 'soul of the cow' (*geush urvan*) can also be understood as the 'soul of the world' (1.29.1). Just as the cow, under the good husbandry of the cowherd, yields beneficent by-products of butter and milk (3.49.5; 1.29.7), so clarity of vision and integrity of word and action promote that which is 'really real' (*haithya*), bringing nourishment and increase to the world, rather than injury and decrease (1.31.15–16). In Young Avestan texts, the pastoral metaphor of the struggle between good and evil played out in the grazing meadows shifts towards more agriculturally-based allusions, suggesting perhaps a parallel shift in lifestyle. Whereas the *Gathas* make no reference to planting seed, in the *Videvdad* the heart of the religious insight (*daena*) of those who worship Ahura Mazda is identified as the sowing of grain: 'the person who sows grain, sows *Asha*' (Vd 3.30–2).

Much of the text of the *Gathas* can be taken, then, at both literal and metaphorical levels. Such poetic metaphor loses much of its beauty – and power – when literally translated, particularly if read as prose, rather than poetry. We can surmise that many of the original allusions of the *Gathas* were lost to subsequent generations at the point when the oral text became fixed linguistically, despite its conscientious transmission. The poetry in the *Gathas* contains a high degree of abstraction and complex compositional techniques, including the symmetrical structuring known as 'ring composition'.[18] Collectively, the poems were referred to as the 'Five *Gathas*' at an early stage (cf. Y 71.6), relating to five single poems of different meters. Three of these poems incorporate several parts, known as *haiti* or 'divisions'. The 17 *haiti* of all five *Gathas* are usually numbered according to their placement within the *Yasna*, the Zoroastrian liturgy of 72 sections (see Appendix 2).

a. Good Thought

The *Gathas* are proclaimed by a self-declared *manthran* (3.50.5, 6); that is, someone whose poetic utterances represent a deep conceptual and existential understanding. The base of *manthran* is the verbal root *man*, 'to think' (as in '*mental* process'). Some translate the word *manthran* as 'prophet', but it belongs more readily within the Indo-Iranian designation of a verbal crystallization of a conceptual vision. The notion of clarity and focus of thought as a central principle percolates through the *Gathas* in many forms. Cognate words include *manah*, meaning 'thought' (rather than 'intention' or 'purpose', as it is sometimes translated); *manyu*, meaning 'inspiration' or 'mental stimulus/mentality', on the poetic level and that of choice, and 'spirit', in the sense of some kind of mythic entity in the *menog* world. *Mazda* is a cognate agent noun from the compound *man* + *dā*, and is most accurately translated as 'the one who keeps mental track' or 'the one who is wise/knowledgeable'. The other epithet that often appears alongside *mazda* in the *Gathas* is *ahura*. One etymology for *ahura* is from a verb meaning 'to engender'.[19] The most accurate translation of the two-part name Ahura Mazda is 'Wise Lord'.

Mazda's good creation includes both the conceptual (*manahiia*) world of thought, and the corporeal (*gaetha*) or 'boney' (*astvant*) world. These two dimensions are not in conflict (1.28.2), but they are distinct in that the former can only be perceived by thought or inspiration, whereas the world of physical beings is apprehended through the embodied senses, particularly of vision and hearing. The Gathic *manthras*, recited 'with agility of tongue and correctly pronounced words' (1.31.19), are believed to resonate between the two spheres.

The *Gathas* are, then, the numinous songs of the *manthra*-maker, who is also described as *vidvah*, 'one who knows' (4.51.8). They are not versified teachings, but rather metric poetry with instructive content regarding the nature of things, which assume an underlying knowledge on the part of those who hear them. It is difficult now to determine the context and meaning of some of the allusions in the *Gathas*.

b. Common Indo-Iranian themes

The fact that Iranians and Indo-Aryans once shared a common linguistic and literary tradition, including that of oral religious poetry, is evidenced in themes, concepts, terminology and the poetic syntax of the *Gathas* that echo those of the *Rig Veda*. This common background not only serves to date the *Gathas*, but also to place them initially within an Indo-Iranian continuum, rather than an Ancient Near Eastern mindset.

That the composition of religiously-inspired poetry was a central part of Indo-Iranian expression may be seen in the plural negative references in the *Gathas* to *kavaiio*. *Kavi* is the descriptive title given to Zarathushtra's supporter, Vishtaspa,[20] and in later Iranian mythology the term was applied to a ruler. But in both Old Avestan and Old Indic, *kavi* referred to an inspired poet.[21] The negative usage in the *Gathas* suggests rival poets, some creating good words, rightly recited with best thought and focus, and others characterized by mediocrity, deriving from an unfocused mind (1.32.10, 14). The *karapan* are also castigated in the *Gathas* (cf. 1.32.12, 4.51.14). They are thought to have been 'mumblers', who recited in an unclear manner. The main distinction between the Gathic and Old Indic understanding of the function of the poet is that in the former, one individual, Zarathushtra, with the patronymic Spitama, is named as the recipient of a vision of the order inherent in the universe – 'things as they are' – whereas in the latter tradition, revelation of reality is bestowed on nameless, timeless sages (*rishis*).

The two language groups also retained similar terms for the act of worship (Av. *yasna*, OI *yajna*), and the implements and constituents of that worship, including the preparation and offering of an efficacious plant (Av. *haoma*, OI *soma*) that grows in the mountains and is believed to descend to earth from a mythical region. Both groups maintained the practice of offering proper fuel to the fire contained in fire-holders placed within a ritual enclosure, strewn with *baresman* (MP *barsom*) or *barhis* respectively.

c. Ritual or Not?

Some of these elements continued in later Zoroastrianism, but it is impossible to know how they relate to the original function of the *Gathas*. Both Zoroastrians and non-Zoroastrian scholars take diverse approaches to this quandary. Zoroastrians regard the *Gathas* as offering a powerful new ethical message in the form of the sustenance of *asha* against the forces of chaos and deceit. Some see this upholding of *asha* as taking place within the established context of a ritual performance that prefigured the structure and purpose of the later *Yasna*, the daily liturgy. Others maintain that the *Gathas* refer only to the mental devotion and support of the auditors. The interpretation of 'worship' in a ritual sense does not, however, preclude an ethical and philosophical interpretation of the *Gathas*. Indeed, such a merging of the physical and metaphysical not only reflects the two dimensions of the corporeal and conceptual, but also allows for thoughts and words to be expressed in concrete deeds, including ritual.

The *Gathas* begin with a reference to the worshippers assembled together to praise Mazda (1.28.9), and retain the centrality of the emblem of fire, introducing a uniquely Iranian word, *atar*, for the fire which functions, like the *manthran*, to cross the space between the human and divine spheres. This concept is expounded in the Old Avestan liturgical text, the *Yasna Haptanghaiti* (Y 35–41), where *atar* is the means for worshippers to approach Ahura Mazda (YH 36.1, cf. 41.5). The composition of the 'seven sections' of the *Yasna Haptanghaiti* is anonymous, and although its language, themes and stylistic features are similar to the *Gathas*, its poetic form is different. The two types of composition seem to come from the same mindset, however, and in the 72-section arrangement of the *Yasna*, the *Yasna Haptanghaiti* is preserved at the center of the Gathic poems, almost as a kernel protected by an outer shell (see Appendix 3).[22]

Yasna Haptanghaiti is presented as a collective recitation to accompany a religious ceremony in which the focus is the veneration of Ahura Mazda and the good creations, in the hope that strength and sustenance will be granted to the worshippers. This unprecedented liturgical text appears to be centered around the preparation and consecration of a ritual offering to the waters, as intimated in the formulaic *apo at yazamaide* – 'We worship the waters' (YH 38.3). Such a ritual is now the culmination of the *Yasna* ceremony and is known as the *ab zohr*, deriving from the Avestan word for 'libation', *zaothra*.

The verbal root *zao*, 'to libate', also gives us a key example of the difficulty of translating the *Gathas*. The agent noun *zaotar* appears once in the *Gathas* in reference to one who is 'upright (*arezush*) according to *Asha*' (1.33.6). This *zaotar* is sometimes translated as 'priest' in the sense of 'one who performs religious ceremonies', or as 'one who offers libations', such as the juice extraction from the *haoma*.[23]

The decision as to where the *Gathas* stand on ritual, particularly with regard to sacrifice, remains a source of debate. Although the *Gathas* and *Yasna Haptanghaiti* enjoin the care and protection of the cow, contemporary Old Indic references provide evidence of animal sacrifice in both the pre-Gathic period and in Indo-Aryan praxis; subsequent Young Avestan, Old Persian and Middle Persian texts attest its place in the post-Gathic period. The interpretation of possible references to elements of ritual in the *Gathas* is inconclusive. For instance, the *Gathas* do not mention the plant *haoma*, although the epithet *duraosha*, which is used exclusively of *haoma* in the Young Avesta, is referred to in conjunction with usage by corrupt *kavis* (1.32.14). This, and another obscure reference to intoxication (3.48.10), has led many to assume that the practice of using *haoma* was castigated altogether. But in the later Avesta, *haoma* is recognized as an integral part of the liturgical and mythical schema, receiving many positive epithets, and identified as an element praised by Zarathushtra (Y 9.16). As many scholars have pointed out, it is curious that followers of the Gathic teachings would retain, or reintroduce, a practice into the liturgy that was so obviously criticized in the *Gathas*, while the *Gathas* themselves formed the core of that liturgy (*Yasna*). Discussion concerning the original botanical identity of *haoma* continues. Nowadays, Zoroastrians in both Iran and India use *ephedra*, a twiggy flowering plant, as the *haoma* (MP *hom*) in their liturgy, or sometimes the juice of a few grains of pomegranate or crushed pomegranate leaves.

d. Original Gathic Themes

1. FIRST THINGS: COSMOLOGY

Despite similarities in Old Indic and Old Avestan terms used to refer to ritual activities, a divergence of cosmology is clear from the earliest stages of the two traditions. Although the notion of sustaining cosmic order, expressed in the terms *Rta* and *Asha* respectively, is central to both ideologies, the *Gathas* introduce the construct of a vertical separation between the world of living beings, who sustain and strengthen order in the cosmos, and those who are ruled by the principles of chaos and deception. The *Gathas* reflect a worldview in which both the conceptual and material spheres of existence are part of the realm of the supreme, creative agency, Ahura Mazda. One Gathic passage (2.44.3–7) delineates Ahura Mazda's generation of the universe within the framework of a series of questions about how the various components of the material world came into being: first *asha*; then the course of the sun and stars, and the cycle of the moon; the earth below and the sky above; the waters and plants; the winds and clouds; good thought (*vohu manah*); light and darkness, sleep and wakefulness, and the passage of the day through dawn, midday and evening; devotion (*armaiti*); the milk-producing cow; the son for the father. This cosmogony is reiterated in the *Yasna Haptanghaiti*, where Ahura Mazda is worshipped as the one who creates (or 'sets in place') the cow, *asha*, the waters and the plants, the lights and the earth, and 'all that is good' (YH 37.1). The cow is the prototype for all animal creation, each of which has a soul (YH 39.1–2).

Such outlines provide an early road map of the order in the universe, and form the basis for a later systematized cosmological schema. The perpetuation of this ordered existence has been promoted for centuries by Zoroastrians through seasonal festivals, the celebration of events in the human life cycle, and the daily recognition of the cosmic order inherent in the rising of the sun and the life-giving light created by Ahura Mazda (cf. 2.43.16). Each recited prayer to Ahura Mazda is made facing a source of illumination of some kind, particularly fire or the sun, and embodies this orderly arrangement in poetic form. Every Zoroastrian ritual is enveloped by such sacred words.

2. ETHICS

Although the constituents of the ordered existence are essentially good and growing, they are constantly challenged. There is reference to an initial destruction of the material world by one of 'bad preference' (2.45.1). Gathic cosmogony introduces the classification of activity in the two spheres as either 'good' or 'bad' inspirations or impulses (*manyu*), which have co-existed from the beginning. This tension is expressed as the division between that which is incremental or beneficent (*spenta*) and good (*vohu*), and that which is detrimental (*angra*) and bad (*aka*). The separation is most clearly conveyed through the notion that the two impulses do not accord at any level of thought, word, action or spiritual understanding (2.45.2). One impulse brings life, the other not-life (*ajyaiti*: 1.30.4). Since it lies within a human being's ability to choose between the two, the split structure of the universe is connected with the moral duty of the individual. The Gathic presentation of *asha* is of 'rightness' as concrete and knowable – that is, as moral order. The individual is encouraged always to choose that which is good in terms of thought, word and action (1.30.2). This choice is encapsulated in the trifold ethic expressed as *humata, hukhta, hvareshta* – 'good thoughts, good words, good deeds' (YH 36.5, 35.2), which remains a seminal *manthra* for Zoroastrians.

Asha is the operational principle of the beneficent path. This term is often translated as 'truth', although in the *Gathas* it is not referred to in terms of a spoken truth, but is used in the sense of that which is real. To adhere to *asha* – to be an *ashavan* – does, however, involve speaking straight and moving on the straight path motivated by having *xratu*, 'wisdom', or *huxratu*, 'good wisdom'.[24] The good thoughts, words and actions of the *ashavan* lead to blessings, increase, peace, wholeness and continuity of life for the individual, the community, and the land.[25] In pursuing this course, the *ashavan* is emulating the increase-producing activity of Ahura Mazda, who brings benefit to the highest degree, expressed in the epithet *spento.tema*, 'most beneficial'.[26]

Respect for and protection of the material creation of Ahura Mazda is an integral dimension of this approach. Both the *Ahuna Vairya* prayer and the *Yasna Haptanghaiti* begin with a veneration of the entire conceptual and corporeal existence. The latter indicates that, although the actions performed as part of the liturgy were particularly for the beneficial provision of peace and pasturage for the cow (YH 35.1, 4), the whole of creation is good (YH 37.1). Young Avestan texts record offerings made to flowing waters and rules to prevent the waters from being polluted (e.g. Vd 5.15–20). This care for the elements, reiterated in internal and external sources from the Achaemenid period onwards, forms part of Zoroastrian eco-awareness today.

The relationship between the *ashavan* and Ahura Mazda is presented as one of dependence, as of the poor on a protector, or a flock of sheep (or worshippers) on a pastor.[27] The word for 'poor' (*drigu*) frames the *Gathas*, appearing in the closing line of the *Ahuna Vairya* prayer, which precedes the first *Gatha*, and again in the closing stanza of the last *Gatha*.[28] In both passages, the name *Mazda* appears, so these two concepts bookend the *Gathas* like supportive pillars. Some post-Avestan cognates of *drigu* expand its meaning to refer to instances in which advocating for the poor is a noble act.[29]

In the *Gathas* the opposite of *asha* is not a simple negation, such as is the case with Rig Vedic *anrta*. The contrary ethos to *asha* is *druj* – the deception that brings chaos to the good, ordered creations of Ahura Mazda (2.45.4). *Druj* confuses the true nature of the working of the world, so that one is unable to make the right choices, as did the *daevas*, the unnamed 'false or erroneous gods', who, in confusion, made bad choices in opposition to *asha*.[30] *Druj* is usually translated as 'the Lie' in the sense of a deception or a misrepresentation of reality. The one who follows *druj* – the *dregvant* – chooses evil thoughts, words and actions (1.32.5). The negative qualities of cruelty, violence, ill treatment, acts of wrath and repression perpetuated by the *dregvant* are identified as *daevic* in the *Gathas*. In later texts, *druj* is identified as the principle that rules in the domain of *Angra Mainyu*, the 'evil/hostile/destructive spirit/inspiration'. The word *daeva* is from the same Indo-European root as Old Indic *deva* used of some of the gods in the *Rig Veda*, and as the Latin *deus*. Criticism of the *daevas* in the *Gathas* seems to mark a move away from certain negative rituals and behaviors associated with them, and towards the elevation of Ahura Mazda as Supreme Being (1.32.3–5).

3. THE *AMESHA SPENTAS*

The idea that the activity of the *ashavan*, in support of the creative work of Ahura Mazda, can reinvigorate the world in the here and now has wider implications. The *Gathas* introduce the notion that the *ashavan* should further certain qualities besides *asha* that are associated with promoting the best existence, such as good thought (*vohu manah*) and humble devotion (*armaiti*). *Armaiti* as 'right mindfulness' is contrasted with *taromaiti*, 'arrogance'. *Asha*, *vohu manah* and *armaiti* often occur together in the *Gathas*, where they seem to be in relationship with Ahura Mazda, as children to a parent.[31] This leads to the consideration that these may be separate 'entities', which, along with other abstract concepts found in the *Gathas*, form part of a complex web of interrelationship with Ahura Mazda. Other abstract concepts in this web include: *sraosha* ('readiness to listen'); *ashi* ('reward'); *airyaman* ('friendship'); and perhaps also *daena* ('[religious] insight'). The *Gathas* refer to *ahuras* in the plural, supporting this notion of a wider group who share the 'lordship' of Ahura Mazda.[32] These abstract concepts are, however, presented more like emanations of Ahura Mazda, deriving, as it were, from the same light, rather than from hypostatized entities.

At this point the group is not a fixed number, nor are they associated with particular elements in the material world, although fire is said to derive its strength (*aogah*) from *asha*,[33] and *armaiti* is described as giving substance to *asha*, benefitting the earth and its inhabitants.[34] A Gathic pairing of waters and plants in correspondence with the attributes of 'wholeness' (*haurvatat*) and 'immortality' (*ameretat*), respectively (4.51.7), seems to be an incipient form of a more concrete relationship that is further developed in later texts. In *Yasna Haptanghaiti*, *asha* is particularly associated with the celestial lights (37.4), and *armaiti* with the firm earth (38.1). The declaration of the worshippers that they are on the side of the cow seems to have a parallel in the declaration of the *amesha spentas* ('the beneficent immortals') that they are on the side of good thought (*vohu manah*).[35]

The phrase *amesha spentas* is not found in the *Gathas*, but does appear twice in *Yasna Haptanghaiti* in inverted order (YH 37.4, 39.3). There its use is open-ended and does not relate to the clearly-defined group of the later Avesta. Although there are explicit Young Avestan references to seven *amesha spentas*, only six are named, since Ahura Mazda is mentioned separately. By this stage, the six entities are listed in order of frequency of their appearance in the Old Avesta, and are more closely interrelated with elements of the good creation:

asha vahishta (best *asha*) is associated with celestial light/fire

vohu manah ('good thought') with living beings, especially the cow

xshathra vairya ('deserved/desired rule' or 'command') with the sky, which is described as surrounding the world like an egg (Yt 13.2)

armaiti ('devotion') with the earth

haurvatat ('wholeness') with water

ameretat ('continuity of life') with plants.

Later, Ahura Mazda is represented by his creative force, *spenta mainyu* – the 'beneficent inspiration/spirit'. In the *Gathas*, *spenta manyu* seems to belong to Ahura Mazda in the sense of an inner force, whereas in the *yashts*, *spenta mainyu* is depicted as more of a separate power belonging to both Ahura Mazda and also to humanity. In a parallel theological development, so the contrary form and function of *angra mainyu*, the 'destructive spirit/inspiration', begins to take shape.[36]

Such a system of ethical and cosmological opposition, as posited by the ancient Iranians, is a constant of Zoroastrian thought in all periods, and also resonates with Europeans from Aristotle and Plutarch, down to Voltaire and Nietzsche.

4. LAST THINGS

INDIVIDUAL ENDINGS

The attributes associated with *asha/druj* and the qualities nurtured by the *ashavan/dregvant* seem to relate to a nascent eschatology in the *Gathas*. Gathic references to a place of reckoning for humans indicate a focus on individual eschatology: at the Crossing-place of the Account-Keeper (*chinvat peretu*), the thoughts, words and behavior of each 'breath soul' (*urvan*) are tallied[37]; the good receive a good reward, but the bad come to a bad end.[38] Fire is an index of reward or punishment, and so, it seems, is molten metal,[39] but the connection is not clear. The rewards in store for the individual who lives a life based on good thought, words and deeds relate to the 'house of song' (*garo.demana*[40]), 'the house of good thought', and the 'best things',[41] which await the *ashavan*. The Gathic word for 'the best', *vahishta*, is not only the descriptive epithet for *asha*, but is also found in phrases such as the 'best thought' (1.30.4). The concept of reaching for that which is superlatively good becomes part of the Young Avestan understanding of the 'best existence' (*vahishta ahu*) for the *ashavans*, which is located beyond the stars, moon, sun and endless lights.[42] The Middle Persian term *vahisht* refers to a physical paradise, a meaning that continues in New Persian *behesht*. In the *Gathas*, the word for 'existence' – *ahu* – is also linked with the adjective *frasha* ('perfect' or 'wonderful'), in the context of petitioning Mazda to help make the world pristine. The notion of the Mazda-worshipper as part of this restorative process is embodied in the term *ahum.bish* – 'the healer of existence'.[43]

In contrast, the path taken by the *dregvant* – that of bad action, bad words, bad religious insight (*daena*) and thoughts[44] – leads to a reserved spot 'in the house of deceit' (*drujo.demana*), where the food is also bad![45] The road to this unpalatable situation follows a descent into destruction, decline and darkness,[46] culminating in a state described as 'the worst existence' where the song is one of lamentation.[47]

UNIVERSAL ENDING

At a universal level, the principle of *asha* permeates the entirety of creation, and is embodied in the good things of the world, in life itself. The phrase *astvat ashem* (2.43.16) can be translated as 'May *asha* have bones/become corporeal.' In context, the wish is for *asha* to be animated and strengthened through the energy of the offerings of the worshipper, so that it has a material impact. The straight path of the *ashavan* leads, then, not just to individual growth and increase, but also to the reinvigoration and healing of the natural world.[48] The concept of 'wholeness' or 'completion' (*haurvatat*) always appears alongside that of 'continuity of life' (*ameretat*) in the *Gathas*.[49] These two qualities represent the ultimate goal of all existence: the state of completion and imperishability that occurs with the restoration of creation – including humanity – to its original, wonderful state.

The Gathic construct is of a moment marking the beginning of creation and an end that does not involve complete conflagration and rebirth from the ashes, but instead final renewal. Such a model is a novel combination of the cyclical dialectic of life, death and rebirth (a concept that develops further within the Indo-Aryan setting) with the linear notion of an end point. The idea of 'last things' is prevalent throughout the *Gathas*, in the use of the adjectives *apara* and *apema*, meaning 'later/future' and 'last/end' respectively. It is expressed in terms of the moment of completion of a horse race,[50] in which one hurtles towards the finish line, just as the world moves inexorably towards its own final 'turning point' (*urwaesa*: 2.43.5). The end-time revisits the beginning in a kind of elliptical model, in which the first antipodal point is the moment at which the initial destruction of the world occurred, and the facing antipodal point is the moment at which the struggle between good and evil received a new impetus – that is, with the advent of Zarathushtra[51] (see Fig. 4). Reference to an initial act of devastation, and subsequent detriment, is balanced by the introduction of the concept that the world will be made *frasha* again, and is even now moving towards that moment (1.30.9, 1.34.15). This notion of a circle within which cosmic activity occurs is incorporated into the use of the 'turning-point' terminology (MP *urwis*) for the ritual space, in which the celebrants and implements of the *Yasna* are arranged.

The Avestan concept of *frasho.kereti* as a final 'miraculous' revitalization of the cosmos is not clearly delineated, but the Gathic idea of a healing of the world contains the seeds of a collective and universal eschatology that is more fully developed in Young Avestan and then Middle Persian literature.

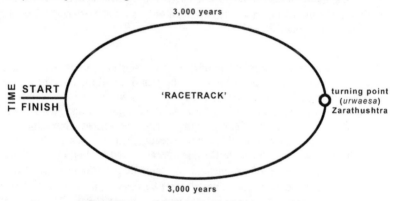

Fig. 4. Diagram of the 'three times' and the 'turning point'.

This representation of the cosmic cycle recalls the way that the kusti is tied around the waist, with a knot in the front and one in the back. The kusti is composed of 72 strands of wool, which are now interpreted as referring to the 72 sections of the Yasna. The action of tying and retying the thread is intended to regenerate the cosmos, as is the priestly performance of the Yasna.[52]

THE SAOSHYANT

Another Old Avestan concept that has central significance within a later, developed eschatological schema, is that of the *saoshyant*, a word which appears six times in the *Gathas*. The term comes from the future participle of the root *su*, meaning 'to swell', 'to energize' or 'to be strong'. We have seen this root before in the adjective *spenta*, meaning 'beneficent' or 'bringing increase'. The title *saoshyant* refers, then, to 'one who will be strong'. Some scholars translate it in the sense of 'one who will revitalize'.[53] The future work of this figure may be construed in broad general terms, referring to anyone whose actions are motivated by good thought and *asha*, and who opposes the forces of cruelty and violence.[54] When the word appears in the singular, it could be an oblique reference to Zarathushtra,[55] but the fact that it occurs in the plural three times indicates the possibility of several future benefactors of the religion.[56] Some regard the function of the *saoshyant* as being technical, possibly ritualistic. The term has also been translated as 'redeemer' or 'savior', which has Christian overtones, but which is not entirely discordant with the way in which the term develops in later Avesta and then Middle Persian texts. These include mention of a single *saoshyant* who will benefit the whole corporeal world, bringing about the final defeat of evil. The use of the future participle indicates an eschatological sense already in the *Gathas*.

5. UPHOLDING *ASHA* IN THE YOUNG AVESTA

Young Avestan texts such as the *Videvdad* contain much material relating to the development of what becomes mainstream theology and praxis in later times. Such material is sometimes dismissed as a later accretion to the religion, or as reintroducing an earlier Indo-Iranian polytheism. The existence of a collection of 21 Young Avestan 'hymns of praise' or *yashts*,[57] which are similar in meter and form to archaic Old Indic poetry, do introduce new elements into the religion – particularly in their elevation of 'beings worthy of worship' (Av. *yazatas*), such as Mithra, Anahita and Tishtrya – while still upholding the supreme status of Ahura Mazda. The *yashts* evolved within Old Iranian oral culture, and many of their themes recur in Old Persian inscriptions. Some of the information in the *yashts* acts as a textual bridge between the Old Avesta and the mythology of the ancient Iranians. Most of the *yazatas* to whom the *yashts* are dedicated are also commemorated in the day-names of the Avestan calendar, which were cited by Greek astronomers in Cappadocia in the Achaemenid period. A common element of the *yashts* is the propitiation of the *yazatas* to ensure material blessings. Such is the case, for example, with Mithra, who, when properly invoked, conducts the worshipper's prayers to Ahura Mazda.

e. Mithra

Mihr Yasht is a long hymn addressed to Mithra, who (as Mitra) also appears in the Vedic pantheon. The word *mithra* does not appear in the singular in the *Gathas*, so it cannot be claimed that there is a direct rejection – or acceptance – of Mithra as *yazata*. Mithra means *contract* – that which is binding in a legal sense – and also *ally*: *bond* is a translation that covers both concepts. *Mihr Yasht* emphasizes Mithra's role as protector and sustainer of the one who keeps the contract. He is an upholder of the principle of *asha* and defender of those who reject *druj*, acting as a judge in rooting out those who break their bond and smashing them with his mace.[58] In *Mihr Yasht*, Mithra rises beyond

Mt. Hara and travels across the sky before the sun, surveying the entire material world from the mountaintops with 10,000 eyes.[59] Mithra is therefore intimately linked with the sun, the greatest natural illumination for both the conceptual and corporeal worlds, which Mithra protects from wrath, destruction and death.[60] The portrayal of Mithra as a mighty warrior on the side of *asha* against *druj* is echoed in the depiction of mortal heroic characters in the *yashts*, and is the manner in which Iranian champions continue to be described in Ferdowsi's recension of the national epic, the *Shah Nameh*, in the early eleventh century CE. In Young Avestan mythology, the conflict is also articulated as that between Iran and Turan, epitomized in battles with the 'Chionians'.[61]

f. *Videvdad*

The struggle between *asha* and *druj* is expressed both metaphysically and physically in *Videvdad*, which revisits the moment of vertical division of the cosmos several times. The word *Videvdad* (often referred to as *Vendidad*) means something like 'the law dispelling the *daevas*', and the whole text concerns identifying and pursuing the sources of evil. It begins with the account of the creation of good 'places and settlements' for Iranians by Ahura Mazda and their initial destruction by Angra Mainyu, who is hypostatized as a separate entity. The text continues with the narrative of the good rule of Yima lasting 900 years, and the threefold expansion of the earth, which was to be succeeded by terrible winters that would decimate life on earth. The next struggle occurs in the description of Zarathushtra's temptation by both the *druj* and Angra Mainyu, as head of the *daevas*, who now include some of the named gods of the *Rig Veda*.[62] Zarathushtra then asks how he can protect the world from the destructive forces of evil, and heal the material world and its inhabitants of the corruption already wrought. The answer consists in the performance of ritual liturgy and a nine-nights' purification (Vd 19.12–26).

Various references throughout *Videvdad*, supported by other passages in the *yashts*, delineate an early image of the mythical Iranian world, suggesting a coherent cosmology. Elements include the Vourukasha Sea, which is the gathering point of all waters, and where a tree of all species grows, which is elsewhere called the Saena tree.[63] *Videvdad* 21 pays homage to the cow as bringing increase; to the rains as bringing new water, new earth, new plants; to the sun which rises hig over Mt. Hara and makes light for living beings; to the moon which has the seed of cattle; and to the stars which hold the seed of the waters. Elsewhere, Mt. Hara is depicted as the primordial mountain, the first in the great mountain chain encircling the earth.[64] The notion of the moon safeguarding the seed of cattle is repeated in the hymn to the moon, *Mah Yasht*, which also refers to the primal 'lone' cow – *gav aevo.data*. The figure of a primordial mortal (*gaya maretan*) does not appear in *Videvdad*, but is found in *Yasht* 13.87 as the first *ashavan*. The final section of *Videvdad* circles back to the initial assault of Angra Mainyu on the good things created by Ahura Mazda, and narrates the devastation wrought by 99,999 diseases. *Airyaman*, the *yazata* of friendship – 'community unity' – is called upon to heal the diseases through a purification ritual. In a previous section, the prayer to *Airyaman* (the *Airyema Ishyo*) is recognized as an efficacious means of combating such threats (Vd 20.11–12). *Videvdad* ends, then, with both the healing of the world and the healing of humankind.

The purity regulations in the central section of the *Videvdad* reflect the understanding of a material division between 'good' and 'evil'. Discussions about how to dispose of 'dead matter' (*nasu*) so as not to pollute the elements of the world, particularly water, fire or the *ashavan*, hinge on the distinction between that which brings growth and increase, and that which brings decay. In *Videvdad*, *nasu* has become hypostatized as a female demon, [*Druj*] *Nasush*, who pollutes the human body, so that it constantly produces dead matter in the form of effluent such as saliva, mucus and women's menses. Cuttings of hair and fingernails are also considered as dead matter (Vd 17), and the body of a corpse is the most polluting of all. The *ashavan* is encouraged always to be on the alert not to let such dead matter near the good creations, and this is why one should not urinate or spit into streams.[65] A female in menses is to isolate herself in a place removed from people, fire and water (Vd 16). Pollution by such dead matter can be removed by cleansing first with bull's urine and then water (Vd 19.20–5).[66] The wearing of the *kusti* is advocated for men and women over 15 years of age as a barrier against the onslaught of evil at both material and conceptual levels (Vd 18.54–9).

Practical action to avert evil includes the killing of 'noxious creatures' (*xrafstra*) considered to be the miscreations of Angra Mainyu,[67] and the building of enclosures (Av. *pairidaeza*) on arid, barren land, in order to contain the pollution of those who have purposely not handled a corpse correctly.[68] The latter passage is followed by injunctions to destroy the abodes of those who adhere to evil, and to sow the seeds of edible plants, to irrigate dry land and to drain that which is marshy – in other words, to make unproductive land fertile once more.

g. Endings in the Young Avesta

1. THE END OF THE ROAD

In *Videvdad*, Mithra is named as one of the judges of the souls of the deceased as they arrive at the Chinvat crossing (Vd 19.28–9). Both *Videvdad* and *Hadokht Nask* expand upon the concept of a pathway leading the soul to a point of judgment, and from there to reward or punishment. These accounts are framed within the context of Zarathushtra asking Ahura Mazda an ultimate question concerning what happens when we die.[69] The soul of the *ashavan* is described as crossing over with the support of a strong, beautiful woman accompanied by dogs, and entering into the abode of Ahura Mazda and the *amesha spentas* (Vd 19.30). This place is called by the Gathic term, the 'House of Song' or the 'Endless Lights' (*anagra raoca*[70]). The woman is identified as the totality of the thoughts, words and deeds – the hypostatized *daena* – of the individual,[71] and the dogs are numbered as two.[72]

Hadokht Nask includes listening to the *Gathas*, and making offerings to the good waters and to fire among the good works of the *ashavan*. Whereas the soul of the *ashavan* is met by a sweet-smelling, southerly breeze as it journeys towards the bridge, the soul of the *dregvant* is met by a stinking north wind. The North, which is on the left as one faces the rising sun in the East, is the source of evil in much Indo-European mythology, hence the subsequent usage of the Latin word for 'left' – *sinister*. The soul of the *ashavan* reaches the Endless Lights by three steps, corresponding to good thought, good speech and good deeds. In contrast, the *dregvant*'s three steps lead to Endless Darkness (*anagra temah*[73]). These states are not so much an upwards or downwards movement, as a journey towards or away from the light.

2. THE *SAOSHYANT*

Young Avestan literature identifies a plurality of *saoshyants*: (successful) priests (Yt 14.1); those who venerate *Haoma* (Y 9.2); those who fight against the 'Lie' (Y 61.5) and against the enemies of the Iranians (Yt 13.38). But *Farvardin Yasht* names three distinct *saoshyants*, the last of whom is called *Astvat-ereta* – 'the one through whom *Asha* has bones/becomes corporeal' (Yt 13.128–9). The *Zamyad Yasht* depicts a single heroic *saoshyant* with this name, who arises out of the Sea Kansaoya brandishing the same weapon that other heroes before him had wielded, particularly Thraetaona (MP Feridun) when he slew the giant dragon (Yt 19.92f.; also Vd 19.5). The Haetumant (Helmand) river flows into this sea,[74] now identified as Lake Hamun in Sistan. This could indicate that the locus for the *yashts* at this stage is in this part of eastern Iran.

The name *Astvat-ereta* echoes the Gathic phrase *astvat ashem*, but is here used to signify a permanent state. His function is to destroy demons until the malice of *daevas* and humans is no more, and evil thoughts, words and deeds are overcome.[75] One of the benefits that the expected *saoshyant* will bring, then, is the end of physical destruction and decay so that the whole material existence will be 'made indestructible'.[76] The concept of bodily resurrection is attested in a passage that speaks of this moment as a time when the dead will rise and be made imperishable through the reviving activity of the *saoshyant* (Yt 19.89). This passage is the most detailed Young Avestan outline of events concerning the renovation of the world. It points to the existence of a developed, complete schema centuries before the Sasanian period, when such universal eschatological ideas were well established.

3. YIMA

This later development of the *saoshyant* as one who ushers in a time of growth and prosperity is prefigured by Yima, a character from ancient mythology, who reverberates through centuries of Iranian storytelling. Yima is paralleled with Old Indic Yama in many ways. In the *Rig Veda*, Yama is the first mortal and the first to die, who then becomes the ruler of the world of the dead. The Iranian narrative develops in a different direction, although Yima remains connected with an underground existence. In *Videvdad* 2, Yima is the first mortal to converse with Ahura Mazda, and to have been shown religious insight (*daena*). Yima declares that he is not prepared to further the *daena* in the material world, but does accept the task of protecting all living things (Vd 2.1–5). Yima is depicted as ruling the world in a golden era, during which there was neither heat nor cold, old age or death (Yt 19.33), and as having the power to free people and animals from death, and plants and rivers from drought (Y 9.4, 5). He also provides humans with imperishable food (Yt 15.16) and is described as the 'good shepherd' (Vd 2.2). His epithet is *xshaeta*, the 'radiant one' (Y 9.4), who glows with divine fortune or glory (Av. *xwarenah*). In *Zamyad Yasht*, the *xwarenah* is described as 'the mighty, gleaming glory created by Mazda' (Yt 19.54). *Yima Xshaeta* becomes 'Jamshid' in Middle Persian.

At some point in each account, however, Yima loses his way, and the balance in which he has held the world swings towards the *daevas*. The *Gathas* allude to some fault (*aenah*; Y 32.8), possibly of violence, on the part of Yima, but it is unclear what this was. *Zamyad Yasht* describes the sin in terms of a lie entering the mind of Yima, at which point the *xwarenah* flies away in the form of a bird.[77] In *Videvdad*, no fault is attributed to Yima, but at the behest of Ahura Mazda, he withdraws to an underground enclosure – a *vara* – supplied with its own light and flowing water, in order to survive the bitter winter that will afflict the material existence following his rule. Yima is instructed to gather the best animals, plants and humans in couples to populate the *vara* and to preserve the world of the living (Vd 2.27–8). Later eschatology paralleled Yima's regenerative activity with that of the *saoshyants*, explaining that the people and animals from the *vara* will repopulate the world after a winter lasting three years (Bd 33.30).

In the *Hom Yasht*, both Yima and his father stay at 15 years old – considered to be the ideal age![78] Yima remains one of the great heroes of Iranian tradition, embodying the ideal of kingly power. His role is crucial to the establishment, sustenance and ultimate victory of the rule of Ahura Mazda in the created world, and as such he is closely associated with mythology relating to *Nav Ruz* (New Year), a festival which itself prefigures the time when the world will be 'made wonderful'.

4. *FRAVASHIS*

Also associated with the world of the dead, and particularly venerated at the time of *Nav Ruz*, are the *fravashis*, who are thought to be efficacious on behalf of the living. The concept of *fravashi* may be related to Old Indic *pitaras*, the 'fathers', a collective term for the souls of the departed. The *fravashis* pre-existed material creation before the birth of humanity, however, and post-exist the individual after death. The *Farvardin Yasht*, addressed to the *fravashis* of the *ashavans*[79] from the primal human (*gaya maretan*) to the victorious *saoshyant*, begins by declaring the *fravashis'* aid to Ahura Mazda at the creation of the world, and of their subsequent protection, particularly through the formation of new 'sons in the womb' to follow the way first mapped by Zarathushtra under the guidance of Ahura Mazda (Yt 13.1–12, 87–91). Although each man and woman has a *fravashi*, they are spoken of collectively as feminine-gendered beings, who fly to defend the material world against assault from evil (Yt 13.45–9, 67–70). The *fra+var* compound in the word (meaning 'to choose for') implies that the *fravashis* always choose for the good, on the side of Ahura Mazda.

In the past, this description often led Europeans to interpret the *fravashi* as a protective spirit along the lines of a guardian angel. This terminology was then adopted by Zoroastrians so that by 1884, one Parsi author referred to the *fravashi* as 'the presiding angel' that 'watches not only over the living, but also over the dead and the still unborn'.[80]

Chapter II

The Ancient Persians: Truth-Tellers and Paradise-Builders

'For this reason Ahura Mazda bore me aid,

as well as the other gods who are,

because I did not side with the Evil one [and] I was not a liar,

I did nothing crooked, neither I nor my family.

I wandered in straightness.'

Darius (DB 4.61–5)[1]

'And when the [Persian] boy reaches fourteen years he is taken over by the royal tutors.... The first of
these teaches him the magian lore of Zoroaster son of Horomazes; and that is the worship of the gods....
The justest teaches him to be truthful all his life long.'

Pseudo-Plato Alcibiades 1.121e[2]

I do not intend here to review the entire socio-political history of the 200-year
rule of the Achaemenids (c. 550–330 BCE),[3] but rather to consider the
fragments of evidence for the form of religious belief and practice at that
time, and whether it can be defined as 'Zoroastrian'. Most historical texts on
the Achaemenids do not dwell on trying to define their religion. This is partly
because scholars feel that to describe the Ancient Persians as 'Zoroastrian'
assumes not only that we know much more about the religion of the former
than we actually do, but also that we have a clearly-defined understanding of
what constituted 'Zoroastrianism' at the time. The religion of the Ancient
Persians was a far remove from the state Zoroastrianism of late Sasanian
times. By the time of Darius I (522–486 BCE), the Persian worldview as
known from internal inscriptions and external sources exhibits many
similarities to that of the Avesta. Achaemenid religion, although not
replicating all of the concepts and expressions of the *Gathas* – for instance,
there is no mention of Zarathushtra in Old Persian inscriptions – displays a
close enough connection with the Old Avesta to be reasonably regarded as
part of evolving Zoroastrianism.[4] Whether the Ancient Persians were always
Zoroastrian, or became Zoroastrian early on, is a separate issue.

Sources

Assyrian references to Medes (*Madai*) and Persians (*Parsuwash*) begin with
an account of Shalmaneser III's campaigns in the region of Lake Urmia in
835 BCE, and in the annals of Tiglath-Pileser III (r. 744–727 BCE). The
domain of the Medes is usually assigned to western Iran, although
archeological sites there attributed to the Medes, such as Hamadan, have
provided nothing conclusive.[5] No documents in Median language have been
preserved, although many loanwords are found in Old Persian. There are no
references in the Avesta to the Medes, whom Herodotus claims were defeated
by Cyrus II, and who are mentioned on the Bisutun inscription as rebelling
against Darius I.

The Persians appear in later Assyrian accounts of subject peoples and of
battle campaigns, such as that at Halule on the Tigris in 691 BCE. By the time
they became an imperial power under Cyrus II in the mid-first millennium
BCE, the Persians had settled in the Elamite regions of south-western Iran.
Before the first Old Persian inscriptions were carved in around 521 BCE, the
earliest tangible evidence of Iranian ideology had found expression in the
monumental art and architecture of Cyrus II's palaces and gardens at
Pasargadae, and in the 'Cyrus cylinder'. These were followed by Darius I's
great rock inscription at Bisutun, the terraced palace complexes at Persepolis
and Susa, and iconography at other sites in greater Iran, such as Babylon,
Daskyleion in Anatolia and Erebuni in Armenia. Cylinder and stamp seals
along with thousands of Fortification Tablets from Persepolis (PFT), mostly
in Elamite, also provide internal perspectives into some of the religious
beliefs and practices of the first Iranian Empire. In many instances,
iconography also acts as visual text, illustrating some of the emblematic
motifs of the time. It must be noted, however, that much of this source
material concerns the ruling elite – kings, nobles, a few officials, priests and
even fewer women.

Herodotus (c. 485–425 BCE), a Greek-speaking Persian subject from
Halicarnassus in Asia Minor, is one of our major sources of information about
the beliefs and practices of the Ancient Persians, which he compares to those
of the Greeks: again, the focus is largely on the practices of the elite. At the
time of the wars between the Persians and Greeks under Xerxes (492–479
BCE), Herodotus was still a child, but is thought to have gained much of his
information from those who took part in the campaigns on both sides. Other
contemporary Greeks from both Asia Minor and the mainland are also
important, if biased, sources of information about the Persians. The
designation 'Persia' is from the Greek form of Old Persian *Parsa*, and the
Greek 'Achaemenid' (*Histories* 3.75.1, 7.11.2) derives from the Persian

proper name *Haxamanish*, used in Darius' propaganda concerning his claim to the throne (DB 1.1.6). *Haxamanish* may mean 'one who has friend(s) in mind' or 'one who has the mind of an ally'. This name for the dynasty is not mentioned at all in the detailed genealogy on the Cyrus cylinder, one of our earliest sources concerning Cyrus, and is absent from subsequent Iranian histories, including the national epic, the *Shah Nameh*.

Contemporary external sources from Babylon and Egypt, including fifth-century Aramaic papyri from a military colony at Elephantine on the Nile, also provide useful information about Achaemenid ideology. Many of the Elephantine documents come from the Jewish community. After Cyrus II's conquest of Babylon in 539 BCE, some Jewish exiles chose to remain there under Persian rule, rather than return to Jerusalem, while others moved further into Persia itself, or to other parts of the Empire, rising to positions of prominence in the imperial court and in the Persian army. The Biblical books of Deutero-Isaiah, Ezra and Nehemiah – and to an extent Esther and Daniel – emerge from and reflect such settings, providing supportive material concerning the thought world of the Ancient Persians.

An Avestan Worldview?

Let us first approach what is known about the Ancient Persians from the perspective of discerning similarities with an Avestan worldview. What emerges from the internal evidence is an idea of the self-perception of Achaemenid rulers as being located at the center of the world of the Aryas, and at the zenith of Iranian history. The Persians seem to have been familiar with the Avestan image of the world in which Iran – as both land and people – held a central position. Their texts, however, are of a different literary genre and language than the Avestan compositions, which were not committed to writing until a thousand years later.

i. Avestan Names

Our earliest evidence for the Ancient Persians comes not from their own voice, but from non-Persian documents, such as a clay cylinder from the Assyrian capital, Nineveh, recording a tribute sent around 646 BCE to Ashurbanipal by 'Kurash, king of Parsumash'. This is the first reference to the name 'Cyrus', which is of uncertain etymology, but may refer to Cyrus I. Old Persian inscriptions relate that this Cyrus' younger cousin Arsama ('having the strength of a hero') gave one of his sons the name Vishtaspa (DB 1.4), whose grandson – a son of Darius I – was also named Vishtaspa. Vishtaspa is the name of Zarathushtra's supporter in the *Gathas*, portrayed as a defender of the faith in the Young Avesta. Herodotus uses the Greek form 'Hystaspes'. The Greek name of Cyrus II's eldest daughter (and Darius' queen), Atossa, is thought to be a version of another eastern Iranian name, 'Hutaosha', the name of Vishtaspa's wife (Yt 9.26 and Yt 15.36). These names do not continue in western Iran beyond the Achaemenid period. According to Thucydides, one of Darius I's grandsons through Vishtaspa was called Pissuthnes, which could be the Greek form of *Pishishyaothna*, a son of Vishtaspa, whose *fravashi* is invoked in Yt 13.103. Such examples appear to place the Achaemenids within the framework of an Avestan narrative from an early period.

Other names of members of the Achaemenid dynasty reflect a similar ethic to that of the *Gathas*. For instance, *Daraya-vahu* (Darius) means 'holding the good', and echoes the Gathic strophe *darayat vahishtem mano* (1.31.7), which translates as 'he has upheld the very best thought'. *Arta-Xsaça* (Artaxerxes) means 'he whose reign is through *Asha*', and may reflect the Gathic strophe *aogo data asha xshathremca* – 'give strength and power according to *asha*' (1.29.10). Early examples of names relating to Avestan religion are also found in Aramaic documents from around the fifth century BCE, which mention such Iranian names as Spantadata (Av. *spento.data*); Artaxwant (Av. *ashavan*); Atarfarna ('the glory of fire'); and Tiripata ('protected by Tishtrya'). There is no Old Persian etymological equivalent of the Avestan term *yazata*, which seems to be replaced with an Old Iranian *Baga*, meaning originally 'portion', and then hypostatized as 'the one who apportions (good things)'.[6] Mazdayasna, Bagazushta ('beloved by God') and Bagapata ('protected by God') occur in Elamite, Aramaic and Babylonian tablets, and the last appears also in Greek sources. Mazdadata, Tiridata ('given by Tishtrya'), and Zhamaspa (Av. *Jamaspa*[7]) are attested in multiple sources.

Mithra was also a common component of names, particularly in the form Mithradata ('given by Mithra'), which is found in the Aramaic papyri and in the Biblical book of Ezra as Mithredath (*Ezra* 1.8). This appellation continues throughout the Achaemenid period. It is the name of Darius III's son-in-law, and appears in Greek texts as the name of a man who betrayed his father, Ariobarzanes;[8] of the Persian soldier who killed Cyrus the Younger;[9] and of the Persian who commissioned Silanion to sculpt a statue of Plato, which was placed in the Academy in Athens in 370 BCE.[10] Other Mithra-prefixed names attest to the popularity of this *yazata*, such as Mithrayazna ('who worships Mithra') and Mitrabarzana ('high Mithra'). Focus on the concept of *asha* as a component of the Achaemenid ethic may be seen in the use of *arta* prefix names, such as Artapata ('protected by Arta'), Artazushta ('beloved by Arta') and Artadata ('given by Arta'). The personal name *Uhumana* appears in a Babylonian legal text from the time of Darius II (423–404 BCE), and is attested earlier in an Elamite *Maumanna* on tablets from Persepolis.[11] These seem to reflect the Avestan *Vohu Manah*, as does the name 'Eumanes', the father of Sisines, a Persian agent of Darius III.[12] Elamite inscriptions also refer to a *Narishanka* as a being who receives material offerings (PFT 1960: 3–4). This seems to relate to the Avestan *yazata* Nairyosangha, an intermediary between the divine and the mundane, linked with *atar*.

Some of the Elamite texts also appear to incorporate an Avestan word *zruwan* into personal names. As a common noun, *zruwan* means 'time'. During the Achaemenid period, it is thought that the concept of time may have morphed into a separate entity, *Zurvan*, perhaps stimulated by Babylonian astrological ideas or Greek mythology of Kronos ('Time') as the father of Zeus and Hades. The concept of 'limitless' or 'infinite' time (Av. *zruwan akarana*) is referred to several times in *Videvdad* 19, where it is associated with the sphere of creation. 'Long time' (*zruwan darega*) – suggesting limited time – is referred to in the *yashts*.[13] Middle Persian cosmological texts systematize the division of time into that which was limited, but of long duration, and that which was without end.

ii. Avestan Calendar

An early 360-day luni-solar calendar is recorded by Greek authors in reference to the Persian predilection for that number as tribute payment of white horses or royal concubines, numbering one for each day in the year.[14] This calendar was then expanded by five epagomenal days into an official religious calendar, which replaced local calendars by the early fifth century BCE, when Greek astronomical texts provide evidence of it operating in Cappadocia. The 12 months were named after *amesha spentas* and other *yazatas*, including Tishtrya and Mithra. The *yasht* to Tishtrya (Yt 8) associates this *yazata* with the waters, particularly the rainfall that wards off drought. In the Achaemenid period, Tishtrya was associated with the star Sirius.[15] The Avestan calendar continued to function in the region until at least the fourth century CE. The Armenian calendar is based on a similar system, and also includes some Iranian month names of Old Persian origin.

The name of the seventh month in the Avestan calendar from Cappadocia is *Mithre*. Greek accounts from the fourth century BCE onwards on indicate an official celebration in honor of Mithra.[16] Strabo later calls this event *Mithrakana* (11.14.9). Another month on the Cappadocian calendar is *Artana*, relating to the Avestan term for the *fravashis* of the *ashavans* (*ashaunam fravashinam*), and referring to March/April. Records from Persepolis inform us that the Ancient Persians made offerings to the *fravashis* of the *ashavans*, referred to in Elamite as *Irtana-fruiritish*.[17]

Allusion to an Achaemenid religious festival taking place at this time of year may be found in the Septuagint translation of the Biblical book of Esther, where the Greek term for Purim is *Phrouraia*, from *phroura*, meaning 'vigil'. This is close in form to *Fravardigan* – the festival celebrating the *fravashis* – which contracted to *frordigan* in popular speech by Sasanian times.[18] The festival of Purim takes place in the last month of the Hebrew calendar, and the Iranian festival of *Fravardigan* is celebrated during the last ten days of the year, ending with *Nav Ruz* at the spring equinox. At Persepolis, carved stone friezes of men bearing flowers may illustrate a ritual commemorating the *fravashis* of the dead preceding the celebration of *Nav Ruz*.[19]

iii. Ancient Persian Cosmology

Although we do not know for sure that the Ancient Persians celebrated *Nav Ruz* with gift-giving and ritual at Persepolis, we do know that they had a clear-cut sense of their own place in the cycle of the cosmos. Eighteen Old Persian inscriptions begin with an account of the creation of the world.[20] Darius lauds Ahura Mazda (OP *Auramazda*) as 'the great god' (*baga vazrka*) who established the cosmos, setting in place the earth, the sky and humankind, and making happiness for humanity (DE 1–11, DNa 1–8). The phrasing of the formula 'this earth and that sky' parallels that of the Young Avesta (Yt 13.153), as does the notion that happiness is created for humans by Ahura Mazda (Visp. 7.3).[21] The king's mandate is to rule the earth in wisdom (OP *xrathu*) as Ahura Mazda's agent, maintaining order, and promoting the happiness, health and perfection (*frasha*) for the kingdom as a whole (DNb 1– 5). The word for 'happiness' (*shiyati*) incorporates the notion of peace, abundance and well-being, such as prevail when the rule of Ahura Mazda predominates. The king's purpose includes protecting the people, their homes and their livestock (DB 1.61–71) from a hostile army (*haina*), famine (*dushiyara;* literally 'bad year') and the Lie (*drauga;* DPd 12–20).

The tension expressed here echoes the structural dichotomy already seen in the *Gathas* and Young Avesta. It extends beyond human conflict and corruption into the natural world, where bad harvests are symptomatic of a lack of order and rectitude. The Ancient Persian emphasis on the cultivation of both crown lands and private estates, as farms, orchards and produce gardens, seems to be partly motivated by the desire to generate the increase and prosperity that denotes a healthy rule. We know from PFT records that women were also involved in such cultivation of the land. The word for a 'garden' in this broad sense is the Elamite *partetash*, from an Old Persian *pairidaida*. The term was translated by the Greeks from Xenophon onwards as *paradeisos* – a 'paradise'. This seminal concept will be explored in more detail later.

Darius makes specific reference to the earth being in turmoil (DNa 30–1), due to the work of an evil being (*ahrika aha*), whose actions are contrary to Ahura Mazda 'and the other gods' (DB 4.61–5). Under these circumstances the Lie proliferates, unless the king, aided by Ahura Mazda, is ever vigilant. Darius represents himself as being an enemy to evil, stating that he and his family did nothing crooked or deceptive – he was not a 'follower of the Lie', but held to the straight path (DB 4.61–5, DNb 5–12). Darius' son, Xerxes (r. 485–465 BCE), informs in several later inscriptions that the form of religious adherence that was not acceptable to the Ancient Persians was *daiva* worship, which can be equated with the Gathic *daevas* – the 'gods who confuse' and who turn others from the path.

Aristotle, the Greek tutor of the man who would overthrow the Persians in the late fourth century BCE, referred to this Iranian teaching concerning the two forces as ancient and original. He is said to have remarked that, according to the *magi* (religious experts), there are two first principles (*archai*), a good spirit (*daimon*) called Oromasdes, identified with Zeus, and a bad spirit called Areimanios, identified with Hades.[22] Aristotle's use of his own philosophical terminology to express the beliefs of the *magi* implies that these two principles do not derive from a common source. This understanding of the two universal principles – one good, the other bad – was also apparently referred to by Eudoxus, the astronomer and friend of Plato, as well as by Theopompus of Chios (378–ca. 320 BCE) in the eighth book of his *Philippika*.[23]

Aristotle ascribed the teaching that the first generative principle of the world was the supreme Good to both the pre-Socratic Greek philosophers, such as Pherecydes, and the *magi* (*Metaphysics* 1091b). Aristotle's biographer, Diogenes Laertius, reports a correspondence between Darius I and the Ionian Greek philosopher, Heraclitus of Ephesus (*Lives* 9.12–14). Heraclitus focused on fire as the single material constituent of existence from which everything is generated, and into which all will be resolved again. Fire was the symbol, then, of universal order. Heraclitus conceived of death as polluting, and introduced the metaphor of opposition (*polemos*) and strife (*eris*), which is the cosmic struggle operating in all things and events. Such emphases are thought by some to have been stimulated by contact with Zoroastrian teachings.[24]

The discussion concerning philosophical interaction between Greeks and Persians in the sixth century BCE continues, but an early connection between the two was evidently made by the Greeks themselves. According to Pliny, both Eudoxus and Aristotle placed Zoroaster and Plato 6,000 years apart, thereby establishing a relationship between the two figures.[25] Diogenes Laertius relates that Xanthos of Lydia (fl. c. 450 BCE) was also aware of this periodization of 6,000 years, but measured this span between Zoroaster's birth and Xerxes' crossing of the Hellespont. Alternate readings of this passage have '600 years', which would cohere with a more realistic time-frame. In his *Philippika*, however, Theopompus is reported to have discussed the to-and-fro dialectic of Iranian mythology as playing out over successive periods of 3,000 years. For 3,000 years, 'each of the two gods is alternately supreme and in subjection', and for another 3,000 years, 'they fight and are at war'. It is not entirely clear whether this is a 6,000- or 9,000-year cycle, depending on how the first part is read. The conflict ends only 'when Hades [Angra Mainyu] is left behind'.[26] The systematization of the cosmic struggle into successive 3,000-year cycles is not found in extant Avestan texts, or in Old Persian inscriptions, but seems to have been circulating as part of an Iranian cosmological schema towards the end of the Achaemenid period.[27] Although it is probably influenced by Babylonian ideas, such millennialism fits neatly within the Zoroastrian cosmic cycle that extends from creation to the perfection of the world at the end of time.[28] The millennial structure is well-established in Middle Persian texts, particularly *Bundahishn*.[29]

iv. Ethics of the Achaemenid Rulers

The dichotomy between Good Rule and Bad Rule pertaining to both a material and spiritual realm is a common notion in both Indo-European and Mesopotamian thought, but in the context of the Old Persian inscriptions it appears to be expressed in more morally explicit terms. The Achaemenid monarchs seem to have placed themselves not just at the center of the world physically and cosmologically, but also ethically. The tension expressed between the two principles of *Arta*, as Order or Rightness, and *Drauga* as the Lie that causes confusion, relates directly to the ethic of the *Gathas*.

External Perceptions

Although there is a lack of internal material concerning Cyrus II – who is also called 'Cyrus the Great' following Herodotus' use of the title 'Great King' – he is perceived in many external texts as a kind of Robin Hood of ancient times. As one of my colleagues pointed out, 'No one ever has a bad word to say about Cyrus the Great'. Just as Robin of Loxley is a heroic figure of legend, so too is the Cyrus to whom is attributed the 'first charter of human rights', and who became a model for subsequent rulers to follow. It is salient to note that Xenophon's purported account of Cyrus II in *Cyropaedia* was translated and read by Renaissance princes in Italy, and later by founders of the American constitution. Although Xenophon was probably describing his own patron, Cyrus the Younger, his fourth-century BCE construct of Cyrus 'the Great King' became a classical Greek cipher for the epitome of Good and

Just Rule.

Xenophon presents the Persian king as one who kept his word and maintained an impartial justice,[30] but whose reign was followed by a time of strife, during which 'cities and nations revolted, and all things began to decay' (*Cyropaedia* 8.2). To an extent, this is how the Greeks felt about subsequent Persian kings, particularly Xerxes, as exemplified in Plato's *Laws*, where he is said to have had an indulgent upbringing and to have 'repeated the bad deeds of Cambyses' (*Laws* 695d–96a). But the image of Cyrus II as the epitome of good rule persisted. Two hundred years after Cyrus' death, Alexander of Macedon (who is said to have read *Cyropaedia*) visited his tomb at Pasargadae, apparently intending to be ritually enthroned in the Persian manner. Curiously there is no mention of Cyrus' name, nor that of any other Achaemenid ruler, in Zoroastrian textual tradition. It has been suggested that here, too, Cyrus has become a cipher, coalescing with the composite archetypal figure of the good ruler, Kavi Vishtaspa, or perhaps with Yima Xshaeta. The description of Yima as a 'good shepherd' (Vd 2.2) is an attribute also associated with Cyrus in Isaiah (44.28), and in *Cyropaedia*, where Cyrus is said to have compared the duties of a good shepherd to that of a good king (8.2.14).

Cyrus II's conquest of Babylon is recorded on both a clay tablet known as the *Nabonidus Chronicle*, and the so-called Cyrus Cylinder. The latter was discovered in 1879 as one of the foundation stones in the ruined walls of Babylon. It represents a key religious and political document, but its promotion as the *first* charter of human rights in the early 1970s has led to vigorous debate.[31] The Akkadian text of the cylinder, ostensibly composed by the Babylonian priests of Marduk, has the markings of a piece of Persian propaganda: in the last part of the edict, Cyrus declares himself to be part of an eternal line of kings with the Assyrian titles of 'king of the world, great king, mighty king'. He claims that he deposed the incompetent Nabonidus, who performed 'improper rituals' in 'counterfeit cult centers', and who 'did evil' against Babylon. (This negligence in religious performance on the part of Nabonidus is also reported in the *Nabonidus Chronicle.*) In contrast to Nabonidus, Cyrus claims that he is a just and upright ruler, who sought the welfare of the city of Babylon, and the restoration of religious sanctuaries there and elsewhere in Babylonia. Cyrus also says that he has removed the 'yoke' imposed on the citizens of Babylon.[32]

The restoration of deported gods and peoples is a common trope in ANE edicts.[33] The thrust of Cyrus' cylinder is not, then, so much in the phraseology, but in the execution of the promises made. Ezra records that Cyrus authorized funds for the reconstruction of the Temple in Jerusalem from the imperial treasury and encouraged Jewish exiles to return to Israel to help in this effort (*Ezra* 1.3–4, 3.7, 6.8). Cyrus also returned the Temple vessels that the Babylonians had confiscated (*Ezra* 1.7–11, 5.14–15, 6.5). Such Biblical texts indicate that this was more than just a poetic or political trope, but reflected an actual state of affairs. Restitution of citizens and their places of worship was a clear departure from the policy of both the Assyrians and Babylonians, which was to kill or exile rebellious peoples, or at least those who might lead them in revolt.

Relocations of people were, however, common at later stages, particularly of Ionian Greeks who had revolted. This partly explains why the Greeks, beginning with Aeschylus (c. 525–456 BCE), distinguish the 'good' rule of the early Persians – Darius is invoked by his Queen as a 'God in wisdom', who 'ruled his people well' in Aeschylus' play *The Persians* (v. 655f.) – from the 'bad' rule of Xerxes, who had brazenly attempted to control the divine powers, and by extension Greek polity, by crossing the Hellespont. In *The Persians*, Xerxes' hubris is punished, and all of Persia suffers. *The Persians* is the world's oldest play – first performed in Athens in 472 BCE – and our earliest account of the Ancient Persians.

There was no forced conversion or assimilation, however, nor any attempt to achieve a cultural uniformity through supplanting the languages of other nations with Persian. The use of Aramaic as the lingua franca by the administrative offices in the western part of the Empire under Cyrus extended throughout the realm under Darius, but each province was encouraged to use its own language and script (*Esther* 3.12).

Parallels between Deutero-Isaiah (*Isaiah* 40–55) and elements of the Cyrus cylinder point to active Persian promotion of Cyrus' redemptive work on behalf of other peoples in alliance with their divinities.[34] This approach seems to have worked, for the act of freeing the Jewish exiles from Babylonian captivity and sending them home to worship 'the God who is in Jerusalem' was perceived as evidence of the hand of God at work through Cyrus (2 *Chron.* 36.20–3). Deutero-Isaiah, which is generally held to have been composed by a Jewish exile in Babylon at around the time of its fall, praises Cyrus as the deliverer of the Jews using the term *mashiach*, 'the anointed one' (*Isaiah* 45.1). It is the only time in the Hebrew Bible that the term *mashiach* is used of a non-Hebrew. It is tempting to see, in this presentation of the Persian king's agency in implementing the divine will, a reflection of the instrumental, incremental action of the Gathic *saoshyant*. If so, that beneficial work has now been expanded to a royal function.

Deutero-Isaiah's expression of a future hope for the restoration of creation presents a more prominent focus on cosmology than in datably earlier Hebrew literature. Here, God is celebrated as Creator in terms new to the Jews, in a terminology that has striking parallels to that of the ninth *haiti* of the *Gathas* (2.44). Its application, however, suggests both awareness of Gathic cosmogony and a negative reaction to it that resulted in the formulation of a Hebrew etiology, in which 'wholeness and evil' are created by one divinity rather than being separate (*Isaiah* 45.6–7). Fire is perceived as a torment and sign of God's wrath, rather than of purification (*Isaiah* 50.11). By the time of Trito-Isaiah (*Isaiah* 56–66), composed around the late sixth to mid-fifth century BCE, the language is that of cosmic eschatology, in which the solar imagery used of God not only reminds us of the ancient Iranian conception of Ahura Mazda, but also recalls prevalent Achaemenid iconography (cf. *Isaiah* 60.1–3, 19–20).[35] Jewish interaction with Persians in the post-exilic period must have been quite sophisticated, partly due to the shared use of Aramaic.

Self-perceptions

The conception of the king as the linchpin, not just of the Iranian world but of the entire realm, is expressed in Darius I's proclamation that he has been made king by Ahura Mazda, and is 'king in this great earth, far and wide, a Persian, of Aryan heritage' (DNa 1.5, 13–14). His kingship is then rooted in a religious, ethnic and linguistic framework. It is thought that Darius was the first Persian to have his words recorded in Persian language. His trilingual inscriptions are expressed in a personal style and are our only concrete evidence for his understanding of religion.

In his great relief at Bisutun, carved around 521–519 BCE, Darius took steps to give clear articulation to Ahura Mazda's endorsement of his rule, as well as to his own elevation to royal status and his Achaemenid Persian identity. Darius sees that the way for him to effect a continued state of peace is by 'being a friend to right, and not a friend to wrong' (DNb 8.6–8, 11f.). This approach indicates that the Ancient Persian rulers were inspired in such ideals by their personal conviction that just governance required keeping those in one's realm happy (DNa 1.3–4). The responsibility for keeping the populace happy did not apparently only rest upon the king. Herodotus provides us with the sense that this was a mutually reciprocal scheme when he records that when they made a ritual offering, the Persian laity did not just pray for their own interests, but for good to ensue for all Persians, particularly the king (*Histories* 1.132).

Old Persian texts maintain the central antithesis between that which is true (*hashiya*) and straight (*rashta*), and that which is a lie (*drauga*) or wrong (*mithah*). The goal of humans is described in an inscription of Darius, in which those who worship Ahura Mazda will receive a boon both during their lifetime and after death (DB 5.16–20). This concept is reiterated in an inscription of Xerxes (XPh. 46–56). A life of rectitude involves performing no injustice (*zurah*) to either rich or poor (DB 4.61–7): *zurah* literally means 'crooked behaviour'. Darius is keen to point out that he is egalitarian in his treatment of his subjects, desiring no wrong for either the weak or the mighty (DNb 8.8–11). This sentiment echoes the Avestan concern to protect the vulnerable *drigu*. Darius then asserts that he is not quick to anger, but is able to keep his temper under control through his power of thought (*manah*).

Order Upheld

The Achaemenid focus on the notion that to choose the good was a moral imperative with far-reaching implications had a marked impact on their non-Iranian contemporaries. Herodotus observed that, besides being taught the necessary skills of horse-riding and archery, Persians were also taught to speak the truth, and that they regarded telling lies as shameful (*Histories* 1.136). Darius makes the same claims for himself.[36] Persian moral doctrine was, according to Herodotus, based on the balance of a person's good and bad deeds – translated as 'services and faults' – in which goodness was signified primarily by valor in fighting (*Histories* 1.137).

Given Aristotle's awareness of the two principles of the Persians, his placement of Zoroaster as living 6,000 years before the death of Plato could be understood as suggesting that the Platonic pursuit of the good is somehow related to an antecedent Persian ethic: Zoroaster and Plato were both symbolic figures in this cosmic struggle for good to prevail, each living at critical points in the cycle of history.[37] This fight for the good is seen as playing out not just vertically, throughout history, but horizontally, across all levels of life, including the elements of the natural world. Herodotus mentions the particular reverence the Persians gave to flowing water, and the care they took not to pollute it by spitting, washing their hands or urinating into a river (*Histories* 1.138). This approach is reiterated in Xenophon's *Cyropaedia*, and substantiates Avestan regulations concerning keeping the waters clean of 'dead matter'. Xerxes' scourging of the Hellespont does not appear to be in line with this charge, but Herodotus notes that this was a reaction to the destruction by a storm of the first bridge built across the waters (*Histories* 7.35).[38] It has been suggested that the development of some of the purity laws in post-exilic Judaism were stimulated by Nehemiah and Ezra's exposure to such regulations at the court of Artaxerxes I.[39]

Elsewhere, Herodotus records his knowledge of the Persian belief 'that fire is a god', and that is why they never burn their dead (*Histories* 3.16). Xanthos of Lydia, who lived just before Herodotus, related the Persians' claim that their rules against burning dead bodies or defiling fire in any other way had come from Zoroaster himself.[40]

Emblems of Good Rule

The art of the Achaemenids provided visual articulation of an imperial worldview that largely focused on the good rule of the king. Some elements of the aesthetic presentation of this ethos continue today. The icon of fire appeared as a central emblem on Persepolis Treasury Tablet stamps, which show attendants in Persian clothing paying homage to the fire. A similar motif is found on the monumental reliefs over the tombs of the Achaemenid kings at Naqsh-e Rostam and Persepolis, beginning with that of Darius I. The recurring depiction of the king, standing on a three-stepped plinth before a blazing fire in a holder on a similar plinth, with a winged disc and crescent moon above and the subject nations arrayed in rows below (Fig. 5), points to the development of a privileged relationship between the king and fire. Such iconography, alongside evidence from contemporary Greek accounts, indicates that both king and fire were thought to stand at the interstices between Ahura Mazda and humanity.

A hybrid iconography that became entirely Persian arose through the adoption and adaptation of concrete features from surrounding cultures, particularly Assyrian, Babylonian and Elamite. One such modified form involved the ancient symbol of the winged sun disc. This first appeared in a Persian context at Bisutun, partly deriving from the Assyrian image of the sun god Shamash, who was also the god of justice. It is tempting to understand the Iranian adaptation as an iconographic expression of the sun as a representation of *Asha*, or even of Ahura Mazda. Both the iconography and identification of this motif are uncertain, however. Sometimes the Achaemenid monarch stands under what appears to be a replica of himself rising out of the solar disk, but at Bisutun, and in some of the earlier cylinder seals, the king's crown and that of the figure above are different. Some suggest that the Bisutun figure could be identified with Ahura Mazda, whom Darius mentions throughout the inscription, but that elsewhere it is the *fravashi* of the king or the *xwarenah*, the '[divine] glory or fortune'. The word *xwarenah* is first used in the *Gathas* in reference to Jamaspa (4.51.18). The identification of the winged figure as Ahura Mazda would conflict with Herodotus' statement that the Persian religion is not anthropomorphic like the Greek (*Histories* 1.131). The figure is now popularly referred to as the *fravohar* (Av. *fravashi*), and is thought by many to represent the 'glory' of Iran.

Fig. 5. King standing before the fire-holder, with the winged figure overhead. Above the tomb of one of the Ancient Persian kings, Naqsh-e Rostam.

Ancient Persian Religious Praxis

i. Place

Textual, iconographic and archeological evidence from this period suggests that most worship was conducted outside. Herodotus regards as noteworthy that the contemporary Persians had no temples, altars or statues, but would climb the highest peaks of mountains to worship their supreme God, who is 'the full circle of the firmament' (*Histories* 1.131). This echoes the idea expressed in the *Gathas* that Ahura Mazda wears the sky like a garment (1.30.5), and incorporates the ancient Zoroastrian practice of facing the sun during prayer.[41] Herodotus adds that other focal points of worship are 'the sun, the moon, earth, fire, water, and winds', suggesting a devotion to the *yazatas*, whose activity in supporting and protecting these beneficial creations is also praised in the *yashts*. In Herodotus' summary of the elements of creation, however, plants and animals are noticeably absent.

The absence of religious edifices would have been as striking to the Greeks as the lack of images. At Pasargadae, however, excavations in the 1970s revealed two large limestone plinths, on which stone fire-holders were apparently placed in the same manner, as illustrated in the iconography above the Achaemenid tombs (Fig. 6). Parts of three such stepped fire-holders were found scattered around the site at Pasargadae. The most complete has a bowl deep enough to hold a long-burning fire. These fire-holders may have originated in earlier forms, such as that discovered in the temple at Tepe Nush-e Jan dated to around the eighth century BCE. That fire-holder, however, was made of mudbrick, with only a shallow fire bowl.[42] The three-stepped fire-holder from the Ancient Persian period is the most enduring icon of the Zoroastrian religion, being continuously illustrated down to the present day. The symbolism of the number three is also recognized as a constant element of belief and observance from the *Gathas* onwards.

Fig. 6. One of the two fire plinths at Pasargadae.

There is no archeological evidence of consecrated buildings from the early Achaemenid period, although the Bisutun inscription mentions that Darius overcame a usurper who had destroyed *ayadana*, a term translated in the Akkadian and Elamite versions of the inscription by the standard phrase 'houses of the gods'. Scholars disagree as to exactly what these *ayadana* were. They could have been sacred places of prayer and offering, such as the plinths at Pasargadae. The term recurs in the Parthian period as *ayazan*, 'place of worship', and at that stage probably refers to a building of some kind. An

Aramaic inscription from Syene dated 458 BCE, during the rule of Artaxerxes I, refers to the construction of a *brzmdn'* by the commander of the garrison there. This term was originally thought to refer to a 'place of ritual', but probably means 'reverence' or 'being on high' – as in Old Avestan *bareziman,* 'height'.

The fourth-century BCE Greek chronicler Dinon is said to have remarked that the Persians sacrifice in the open air, and that their only images of gods are fire and water.[43] The word for 'images', *agalmata,* can refer to an object of worship as well as a cult statue, but it is this very word that Herodotus, and later Strabo, uses when explaining that the Persians erected no statues. Strabo repeats the notion, however, that these two elements were revered by the Persians above any other (*Geographia* 15.3.14).

a. Place of Fire

There is no Avestan term for a fire temple, although *Videvdad* refers to a 'lawful place' where fire may be set.[44] Frequent references in the Persepolis tablets to 'guardians of fire' (*atarvakhsha*) indicate a ritual setting, but do not explicitly mention worship centered on fire. Diodorus Siculus (fl. 49 BCE) records that at the death of his friend Hephaestion, Alexander ordered all the inhabitants of Asia to extinguish with care 'the fire the Persians call sacred' until the funerary rites were over, according to the Persian custom at the death of their king (*Diodorus Siculus* 17.114.4–5). This reference to the Persian custom of quenching the fire relates to the royal fire of the deceased king, and implies that Alexander treated his friend as a king. Royal dynastic fires are recorded in Parthian and then Sasanian times.

A cult legend relating to the Persian reverence for fire appears to form the background to a narrative in 2 *Maccabees,* composed sometime in the second century BCE. The story concerns the reaction of the Achaemenid king Artaxerxes I to the discovery of the place where Jewish Temple priests had hidden the altar fire to keep it safe during the Babylonian exile. Upon being told that a fiery liquid had replaced the original Temple fire, the Persian king 'had the place enclosed and pronounced it sacred' (2 Macc. 1.19–34). This liquid is called *nephthar* in Hebrew and is also referred to by the Persian form of a Babylonian word for crude petroleum, *naphtha.* Strabo describes the existence of a fountain of *naphtha* next to 'fires' and a 'temple of Anea', near Arbela in northern Babylonia (*Geographia* 16.1.4).

The idea of enclosing fire may well have first become established in eastern Iran, for it is there that we have evidence of the earliest fire temples, dating back to the Parthian period (Kuh-e Khajeh in Sistan and Mele Hairam in southern Turkmenistan). These seem to be based architecturally on

Achaemenid precedents, such as the temple excavated at Dahan-i Ghulaman, also in Sistan, and Building 2 at Altin Tepe in northern Afghanistan. The former dates to the early fifth century BCE; the latter was apparently destroyed by the Greeks in 329/8 BCE. A prototype for these edifices may have been the square columned hall in the *apadana*, built by Darius I at Susa.[45]

b. Place of Waters

Although from Herodotus onwards, fire is referred to by 'outsiders' as central to Zoroastrian ritual, worship of the waters has also been important from the earliest times. Persepolis tablets inform us that offerings were made at a place identified by the Elamite word *hapidanush*, which translates as 'water reservoir' or possibly 'river'.[46]

c. Place of Images

In the *yasht* dedicated to Mithra, the *yazata* is associated with the sun, the greatest natural fire, and it is often proposed that references by Strabo and Dinon to the Persian worship of fire and water are linked to worship of Mithra and Anahita respectively. Berossus, a Babylonian historiographer, writing in Greek in the early third century BCE, reports that, originally, neither the Persians or Medes made offerings before images of wood or stone, but that during the time of Artaxerxes II (405–359 BCE) an image cult was promoted.[47] An inscription of Artaxerxes II at Susa invokes by name both Anahita and Mithra after Ahura Mazda. This is the earliest reference to 'Anahita' outside the Avesta. Berossus states that this Persian king erected statues of *Aphrodite Anaitis* in Babylon, but suggested that such practice should also be adopted in the main administrative centers across the Empire from east to west.[48]

Later classical sources also attest the existence of temples to Anahita at this stage. Plutarch (46–120 CE) wrote that Artaxerxes II was inaugurated by Persian priests at Pasargadae in the sanctuary of 'a warlike goddess', whom he conjectured to be Athena (*Artaxerxes* 3.1–4). This sanctuary has not been found, nor has one in Ecbatana 'dedicated to Anaitis', whom Plutarch equated with Artemis (*Artaxerxes* 27.3). Plutarch's comparisons, and Tacitus' later reference to a shrine at Hierocaesarea in Lydia, dedicated 'to the Persian Diana' in the time of Cyrus (*Annals* 3.62), indicates that non-Iranians attempted to find parallels between their own perception of the divine and that of the Persians.

From the Young Avesta onwards, Anahita is an important *yazata*, identified as the beneficent female hypostasis of the mythical world river that plunges from Mt. Hara into the Vourukasha Sea, and is the source of all the waters of the world (Yt 5.3–5). In the *yasht* dedicated to the waters (*aban*), Anahita is invoked by the epithets *aredvi sura anahita* – 'moist, mighty, pure' – and praised as a source of increase and well-being. She brings fertility, making 'the seed of all males pure' and 'childbirth easy for all females' (Yt 5.2, 5, 87). A vivid description of Anahita (Yt 5.7, 126–9) may indicate that an image-centered worship was in place before the final recension of the *yasht*, but it could also be a composite representation of her various attributes using Avestan motifs. The description is similar to that of the female embodiment of the good thoughts, words and deeds of the *ashavan* in *Hadokht Nask*. The evolution of the Zoroastrian religion certainly included the development of worship of Anahita, but it is uncertain to what extent this was iconic.[49]

An inscription from Cappadocia refers to a sanctuary to *Anaitis Barzoxara* ('Anahita of high Hara'), but to date none of the temples to Anahita identified as existing during the Achaemenid period have been positively identified, nor has any statuary, although some scholars claim that she is represented on coins and stelae from Asia Minor, and as the crowned or haloed woman with a flower on a few Achaemenid seals. Some of these depictions resemble the Mesopotamian goddess Ishtar, and others show Greek or Anatolian components, indicating that if they are portrayals of the Avestan *yazata* of the waters, her iconography had fused with that of local female divinities. This fusion – and confusion – of divinities is epitomized by Herodotus, who identifies worship of a Semitic sky goddess, 'Ouranie', with 'the Assyrian Aphrodite Mylitta, and the Persian Mitra' (*Histories* 1.132). In the Indo-Iranian context, Mithra is a male *yazata*, but the connection with Venus (Aphrodite) may have to do with his location high above Mt. Hara.

Berossus says nothing about Mithra, the other *yazata* named by Artaxerxes II. Artaxerxes III (r. 359/8–338 BCE) invoked only Ahura Mazda and Mithra. Plutarch relates that Darius III (r. 336–330 BCE) venerated the 'light of Mithras', but makes no reference to an image (*Alexander* 30.7). The plethora of names with 'Mithra' suggests that the *yazata* had become more central to worship by Achaemenid times. The development of focus on Anahita and Mithra is sometimes regarded as the accretion of older, or western, Iranian practices to 'Gathic' Zoroastrianism, but it could be that both *yazatas*, as hypostatic representations of the good waters and fire respectively, acquired more explicit positioning through the incorporation of the later eastern (Young) Avestan texts, particularly the *yashts*, into Achaemenid praxis.

d. *Daivadana*: Place of the 'false gods'

The primacy of Ahura Mazda and the 'Gathic ethic' is emphasized in an inscription at Persepolis, where Xerxes records how, in one of the countries that was in turmoil, he had destroyed a *daivadana*, a 'place of *daivas*', and had established 'worship of Ahura Mazda according to *arta*' in its place (XPh. 28–41).[50] The Greek mistrust of Xerxes spills over into later European interpretations of this passage, which infer that the *daiva* sanctuary was in Babylonia, Egypt or Greece. The *daivadana* could then be identified as one of the two great temples known to have been destroyed by Xerxes: the Esagila in Babylon or the Acropolis in Athens. There is no evidence, however, to suggest that Xerxes celebrated Mazda-worship at either place. Instead, the use of the word *daiva*, and the supplanting of the worship of *daivas* with that of Ahura Mazda and *asha*, suggests that this refers to a residual Iranian cult that had perpetuated worship of the *daevas* denounced in the *Gathas*.

ii. Religious Experts

The establishment of temple worship during the late Achaemenid period – whether iconic or aniconic – was an important ecclesiastical development within the evolution of Zoroastrianism, since it expanded the function of the ritual experts. Babylonian texts from the early fifth century BCE record the existence of a group of Iranian functionaries living in Mesopotamia at the time, who were called *magi* (Akkadian *magush*; OP *magu-*). The word is of uncertain etymology and was not used to refer to a religious specialist by eastern Iranians, but is well attested in western Iran from this time on. Herodotus identifies a tribe of the Medes as *magi*, but also uses the name to refer to the religious experts of both the Medes and the Persians. These *magi* were said to pour libations, to make offerings to the gods, to interpret dreams and to foretell the future (*Histories* 1.103, 107, 119f., 133, 7.43). Xenophon later presents the *magi* as experts in everything religious, whose establishment as a priestly order was thought to date back to the time of Cyrus II.[51]

Tablets and seals found at Persepolis tell us that *magi* were active in the neighborhood.[52] Although some of their functions set them apart, the *magi* also performed administrative tasks. According to letters from the archives of the Eanna temple in Uruk, the *magi* were responsible for checking on supplies in the temple stores, as well as supervising temple workers. In Babylonian legal documents, *magi* appear as witnesses alongside Babylonians. They could also own land.[53]

According to Herodotus, the *magi* had distinctive practices including the killing of certain animals, including ants, snakes, flying and creeping things (*Histories* 1.140). This abhorrence of 'creeping things' mirrors the detestation of 'noxious' animals – *xrafstra* – in *Videvdad* (3.10, 14.5–6), a text which scholars consider to have reached a fairly fixed form by this time.

a. Libations

PFT references inform us that the *magi* received rations of grains and jugs of wine as payment for performing 'libation services' (Elamite *dausha* or *daushiya*), as well as for more mundane employment. It is not altogether clear whether the provisions were for the ritual activity itself, or to feed those responsible. What is clear is that libations were performed by officiants with Iranian names at several named bodies of water, apparently specific rivers or lakes. Both the term *daushiya* and the action associated with it parallel Avestan *zaothra* ('libation'), and it is assumed that the Persian *magi* practiced such offerings for both past and future benefits brought by the waters.

The preparation and consecration of a ritual offering to the waters appears to be at the center of the oldest Zoroastrian liturgical text, the *Yasna Haptanghaiti*. *Nerangestan*, a late Avestan text with a Middle Persian exegesis, refers to 'the coming forwards of the good waters' as part of a ritual libation (Ner. 48). Such early references indicate that an act of offering to the waters was part of Zoroastrian praxis in the Young Avestan period; that is, during Achaemenid times, if not earlier.[54] In *Videvdad*, worship of the waters is considered to be an essential element of Zoroastrian practice, alongside the recitation of the *Gathas* and the wearing of the *kusti*: these activities are all said to prevent the increase of the power of death (Vd 18.8–9).

Xerxes is recorded as making an offering to the waters at dawn before crossing the Hellespont to do battle with the Greeks (*Histories* 7.54). Standing on a bridge strewn with myrtle boughs (as *baresman*?), the Persian king poured a libation from a golden goblet into the sea, and facing towards the sun, prayed that he might be victorious. Once he had finished his prayer, Xerxes flung the cup into the Hellespont, followed by a golden bowl and a Persian short sword. These offerings of symbols of strength before battle cohere with the warrior aspects of the *yazatas* of the waters, Anahita and Tishtrya, who are said to overcome both the mortal and elemental enemies of Iran (Yt 5.53, 86; Yt 8).

b. Other Acts of Offering

That the *magi* performed a range of acts of offering is confirmed in PFT references to their involvement with the *lan* ceremony. *Lan* is an Elamite term thought to be a general reference to 'offering' or 'oblation', which could include the *daushiya*. The *lan* was not made exclusively to Ahura Mazda, but also to identifiable *yazatas* such as Spenta Armaiti (*Ishpandaramattish*) and Nairyosangha, and to named mountains and rivers, as well as to the Elamite god Humban and to 'all the gods', who may or may not be purely Iranian. Both Iranian and Elamite officials received rations for the *lan*, including those with ritual functions, named as *magi* (Elamite, *makush*) and *shatin* respectively. The fact that the *lan* was offered to divinities of both cultures, and by priests from both traditions, suggests an overlap of purpose and performance. The Iranian term *atarvakhsha* ('guardian of fire') is only mentioned in connection with the *lan* ceremony. Rations received for *lan* include small livestock, dates, apples and figs, grains and flour, wine and beer.

A fifth-century BCE papyrus, found at Derveni near Salonica, describes in Greek a ritual on behalf of the souls of the deceased in which the *magi* perform a sacrifice, 'as if paying compensation', and then make libations of water and milk over the sacrifice, and offer countless cakes, 'because the souls, too, are innumerable'.[55] The illustration of such a scene of sacrifice at the burial place of the deceased may be seen on a contemporary funerary stele from Daskyleion, now in the Istanbul Archaeological Museum (Fig. 7). It depicts two *magi* wearing mouth covers, each holding a thick *baresman*, standing before what appears to be the door of a building – perhaps a tomb – with the head of a bull and a horned sheep on a plinth at their feet. The mouth cover is seen on many illustrations of the *magi* during this period, and seems to represent the *paitidana* advocated in *Videvdad* (14.8, 18.1), worn during an act of offering so as not to pollute the fire. By the Achaemenid period, the *baresman* strew also evidently included a bundle of grass, twigs or metal rods held in the left hand

Fig. 7. Two priests in front of a tomb. Funerary stele, Daskyleion.
Istanbul Archaeology Museum.

The practice of animal sacrifice by the Persians alluded to in the Derveni text appears also in the PFT, and is described by Greek sources from Herodotus onwards. Offerings of horses, cows and sheep are spoken of in the *yashts* as a means of pleasing the *yazatas*.[56] Such sources provide evidence that animal sacrifice formed an integral part of the evolving Zoroastrianism of this period, although there may have been a distinction between animals killed for consumption and those sacrificed for less mundane reasons, such as victory in battle. Xenophon describes Cyrus' sacrifice to 'the gods whom the *magi* named' (*Cyropaedia* 8.1.23) including Ahura Mazda ('Zeus the god of his fathers;' 2.4.19) and the sun, to which horses were offered (8.3.12, 24).

Arrian, later supported by Strabo (15.3.7), records that the *magi* who looked after the tomb of Cyrus II were given a sheep, wine and flour every day for their sustenance, and a horse every month to sacrifice until the conquest by Alexander (Arrian *Anabasis Alexandri* 6.29.7).

Herodotus records that after a sacrifice performed by the laity, pieces of the cooked meat were presented on 'tender grass' (the *baresman* strew), which a *magus* would then consecrate through invocation (*Histories* 1.132). This suggests that although the priestly system was becoming more formalized, the laity remained intimately involved in ritual praxis. The lay prayer offered at the sacrifice for good to ensue to all Persians, including the king, reflects the symbiotic link between ritual offering and the increase of good. That no Persian act of offering could be made without a *magus* being present 'to chant a theogony' (*Histories* 1.131) suggests the existence of a liturgy that recapitulated the myth of the birth and regeneration of the cosmos, such as became crystallized in the *Yasna*. Theopompus supports this thesis when he attributes a teaching to the *magi* 'that the world would endure through their invocations' (Diogenes Laertius *Lives* 1.9). An earlier reference in the Derveni papyrus mentions 'the incantations of the *magi* as being powerful enough to change the spirits (*daimones*) who hinder'.[57]

Were these *magi* also *manthrans*, and cognizant of the *Gathas*? If it is accepted that Darius and subsequent Achaemenid kings were familiar with an Avestan worldview such as presented in the *Gathas*, then the *magi* attached to the court, and to the temples around the realm, were presumably the ones who memorized and transmitted parts of the Avesta as it then was.[58] The fact that many of the activities of the *magi* reflect Avestan prescripts supports this, but their knowledge of the Avesta itself would have relied on an aural recollection and oral communication of the texts, which by that time would have been equivalent to first hearing and then repeating a different dialect, if not a foreign language.[59] Although some Old Persian phraseology parallels that of the Avesta – such as the use of *yashta*, meaning 'one who offers' – the predominance is of vernacular Persian religious vocabulary (such as *baga*), rather than specific Avestan terms.

c. *Haoma* Ceremony

Evidence for a continued significance of *haoma* is found in a personal name equivalent to Iranian *Haumdata*, attested in Aramaic papyri from Elephantine, Elamite texts from Persepolis and on Babylonian documents. This name is also possibly attested in an Aramaic inscription on a pestle and mortar from Persepolis. The discovery of the Aramaic inscription *hawan* on over 20 such pestles and mortars suggested initially that rituals involving *haoma* were performed at Persepolis. Avestan *hawana* is the mortar used to press *haoma*

(Vd 14.8). The Parsi term for the metallic mortar – *havanim* – is based on a Middle Persian form of the word. The mortar is used to pound the *haoma* in the *Yasna* ceremony, which always takes place in the *havan gah* – 'the time of pressing' – that is, early morning. But the green chert pestles and mortars found in the Persepolis Treasury were not used in any ritual: the ink writing on the objects was still apparent, and many of the mortars were the wrong shape for constant pounding. Current consensus is that these were decorative objects received as tribute or tax payment over 40 years, and that the Aramaic *hawan* is just an inventory description. A seal found at Persepolis shows an almost identical mortar and pestle on a table in front of a fire-holder, before which stands a man with a bundle of sticks (*baresman*) in his right hand and a long stick in his left.

In the *Mihr Yasht*, Mithra is described as receiving worship with many of the ritual prayers and implements associated with the later *Yasna* liturgy: he is worshipped 'with milk mixed with *haoma*, with *baresman*, along with 'skill of tongue, *manthras*, with speech and action, and libations (*zaothra*), and with properly-spoken words' (Yt 10.6). Yt 10.91 describes a man who, having washed his hands and all the implements first, worships Mithra 'holding wood, *baresman*, milk, and the *haoma* mortar (*hawana*) in his hands', and who recites the *Ahuna Vairya* prayer. Some of these rituals and implements are reiterated in *Videvdad* 14.4.7–8.

d. The Wisdom of the *Magi*

The ability of the *magi* to interpret dreams and to foretell the future (*Histories* 1.103, 107ff., 119f., 133) was an attribute that particularly influenced the later classical depiction of the *magi* as sages skilled in astrology, divination and related 'magical' subjects. The Greek words for magic – *mageia* and *magike* – derive from *magi*, although some Greek and Roman authors declared that the latter knew nothing of the 'dark arts' or sorcery, but rather were the source of a cult of wisdom and power.[60] Others, however, placed all magic together as an importation from 'Chaldea', a place that represented a blending of Iranian and Mesopotamian traditions following centuries of close proximity.[61]

Classical Greek accounts of meetings with Persian *magi* indicate that they were more prevalent than has previously been credited. A fragment of prose drama, entitled 'Zoroaster' by Heraclides of Pontus, who lived in the fifth century BCE, indicates not only awareness of the *magi* by the Greeks around the Black Sea, but the possible presence of *magi* in Sicily.[62] A connection between Empedocles, the fifth-century Greek philosopher from Sicily, and the Persian *magi* was made by his contemporary, Xanthos of Lydia. According to Herodotus, the Orphic poet Onomacritos (c. 520–485 BCE) was sent on a mission to Xerxes' court in Susa (*Histories* 7.6), and the Persian *magi* are said to have taught Democritus (b. c. 460 BCE) at Xerxes' bidding (Diogenes Laertius, *Lives* 9.34).

Intimations of Paradise

Ancient Persian funerary practices are described by contemporary Greek authors. Some resemble those advocated in *Videvdad* concerning the exposure of the body to birds and animals, so as not to pollute the elements of creation, particularly fire, earth and water (Vd 8.3–10). Herodotus' brief description of such a rite of exposure, which to him was 'something of a mystery', states that only the *magi* and a few other male Iranians practiced this, but that, in general, the Persians embalm and then bury their dead (*Histories* 1.140). The fact that Cyrus II and subsequent Achaemenid kings were interred in stone tombs suggests that an eastern Iranian practice of exposure existed alongside a western custom of primary burial. The rock-cut tombs contain a number of cists, which may have also been intended for the king's wife or high-ranking consort. Some of the tombs dating from the fourth century BCE were too small to hold an articulated body, and are therefore thought to have functioned as 'bone-holders' or *astodans*. The term *astodan* was found in an Aramaic inscription on one such tomb.[63]

Cyrus II's tomb at Pasargadae, and those of Darius I and later Achaemenid kings at Naqsh-e Rostam and Persepolis, may indicate that primary burial was a concession to the imperial family, who were already in the 'favor of Ahura Mazda' (Fig. 8). It could be argued that the thickness of the cut stone tombs, or those in living rock, would not allow the body of the king to pollute the elements. *Videvdad* allows for burial on a temporary basis and for the building of burial houses for use during the winter months (Vd 3.36–9; 5.10–14). In both cases, however, the body was supposed to be exhumed and exposed afterwards. Some scholars maintain that Ezekiel, whose preaching in Babylonia is dated to the early sixth century BCE, may have come into contact with Zoroastrian concepts relating to death, if not an actual site of 'dry bones' (*Ezek.* 37.1–6).[64]

Fig. 8. The Tomb of Cyrus, Pasargadae.

An inscription of Xerxes at Persepolis expands on the concept mooted by Darius (DB 5.16–20) that what is done in this life has repercussions in the next. It states that the person who behaves according to the law (*data*) and order (*arta*), established by Ahura Mazda, becomes happy while alive, and, when dead, *artavan* (XPh 46–56). The use of the term *artavan* (cognate with *ashavan*) implies that following an orderly existence – a life lived straight – leads to being 'blessed' after death, in the sense of being admitted into the abode of Ahura Mazda.

This notion relates to the eschatological function of the king as an active agent of Ahura Mazda. The Old Persian use of the word *frasha* ('excellent'; OAv. *frasha*, 'perfect' or 'wonderful') appears in a range of contexts relating to the creative activity of Ahura Mazda (DNb 2), the work of the king (DSa 5) and the construction of a palace complex or building (DSf 56, DSj 6, DSo 4). In an Achaemenid world-view, the king's efforts to make the material world 'excellent' replicate the perfection inherent in the creative work of Ahura Mazda. Does this consciousness of royal beneficial function (on the lines of an Avestan *saoshyant*?) find its first expression in Persian propaganda to the Jewish exiles at the time of Cyrus II, which is then reflected in Biblical texts, such as Deutero-Isaiah?

Ancient Persian expressions of ethical action, leading to a final time of happiness, seem to find resonance in Greek preoccupations with the Persian *paradeisos*, 'paradise', as a place of delight and entertainment. The word derives, via an early Semitic borrowing, from Old Persian *pairidaida* (Av.

pairidaeza), meaning 'enclosure'. The Elamite form, *partetash*, refers to an orchard, as well as a storage area for produce such as grain and fruit. In an inscription of Artaxerxes I, the palace at Susa is described as a *para.dayada* (A2Sd3), which may be the only Old Persian example of the word, miswritten.[65] One of the earliest Greek references to a Persian *paradeisos* is found in Xenophon's *Anabasis*, where it is described as full of fruit-bearing trees (5.3.9–12), animals and waters (1.2.7). Xenophon's descriptions of paradises belonging to Persian kings and nobles, and the lack of a Greek word to describe them, indicate that they differed vastly from Greek gardens in both scale and attribute. These *paradeisoi* were 'full of everything good and beautiful' that could be grown from the earth (Xenophon, *Oekonomikos* 4.13).

An archeological model for such a Persian *paradeisos*, albeit on a small scale, may be found in Cyrus' palace complex at Pasargadae, which was landscaped and irrigated on the lines of what became the classic fourfold garden.[66] Persians from Cyrus onwards may have connected the cultivation of a physical garden not only with the final perfection of the material world, but also with a place of best existence for the soul after death. This is suggested by the ornamentation of a petaled flower on the top of Cyrus' tomb, which could represent *Ameretat*, as a symbol of continuity of life.[67] It could also be implicit in successive Old Persian references to evil as 'rotten' or 'foul-smelling' (*gashta*),[68] as in food that has gone bad, which relates to the stench (Av. *gaiti*) that assails the soul of the *dregvant* (HN 2.25). This stink later characterizes the spirit of evil – as *gannog menog* – in Middle Persian texts.

Paradeisos became a trope for the Greeks. The theme of a physical place of delight and abundant life is paralleled in Greek myth with an underworld of gloomy shades and death. In some of Plato's writing, this mythology also includes the concept of the soul wandering through the afterlife. This is the particular focus of the 'Myth of Er' in the tenth book of Plato's *Republic*. Until recently, the 'eastern' background to Plato's myths have been ignored, although during the Renaissance, Gemistos Plethon boldly declared that the philosophy of Plato was not original with him, but derived from Zoroaster through the Pythagoreans. We saw earlier how Aristotle had recognized both Zoroaster and Plato as important figures in the cosmic drama. The *Myth of Er* is told as a story that had formed part of an oral tradition heard by Plato. In the story, Er visits Hades and observes that humans either pay the penalty for every wrong done, or are rewarded for the good they have done: judges deliver judgment on the 'just', who take the right-hand road leading up through the sky, and the 'unjust', who follow the left-hand road leading downwards. After a thousand years, the souls return to draw lots for their next life under the guidance of Lachesis. In a speech to the assembled souls, Lachesis absolves God as 'guiltless' in that good can only generate good, and no evil, and that it is up to each individual to increase his or her own virtue.

Some of these ideas, and those in the 'Myth of Judgment' in Plato's *Gorgias*, resonate closely with Zoroastrian concepts in both Old and Young Avestan, and it has been suggested that Plato may have encountered similar myths of Iranian origin, perhaps through Pythagoreans in Sicily.[69] According to Clement of Alexandria, Plato identified Zoroaster with Er, 'the son of Armenios, the Pamphylian', who 'told the story of what he had learnt from the gods on a trip to Hades' (*Stromata* 5.14). The story of Er could have originated in the Iranized form of an Armenian legend concerning 'Ara'.[70] Other themes from Plato's story – particularly those of an eyewitness account of moral reward in the afterlife – appear in the Middle Persian Zoroastrian *Arda Wiraz Namag*, which includes ancient Avestan elements, such as crossing the Bridge of Accounting. Some philosophers, and a (very) few classicists, consider the possibility of once again treating Plato as a religious thinker, who was genuinely interested in non-Greek teleologies.[71] Such stories, taken not from Greek but from 'barbarian' cultures, bolstered early Christian apologists, who saw evidence in them for their own doctrines concerning the immortality of the soul in a place of reward or punishment, and a physical resurrection.

The concept of *paradeisos* is connected with eschatological anticipation in Jewish and later Christian contexts. The term is used to translate a seminal concept in the post-exilic reworking of the Jewish religion, being consistently (though not exclusively) adopted by the Greek translators of the Septuagint to render the Hebrew word for 'garden' (*gan*), including reference to the Garden of Eden in *Genesis* 2.9–10. Theopompus recorded the *magi*'s teaching that the culmination of the cosmic struggle would be an end time associated with tranquility and sustenance of life: he notes that, according to the *magi*, at the end, 'Hades [Angra Mainyu] will be dismissed' and humanity will be happy, 'neither needing food nor casting shadows' (Plutarch, *On Isis and Osiris* 47). This last feature is reminiscent of Yima's *vara*. Plutarch's record is supported by Diogenes Laertius, who remarked that, according to Theopompus, the *magi* spoke of a time when 'men will come to life again and be immortal' (*Lives* 1.9). Such statements reflect a developed Iranian eschatology – including a physical restoration of humanity – by late Achaemenid times.

Encounters with the Other

The defeat of Babylon was a crucial event in the religious history of several peoples, whose texts incorporate Cyrus into the redemptive activity of their own divinities. In these texts, Cyrus is perceived, probably through his own self-promotion, as taking an active role in the sacred history of each subject state, through partnership with their gods, who bless his rule. The portrayal of Cyrus' conquests and restoration of order as through the respective agency of Bel, Nabo and Marduk of Babylon, the 'great gods' of Ur,[72] the moon-god Sin or of the 'God of heaven' of the Jews (*Ezra* 4.3–5), alongside PFT accounts of Persian ritual experts making offerings to non-Iranian gods, raises the question as to whether the Achaemenids also recognized the deities of other peoples, to the extent of worshipping them to gain their support? Darius continued Cyrus' policy of personal involvement with non-Iranian faiths, performing rites at the Egyptian imperial temple at El-Kab, and appearing in pharaonic style on the murals of a huge temple to Amon-Ra at El Kharga oasis. His predecessor, Cambyses, far from killing the Apis bull, as described by Herodotus (*Histories* 3.27), worshipped it with due rites, as depicted on a funeral monument for the bull at Saqqara. Cambyses' chief physician, Udjahorresnet, described the king's rule in Egypt in the manner of a wise pharaoh.

The rule of the Persians acted as a catalyst for the development of self-definition and a degree of local autonomy in religious matters among some of the subject states. Around 519 BCE, Darius commanded the Persian satrap of Egypt, Aryandes, to assemble experts to codify the pharaonic laws, resulting 16 years later in an Egyptian code of law inscribed in both Aramaic and Demotic on papyrus rolls. In keeping with this policy of preserving a law based on local cultural and religious distinctions, Artaxerxes is said to have called upon Ezra, 'a priest and expert in Torah', to regulate Jews living in Judah and the Trans-Euphrates province 'according to the law of your God' (*Ezra* 7.12–14, 25–6). It was under Persian rule, then, that Ezra promulgated the Torah and established it as the 'law' of the Jewish people within the empire, which was then considered as part of Persian royal law. The Aramaic *dāth* derives from the Old Persian *dāta*, meaning 'law' or 'regulation'.

Such examples illustrate an Ancient Persian attitude that there is a straight path that needs to be encouraged in other nations, so that order, rather than confusion, will be maintained alongside Achaemenid rule. From this perspective, it is immaterial whether Cyrus and his successors actually *believed* in the deities of the vanquished peoples, and tried to gain their favor, while simultaneously considering Ahura Mazda the supreme god of the Iranians. At Bisutun, Darius I emphasized, however, that he received the support of Ahura Mazda 'and the other gods' because he was not 'disloyal', nor a 'follower of the lie' (DB 4.61–3). In this context, it must be noted that the Zoroastrian religion subsequently continued in places with strong cultural and political ties with Iran, such as Armenia, Bactria and Sogdiana, but not elsewhere. From the earliest times, then, the religion was linked with ethnicity.

After a series of kings, including Artaxerxes III, who restored Egypt to Persian rule, but was poisoned around 338 BCE, the empire under Darius III (Codomannus) was unable to stop the invasion of Alexander of Macedon, called 'great' by the Greeks, but *gizistag* or 'accursed' by the Zoroastrians.

There are few internal sources from the time of the last kings of the dynasty, but classical authors provide certain details of episodes during Alexander's conquests and the time of the early Seleucids. In the *Shah Nameh*, the poet Ferdowsi ignores the Achaemenids, but incorporates Alexander as a wise warrior who emulates the Iranian mythical hero Esfandiyar. Perhaps the apparent loss of historical memory concerning the Achaemenids occurred partly as a result of the popularity of 'heroic legends' from eastern Iran, which, from the Parthian period onwards, became superimposed on narrative traditions from western Iran.[73]

Chapter III

A Zoroastrian Presence from Seleucia to Sistan: The Parthian Period

'We have accepted this holy religion from Ohrmazd, and we will not give it up.'
Ayadgar-i Zareran 18

'They [the Persians] also tell many fabulous stories about their gods,... such as the following: Oromazes, born from the purest light, and Areimanios, born from the darkness, are constantly at war with each other.'

Plutarch, On Isis and Osiris, 47[1]

Zoroastrian Middle Persian texts remember Alexander as *gizistag* – the 'accursed' – because he is said to have destroyed fire temples, burnt religious writings and murdered *magi*. In around 327 BCE, Alexander besieged and captured a fortress in Sogdiana, where the local Bactrian chief, Oxyartes, had placed his wife and daughters for safekeeping.[2] One of those daughters was named Rokhshana, whom Alexander later married. This union both symbolized and galvanized subsequent Greek intermingling with local Iranian culture. When Alexander died in 323 BCE, his empire was partitioned among his Greek generals into three kingdoms. Most of western Asia was ruled first by Seleucus and then by the Seleucid dynasty until the mid-third century BCE. The Seleucids made marriage alliances with local ruling dynasties, while adopting much of the existing Persian infrastructure. In turn, Greek culture also had a significant impact on Iran, particularly in terms of social custom and aesthetics – some higher-class Iranians became clean-shaven – and Iranian bureaucrats used Greek rather than Aramaic as their language of diplomacy. Aramaic script continued, however, in Sogdia and Parthia, and in a modified form in the Kharoshthi script of Gandhara. Greek deities and heroic figures, such as Nike, Herakles, Apollo, Artemis-Nanaia and Tyche appear on Arsacid copper coins, although they could also be representations of Iranian *yazatas*.

Not much is known of the development of the religion of Iranians living under Seleucid control, but we do have a few fragments from the autonomous south-western province of Persis – the Greek name for the region of Fars – which existed between Alexander's death and the arrival of the Parthians. The rulers of Persis were known as *frataraka*, a title meaning 'forerunner', referring in this case apparently to the representative of the gods.[3] Coins of the *frataraka* dynasty are Iranian in type, using first Aramaic legend and then Middle Persian script. Some early coinage depicts a *magus* standing before a building similar to the two free-standing towers found at Pasargadae and Naqsh-e Rostam, with a winged figure floating above. This design echoes the triangle of king/fire-holder/winged figure on Achaemenid tomb facades. The name Ardaxshahr appears on both early and later Persid coins, and that of Dara (Darius) on the latter. This echo of Achaemenid king's names, along with the representation of fire, implies an attachment to the previous Persian tradition.[4]

Later coins from Persis show a bearded man holding *barsom* in front of either a fire-holder, or a sun and crescent moon motif. The figure of a *magus* holding the *barsom* survives on a stone jamb in a *frataraka*-era building near Persepolis. A stepped plinth inside the building suggests that this was a place of worship, although we cannot know whether the pedestal held an image or a fire-holder. A similar image of a *magus* image with *barsom* is depicted on a cliff wall underneath a rock-cut tomb, from the same period at Dokhan-e Davoud in Kurdistan (Fig. 9).

In the mid-third century BCE, the former Achaemenid satrapies of Bactria and Sogdiana were incorporated into the independent Greco-Bactrian kingdom of Diodotus at about the same time that the Arsacid Parthians overthrew the Seleucids to the west. From later, somewhat contradictory sources, we gather that the Iranian-speaking Parni, or Aparni, a nomadic Scythian (or possibly Bactrian) tribe, had invaded the Greek-controlled satrapy of Parthia to the east of the Caspian and established themselves there. We know nothing of the Parni religion prior to their arrival in Parthia. The dynasty was named after an eponymous leader, Arshak, which may relate to a Babylonian form of the Achaemenid *Artaxsaça*, 'Arshu'.[5] Ostraca, from the early capital of Nisa in Turkmenistan, mention the name *Ar[tax]shahrakan*,[6] echoing '*Artaxsaça*', and suggesting a continued importance for the concept of 'reigning through *Asha*' and also a possible identification with previous ideology. This notion is su ported by iconography on the earliest coins of Arshak 1 (c. 238–211 BCE), where the seated archer on the reverse recalls the standing or bent-kneed royal archer on Achaemenid coinage.

Fig. 9. Seleucid-era relief of magus holding barsom, *Dokhan-e Davoud, Kermanshah.*

All the early Parthian kings used the dynastic name of *Arshak* in the Greek form 'Arsaces' on their coins. These coins were initially Seleucid-issue, suggesting that to begin with Parthia held a vassal-type relationship with the Greeks. Parthian kings from Mithradates I (c. 171–138 BCE) up to Ardavan II (r. 10–38 CE) referred to themselves as '*philhellene*' on their coins. Although this epithet may have served as a political device, Parthian 'enthusiasm for things Greek' is evidenced by a contemporary report that king Orodes II (r. 57–38 BCE), and the vassal king Artavasdes of Armenia (r. 53–34 BCE), organized banquets and drinking parties for each other, at which Greek compositions were produced (Plutarch, *Crassus* 33). Both knew the Greek language and were familiar with Greek literature. Plutarch records that the two kings were watching a performance of Euripides' *Bacchae*, and had just witnessed the scene prior to the arrival of Agave bearing the head of her son, Pentheus, when a servant arrived with the head of the Roman general, Crassus. The Parthian general Suren had killed Crassus at the battle of Carrhae, and the head was incorporated as a prop in the next scene.

Such examples of the adoption of Greek culture alongside the paucity of internal evidence from Seleucid and Parthian Iran led to the view that the Zoroastrian religion was largely abandoned during this period. This negative perspective was promoted in Middle Persian texts, particularly *Denkard*, which describes the restoration of the *weh den* ('good religion') under the Sasanians after a long period of neglect following the conquest of the Greeks. During the later Sasanian period there appears to have been a concerted effort to minimize Parthian achievements. This approach seems to have impacted Ferdowsi's New Persian version of the Iranian national epic, for although he traces the 'Ashkani' lineage either to one of the mythical Kayanian kings of eastern Iran, or to the legendary archer, Arash, he dismisses the dynasty in a few lines, declaring that they ruled only for a brief period, and were of such negligible influence that their lives and deeds went unrecorded.

Sources

Data from the past few decades has contradicted such a dismissal of the lengthy rule of the Parthians as a dark age in Iranian history, during which 'Hellenism' infiltrated deeply into Iranian social and religious practice. Ostraca from Nisa; rock carvings in Khuzistan; parchment records of vineyard sales from Kurdistan; discoveries of offerings in Kashan cave-mines; ancient fire temples and inscriptions on the borders of the realm; heroic tales preserved in Sogdian, New Persian and Arabic; and numismatic evidence, all provide insights into the Zoroastrianism of the Parthian period. Regional adherence to Avestan beliefs and practices is also attested in some of the edicts ascribed to the Mauryan king Ashoka (c. 272/68–231 BCE).

By the end of the third century BCE, the Greco-Bactrian kingdom, with its mix of Greek rulers and Iranian subjects, extended as far west as Merv and into the south-eastern region of the Hindu Kush. After the fall of the Mauryan Empire, Buddhism continued to flourish under Indo-Greek rulers such as Milinda (Greek, Menander, d. 130 BCE). Although Greek was the administrative language, it seems that much of the region retained its Iranian language and religious worldview. A plaque from Ai Khanum, in north-eastern Afghanistan, depicting a chariot and priests, is characteristic of Ancient Persian forms; some of the personal names attested there – particularly Oumanos (Av. *Vohu Manah*) – suggest the survival of local Zoroastrian beliefs. Variations on the use of Vohu Manah as a personal name are found in Asia Minor also, including an inscription at Smyrna dated just after 242 BCE. Strabo refers to an 'image of Omanos' being carried around in procession by the Persians in Cappadocia (15.3.15). This name is generally now accepted as an Old Persian form of Vohu Manah, although Strabo's identification of the image as this *yazata* is probably incorrect.[7]

It was not until 141 BCE, under Mithradates I, that the Arsacids pressed westward to capture Seleucia and became a major power, ruling over a huge area that included many established cities between Mesopotamia and Margiana. The Seleucids retreated to Syria and Asia Minor, where they ruled for another 150 years. The characteristic Iranian title 'king of kings' first appears in Greek on the coins of Mithradates II (r. c. 123–88 BCE). Additional legends in Parthian appear on coins of Valakhsh I (r. c. 51–78 CE) and are also found on coins of Elymais from the same period, indicating its adoption as an administrative language at that time. Parthian is a Western Middle Iranian dialect closely related to Middle Persian, although its sound system is closer to Old Iranian.

During the reign of Mithradates II, new trading routes opened up between Parthian Iran and China, paving the way for centuries of interaction between the two cultures at an ideological as well as mercantile level. The Han imperial envoy Zhang Qian established contact with Parthia and Sogdiana in the late second century BCE, and his reports encouraged commercial relations between the two powers. Chinese historical sources provide information concerning Han relations with Parthia[8] and Chinese Buddhist missionary texts provide important clues as to Parthian, and then Sasanian, forms of Zoroastrianism, as does the syncretistic art of Kushan Gandhara.

In Sogdiana and Bactria, Greek rule had been replaced by that of the Saka, including nomads from the Tarim Basin known as the Yuezhi, thought to be the ancestors of the Kushans. Some Sakas were displaced southwards to the area subsequently called 'Sakastan' (Sistan), which was briefly under Indo-Parthian rule until the Kushans rose to power in the first century CE, conquering what remained of the Greco-Bactrian kingdoms and moving south across the Hindu Kush as far as Kaushambi in northern India.[9] The Kushans controlled trading routes throughout this region for the next 300 years, and it was along these routes that Buddhism spread.

This period is marked by a confluence of cultural exchanges between Central Asia and India, which coalesced to form a remarkable syncretism of iconography and ideology that was conveyed from India through Central Asia to China, as the power of the Han dynasty waned. The Kushans also maintained close relations with Iran: the clothes on images of Kushan Buddhist devotees from Gandhara are Iranian in style, as are those on a statue of Kanishka, the most significant Kushan ruler (c. mid-second century CE). Early Kushan texts in Bactrian, a Middle Iranian language written in Greek script, contain Iranian terms as well as references to Ahura Mazda and *yazatas*, such as Mithra, Sraosha, Verethragna and Vayu.[10] Based on the preponderance of such references on Bactrian inscriptions and coinage from the time of Kanishka, it seems that, although the Kushan king's personal adherence was to Buddhism, the official religion of the time was an eastern Iranian variation of Zoroastrianism.[11]

Our general understanding of the development of Zoroastrianism under the long rule of the Parthians is also supplemented through contemporary books of the Hebrew Bible, particularly Esther and Daniel; deutero-canonical writings such as Maccabees and Tobit; and some early Christian allusions. The Book of Esther, which is thought by many to have been composed in the Seleucid/Parthian period, was first translated into Greek in around the second century BCE, and indicates that many Achaemenid court ceremonies and institutions remained familiar.[12] 2 *Maccabees* provides a valuable account of Zoroastrian–Jewish contact in the Parthian period. Written in Greek, it describes the persecution of the Jews by the Seleucid Antiochus IV Epiphanes, and the victory of Judas Maccabaeus over the Seleucid general Nicanor (d. 161 BCE). Antiochus' death in 163/4 BCE gave rise to further Parthian conquests. The Jewish philosopher Philo (c. 20 BCE–50 CE) and the Jewish (Roman) historian Josephus (c. 37–100 CE) both document the relations between Jews and Parthians. Josephus narrates the conversion to Judaism of a Parthian prince, Izad of Adiabene, and his mother Helena in the first century CE (*Antiquities* 20.17–96), and Talmudic texts mention Parthian Jews whose culture was thoroughly Iranian. The Talmud alludes twice to a *resh galuta* – 'head of the exilic community' – holding a prominent position first in the Parthian and then in the Sasanian court. The exilarch was of Davidic origin and represented the Jewish minority, carrying out functions of a political-administrative nature.

The main source of external information about Parthian religion, including the development of fire temples, comes from Greek and Roman sources, such as the topographer Strabo (c. 63 BCE–24 CE), who seems to have relied on an earlier *Parthian History* by Apollodorus of Artemita as his primary source of information. Strabo and subsequent authors, such as Pausanias and Dio Chrysostom, all write as if they had had personal encounters with *magi*. Strabo was from the Pontus region, where the impact of the Iranians was still felt, particularly in terms of their religion, although he was more interested in ritual than doctrine. Plutarch (46–120 CE), a philosopher, who later became a priest of the temple at Delphi, was less concerned with the historical analysis of the defeats of both Crassus and Anthony (whose biographies he had written) than the moral substance of the people who had achieved such victories.

Preserving an Avestan Worldview

A Zoroastrian tradition recorded in *Denkard* Book 3 states that the teachings revealed to Zarathushtra were initially collected by Vishtaspa, then copied out; the original was kept in an archive until it was confiscated by Alexander, although other copies remained in circulation. *Denkard* Book 4 elaborates that during the reign of 'Valakhsh the Ashkanian' (usually identified as Valakhsh I), the collection of all the *Avesta* and *Zand* (exegesis), that had survived in both oral and written form, was undertaken within the Iranian provinces, to counteract the chaos and corruption of the religion resulting from the Greek invasion. It has been suggested that there could have been a Parthian *zand* on the Avesta that had survived in each province and that the Avesta could have been first written down in Parthian. *Denkard* 3 notes that the Greek invaders translated the *Avesta* into their own language, suggesting that there might also have been a Greek version of the Avesta. Pausanias, writing in the mid-second century CE, states that the *magi* in Greek-speaking Lydia read from books while performing ceremonies (*Graeciae Descriptio* 5.27.5–6).

Strabo, and later Bishop Basil of Caesarea (329–79 CE), both attest, however, to an oral tradition in Cappadocia, and local, oral versions of the Avestan texts and commentaries could also have existed in Bactria, Media and Persis.[13] Christian Syriac texts refer only to an oral transmission of the Avesta throughout the Sasanian period. That does not preclude a written transmission elsewhere at the same time. Such a transition stage in textual development may be exemplified in the *Nerangestan*, a Young Avestan text with Middle Persian commentary. *Nerangestan* is an exposition on the rituals and includes some Parthian vocabulary. It is important to note, however, that the Sasanian Avesta retains characteristic Old Persian elements, particularly of pronunciation, which indicate a continuous oral transmission of the Avesta – at least in south-west Persia – from Achaemenid times.

In the late fifth century, Herodotus had reported the 'theogony' chanted by the *magi*, and later Greeks may also have encountered such oral recitation by Zoroastrians, particularly of the short Avestan prayers. Aristotle's discussion on the universal nature of justice in the *Nicomachaean Ethics* includes what could be an allusion to the concept of *Asha* in the statement 'fire burns both here and in Persia' (1134b). His concept of virtuous action leading to the happiness of each person uses the Greek word for virtue, *arete*, which is cognate with Iranian *asha/arta*.[14] When Aristotle states that happiness (*eudaimonia*) is the highest good (1097b), attained through and in accordance with the highest virtue, which will be that of 'the best thing in us' (1177a), could he perhaps be evoking the *Ashem Vohu* prayer to prove a subtle point?

i. Avestan Names and Calendar

Evidence of the continued use of Avestan names and the Avestan calendar by the Parthians comes from inscribed Parthian ostraca found at Nippur to the south-east of modern Baghdad, and in a wine cellar in Nisa, as well as a Parthian legal document from Avroman in Iranian Kurdistan. Although there is no hard evidence that Nisa was either a Parthian royal or religious center, the 2,000 chits from there – which refer to consignments of wine, land tenure, the names and titles of the transactors, and regnal dates – bear witness to the Iranian background of the local people between around 100 BCE and 10 CE. The majority of personal names are Zoroastrian in character, reconstructed as Ohrmazdik, Tiridat, Artavahishtak (*Asha Vahishta*), Spandarmatak (*Spenta Armaiti*) and Denmazdak (*Daena Mazdayasni*). Many names on the Nisa ostraca include reference to Mithra, such as Mihrbozan, Mihrdatak and Mihrfarn. Indeed, the Parthian name for Old Nisa may have been Mithradatkirt. Calendar references on the ostraca are to Avestan months, such as Spenta Armaiti, Asha Vahishta, Haurvatat and Ameretat, and day names, such as the day of Mihr (Mithra); that is, to the traditional religious almanac, rather than the Seleucid calendar.

Numismatic legends also point to the Zoroastrian character of the names of Parthian and Armenian kings, particularly Tiridates and Mithradates. Mithradates was a name popular among the kings of Pontus, a region in north-east Asia Minor bordering the Black Sea, which some scholars maintain may have been the cradle of Roman Mithraism. The character of Mithradates VI of Pontus (r. c. 119–63 BCE), who fought against the might of Rome, was so well known in Europe that Racine wrote a book about him and Mozart a three-act opera. Strabo's family in Pontus had been closely allied with both Mithradates V and VI.

ii. Iconography

At the beginning of the Common Era, it seems that Persian reverence for Mithra was widely known. Plutarch identifies Mithra as a 'mediator' (*mesites*) between 'Oromazes' and 'Areimanios' (*On Isis and Osiris* 46). Although this does not directly correspond with the role allocated to Mithra in the Avestan texts, where he is always on the side of Ahura Mazda, it does relate to his role as judge, and also as the contract that is binding on both the *ashavan* and the *dregvant* (Yt 10.2). In Parthian, Middle Persian and Sogdian, various reflexes of the name Mithra occur meaning 'sun', and Strabo mentions that the Persians 'worship the sun, whom they call Mithres' (15.3.13). In the first century BCE, Graeco-Iranian depictions at Nemrud Dagh in south-eastern Anatolia show a syncretistic 'Apollo-Mithra-Helios Hermes' as a radiate divinity, carved in late Greek style, but wearing the Persian high headdress, or *tiara*. This is the earliest portrayal of Mithra. A relief at Arsameia below Nemrud Dagh shows a king shaking hands with a solar deity, who wears local costume, and is crowned and radiates. Such iconography seems to have become the model for Mithra in Roman typology, and a royal cult of Mithra in Commagene could be the means through which an antecedent of Mithraism was transmitted to Rome.[15] The onomastic inscription on the tomb of Antiochus I Theos of Commagene (69–34 BCE) indicates the particular elevation of Ahura Mazda and the *yazatas* Mithra and Verethragna among western Iranians at this point in time.

Coins of the Kushans depict Mithra with a beard and a solar nimbus, wearing an Iranian tunic, cloak and boots. He stands in warrior stance with one hand on a sword or spear, the other holding a torque or a ribboned diadem, which probably symbolize the *xwarenah*.

Representations of other Iranian *yazatas* in Greek style occur in the coins of Kanishka and his successor, Huvishka (late second century CE). The names are in Bactrian, written in Greek script, and can be identified as: Ahura Mazda; Vayu ('wind'); Xwarenah; Vohu Manah; Ashi Vanguhi ('good recompense'); and Verethragna. The Rabatak inscription relates that Kanishka gave orders to make images of some of these Zoroastrian *yazatas*, but to date none have been found.[16]

Parthian Cosmology

In the mid-Parthian period, Plutarch provides us with a summary of what he knows of Iranian cosmology, apparently relying on some of the many myths that the Persians told about the gods (*On Isis and Osiris* 46–7). Plutarch was intrigued by any scheme that distinguished between good and evil principles, stating that the wisest of men believe that the two are distinct. He seems to have been particularly fascinated by the opinion of 'Zoroaster the Magus', who spoke of the 'better' principle as a god, and the other as a '*daimon*'. This construct is reminiscent of a passage in the *Gathas*, which declares that of the two *manyu* who have existed from the beginning, the one is better and the other bad (1.30, 3). If this is the case, Plutarch must be familiar with a solid oral – or textual? – translation.

This is the first time in Greek literature that the title *magus* is given to Zoroaster, whom Plutarch dates at 5,000 years before the Trojan War. According to Plutarch, Zoroaster spoke of the cosmic division between a divinity who is god (*theos*), named Oromazes, and a spirit (*daimon*) named Areimanios, who are at war with each other. The former 'was most comparable to light' and was 'born from purest light', whereas the other was 'more like darkness and ignorance'. Oromazes is attributed with creating six gods: the first three of good thought (*eunoia*), truth (*aletheia*) and good laws (*eunomia*); and the next three as creator of wisdom (*sophia*), of wealth (*ploutos*) and of 'pleasure (*hedeos*) in what is good (*kalos*)'. Plutarch continues that Areimanios created a similar number in rivalry, and then Oromazes grew to three times his size and moved 'as far away from the sun as the sun is away from the earth'. Having adorned the heaven with stars, Oromazes established the star Sirius (Tishtrya) in the role of guardian and placed 24 other gods in an egg, which was pierced by the 24 rival divinities of Areimanios.[17] At this point evil became 'mingled with good'.

Plutarch concludes with Theopompus' statement about the two cosmic forces alternating in power for 3,000 years, and then engaging in war for the last 3,000 years. His account provides us with a comprehensive description of Zoroastrian cosmology, which is not presented systematically in any extant Iranian text until the Middle Persian *Bundahishn*. In the *Bundahishn*, Ohrmazd (Ahura Mazda) creates the world in two stages of 3,000 years, first in its *menog* state including all the spiritual beings needed to combat evil, then its *getig* state. After this period, Ahriman (Angra Mainyu) pierces the world at *Nav Ruz* and 'rushes in', mingling evil with good. This time of 'mixture' lasts for another 6,000 years, but the advent of Zarathushtra at the end of the third millennium sets the scene for the final period of battle, and the ultimate separation of good and evil.

Ahura Mazda's location beyond the sun echoes the Young Avestan setting of the 'endless lights' beyond the sun (Vd 11.1–2, 10). The numerical and functional references to the *amesha spentas* and the *yazatas*, and the fact that some, at least, of the narrative was said to be known to Theopompus in the fourth century BCE, supports the hypothesis that there was a developed Zoroastrian schema not only long before Middle Persian accounts, but well before it was known to Plutarch.

Plutarch recognizes that the Iranians upheld the vertical division between 'good' and 'bad' in their dress – they wore white to ward off 'the powers of darkness'[18] – and in their taxonomy of animals and plants: some plants belong to the 'beneficent god', others to 'the evil *daimon*;' some animals, such as 'dogs, birds, and hedgehogs', belong to the former, but 'water rats' to the latter (*On Isis and Osiris* 46). It was considered a good act to kill 'bad animals'.

A Time of Good Rule

i. Parthian Heroes

Evidence of Parthian self-promotion of their own good rule may be found in some of the Iranian legends which were elaborated and transmitted in Parthian, but which now exist in Middle or New Persian recensions. One 3,000-word heroic text, preserved by the Parthians and written down in the Sasanian period, is the *Ayadgar-i Zareran* – the 'Memorial of Zarer' – an account of the war between Vishtaspa and the Chionian king, Arjasp. The story concerns the first battle of the faith, which the sage Jamaspa predicts will lead to the fall of many Iranian heroes, including the dedicated defender of the faith, General Zarer, before the Mazda-worshippers will prevail. Jamaspa is said to have received this ability to foretell the future, along with knowledge of all sciences through the scent of a flower that he had received from Zarathushtra.

This story probably belonged to the repertoire of Parthian minstrels,[19] who developed an early version of Iranian mythico-history. The Iranian heroes of these early epic poems seem to epitomize the earthly battle for good over evil in the form of the earthly enemy, the Turanians. The core of the Parthian military force consisted of several noble families, including the house of Suren. It is around this time that the eastern Iranian Saka hero, Rostam, is thought to absorb elements of the myth of Herakles, who in Parthian times was associated with Verethragna, the *yazata* of victory.[20] The first-century BCE syncretistic onomastic, 'Artagnes (Verethragna)-Herakles-Ares' at Nemrud Dagh, is evidence for the identification of Verethragna with Herakles, which is reasserted in a bilingual Greek and Parthian inscription of Valakhsh III (105–47 CE) on a bronze statue from Mesene. Iranian heroic stories were first collected in the *Khwaday namag*, a Middle Persian prototype for the *Shah Nameh*.

The narrative poem *Vis and Ramin* can also be traced back to the Parthian period, possibly to the ruling Godarz family. The geographical setting for the poem, between Merv in the north-east and Hamadan in the west, and the names of some of the characters, support a Parthian origin. The story is about the enduring love between a royal prince Ramin, who is an accomplished minstrel, and Vis, the wife of his brother King Mobad. In the narrative, Vis and Ramin eventually become co-rulers, reigning with justice in a state of ecological, emotional and economic harmony. The story, transcribed into New Persian in the eleventh century CE by Gurgani, is similar to, and may be a prototype for, that of Tristan and Isolde, which came to the West with minstrels who had access to both Crusader and Saracen camps in the Holy Land.

ii. Jewish Perception of Parthian Rule

According to Josephus, Cyrus II had been 'moved by God' to encourage the Jews to return home and to rebuild the temple in Jerusalem (*Antiquities* 11.1.1–2). This perception of Ancient Persian rule as instrumental in the unfolding of Jewish religious history had endured well into the Parthian period, where such beneficence contrasted sharply with the destruction wrought by the Romans. Jewish chronicles from the Middle Ages mention the

Parthian period as one of the best in their history, during which the Jews maintained close and positive contacts with the ruling Iranians.

Unusual frescoes discovered in the synagogue in Dura Europos (Syria) indicate that the official royal art of the Parthians remained influential into the early Sasanian period, and that the Jews still perceived Iranian rule in a favorable light.[21] The synagogue was dedicated in 244/5 CE, but was shortly after buried under the reinforced Roman ramparts, along with a Mithraeum and Christian house church. In the scenes of the story of Esther, the Persian king Ahaseurus (Xerxes) sits on the Throne of Solomon, wearing the Parthian costume of belted tunic, wide trousers and long-sleeved coat.[22] Mordechai, astride a white horse, is similarly dressed. These depictions of Biblical figures echo those on Parthian coins and statuary, and indicate the endurance of Parthian notions of just rule.

iii. 'Good Command' in Buddhist Rock Edicts

A sense of the prevalent Iranian worldview on the eastern borders of Iran is found in some mid-third-century BCE edicts of the Buddhist king Ashoka from Afghanistan and Pakistan. The existence of at least half-a-dozen rock-carved edicts, written in the Aramaic of the type used in the Achaemenid chancellery, indicates that some of the Iranian-speaking *Kambojas* of the Gandhara/Swat Valley area had continued with their indigenous Zoroastrian tradition.

The central theme promulgated in these Aramaic edicts is *dhamma*, meaning, in this context, 'social and moral code of conduct'. *Dhamma* is translated in an Aramaic text at Taxila by the Iranian term *hunishtan*, meaning 'good command'.[23] The Prakrit word for an ascetic, *sramana* (literally 'one who exerts effort'), is translated by the Iranian term *arzush* (Av. *arezush*), meaning 'upright'. Such expressions relate to the ideology of the *Gathas*, as do two Aramaic versions of edicts at Kandahar, which explain that following good order leads to the diminishing of evil in the world. The parallel Greek and Indian Prakrit versions give a positive description of the effects of *dhamma*, but no pairing of the notion that furthering good results in the decrease of evil. One Buddhist *jataka* includes the remark that the *Kambojas* considered the killing of insects, snakes and frogs to be a religious duty.[24] This is in accord with the precepts in the *Videvdad* and the behavior of the *magi*, as mentioned by Plutarch.

The Ashokan Aramaic inscriptions represent the first time that Zoroastrians had encountered direct proselytizing from another religion. It has been suggested that in its turn, the Zoroastrian presence in the region led to a greater receptivity of Mahayana Buddhist themes such as the concept of

Maitreya, the future Buddha and the *bodhisattva* Kshitigarbha, who conducts the souls of the dead away from evil.[25]

In their legends, the Saka of the Khotan region traced their conversion to Buddhism to the time of Ashoka, although this probably did not occur until several centuries later. Khotanese Saka Buddhist texts retain many older Iranian beliefs, perhaps the most significant being the Avestan concept of the *xwarenah* (MP *xwarrah*) – the '[divine] fortune or glory' – that rests with the Iranian hero or ruler who follows the straight path. This morphs into the *pharra* of Khotanese texts, which, in some contexts, is similar to the Old Iranian meaning, but elsewhere refers to the stages of a monk following the Buddhist path. That the Iranian notion of a path leading to the endless light of Ahura Mazda was known to the Khotanese Saka may be reflected in their word for the sun in the sky – *urmaysde*. This echoes the Gathic description of Ahura Mazda as having 'the appearance of the sun' (Y 43.16).[26]

Emblems of Good Rule

i. Xwarenah

A stylized representation of the *xwarenah* appeared on Kushan coins from Vima Kadphises onwards, in the form of flames on the shoulder of the king, and on sculptures of the Buddha from Shotorak and Paitava in the Hindu Kush near Kabul. This motif is later portrayed on coins of the Sasanian king Valakhsh (484–8 CE).[27] On the reverse of some of the coins of Kanishka is an anthropomorphic representation of fire – *Atar* (Bactrian *Athsho*), depicted as a man with flaming shoulders.

The flaming shoulder motif is expanded in a few Kushan coins depicting Kanishka on the obverse, with Buddha, Shakyamuni Buddha or Maitreya on the reverse, entirely surrounded by a flaming aureola. The halo motif also appears on some of the earliest extant representations of the Buddha, including that on a casket from Bimaran, Afghanistan, usually dated to the mid-first century CE. The connection between this iconography and the Zoroastrian emblem of fire is made explicit in a second- or early third-century CE painting from the early Kushan-era Buddhist *vihara* of Kara Tepe, near Termez in southern Uzbekistan. Under an image of the meditating Buddha, who sits within a circle of flames, is a Bactrian inscription that reads 'Buddha-Mazda'. The fusion of the symbolism of the glory of Ahura Mazda with the image of the Buddha could denote either a Zoroastrian modification of Buddhist iconography, or the Buddhist incorporation of Ahura Mazda as an attendant local deity.[28]

ii. Ring of Investiture

This endowment with the divine fortune or glory is also depicted in the ring of investiture, which the Parthians adapted from earlier inhabitants of western Iran. High up on a rock face in a schoolyard at Sar-e Pol-e Zohab, in Kermanshah province, is a late third millennium BCE carving of Annubanini, ruler of the Lullubi, receiving the ring of divine authority from Ishtar. Directly underneath this scene is an eroded Parthian relief showing a mounted Parthian king, identified in an inscription as Godarz II (c. 40–51 CE), who offers the ring in his right hand to a local ruler (Fig. 10). In a late Parthian relief from Susa dated 215 CE, king Ardavan IV sits on a throne as he offers the ring to the standing local satrap, named Khwasak. Coins of Pacorus I (c. 39 BCE) depict the ring of investiture proffered by a Greek-style winged goddess. This motif endures until the early second century CE, and the ring is sometimes also offered by a male figure. These, and other symbolic imagery on the coins, may represent Iranian *yazatas*.[29] The identification of Iranian *yazatas* hypostatized in Greek form is clear on contemporary Kushan coins. Although Greek iconography impacted early Parthian plastic forms, other ancient Iranian themes apart from investiture appear as the dynasty progresses, including combat and religious scenes. Parthian-era rock reliefs at Izeh in Elymais indicate that local rulers were influenced by Parthian motifs, iconography and style.[30]

Fig. 10. Relief of a mounted Parthian king, Godarz II (c. 40–51 CE), offering the ring of power (arrowed) to a local ruler.

Parthian Religious Praxis

In *Vis and Ramin*, Gurgani nostalgically recreated the atmosphere of Zoroastrian Iran. It begins with a springtime feast at the court – a reference to the celebration of *Nav Ruz* – and refers to the festival of *Mihragan*, as well as to fire temples. Vis' marriage to her brother Viru remains unconsummated because of Vis' menstruation, which makes her unapproachable. Such information, supported by remarks in Strabo and other contemporary Greek writers, indicates that many of the observances of *Videvdad* were in practice during Parthian times. The endogamous marriage customs of the Persian royal dynasties are also introduced. Vis and Ramin share the same wet-nurse, making them honorary siblings. A Greek document from Avroman attests to this Parthian practice of near-kin marriage, which is advocated in a few Young Avestan texts.[31]

i. Fire Temples

The Parthian term *ayazan* appears on the Nisa ostraca, relating to Old Persian *ayadana*, meaning 'sanctuary'. Archeological excavations have uncovered evidence of Iranian fire temples dating back to this period, indicating a steady growth in the cult of fire, as also attested in both external and internal literary sources. One such external source is Isidore of Carax, a Greco-Parthian who lived in the Mesene (southern Iraq) at the beginning of the Common Era. His *Parthian Stations* describes the road crossing the Parthian empire from the Euphrates to Arachosia, and the significant sites along the way.

Isidore records that an 'eternal fire' burnt at 'Asaak in Astavene', where Arsakes had been crowned. Such a description apparently denotes the regnal fire, which would have been extinguished at the death of the king. By the end of the Parthian period, Arsacid vassal kings had established dynastic fires of their own. The first Sasanian king, Ardashir, is attributed with carrying these local fires 'back to their places of origin' because they had not been authorized by 'the kings of old'.[32]

By Sasanian times, three great hilltop fires in the regions of Pars, Media and Parthia were already considered to be ancient: these were named as Adur Farrobay, Adur Gushnasp and Adur Burzen-Mihr respectively, and their establishment was associated with the origins of the world (Bd. 18.8–17). The location of Adur Gushnasp has been verified as Takht-e Suleiman in Iranian Azerbaijan, where the discovery of a Sasanian seal identified the owner as a priest of the 'house of the fire Adur Gushnasp'. The foundation of the fire temple there dates from the Sasanian period.

In the second century CE, Pausanias noted that the Persians of Lydia had temples in the cities of Hierocaesarea and Hypaipa, with an inner chamber where priests would place dry wood on an altar heaped with ashes, causing a blazing fire (Pausanias 5.27.5–6). According to the specifications in *Videvdad* 14.2, any fuel offered to the fire had to be hard and dry. Strabo had commented earlier that the Persians placed 'dry pieces of wood without bark' upon the fire, and described the *pyraitheia* in Cappadocia as large enclosures with an altar in the middle, heaped with ashes upon which the *magi* maintained an ever-burning fire (15.3.14–15).

No temple has yet been found in any of these named places, but the discovery of fire temples at Kuh-e Khajeh in Sistan and at Mele Hairam in modern Turkmenistan, point to an established fire cult in eastern Iran during the Parthian period (Fig. 11). Later Middle Persian and Muslim references to a fire at Karkoy in Sistan would also support this. Of the two temples built one over the other at Kuh-e Khajeh, the earliest one appears to date from the mid- to late-Parthian period, the second towards the end of the Sasanian era. Both temples had a central rectangular hall, off which was a small square room with four columns and a still smaller room, which is thought to have been the fire sanctuary, or *atashgah*, where the fire was kept, apparently concealed from view of the public and taken to the columned room for ceremonies. Both rooms were surrounded by a circumambulatory corridor, an innovative division of space first evidenced in the enclosure of the courtyard of Building 2 at Altin Tepe.[33]

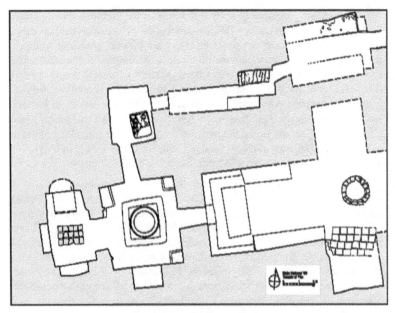

Fig. 11. Plan of fire temple, Mele Hairam.

The squared four-columned structure originated in Achaemenid times, as exemplified in the square hall in the *apadana* at Susa, but its use as a religious sanctuary post-dates the Ancient Persians. In Sasanian times, it seems that this structure was often substituted by the four open arches of the *chahartaq*, topped with a free-standing dome. The *eyvan*, a vaulted arch opening into a courtyard, which is also found at Mele Hairam and Kuh-e Khajeh, became a prominent feature of Iranian architecture. Some art historians consider the monumental niches of the sixth-century Kushan site at Bamiyan to have been adaptations of the *eyvan*.

The existence of Parthian temples in eastern locations, close to the emerging Kushan Empire, may also have had an impact on the development of the form of the Buddhist *stupa*. Circumambulatory corridors appear in the Kara Tepe *vihara*, constructed around the mid-second century CE, and then become a standard feature of Buddhist architecture. The Parthian cult of fire also seems to have been replicated to an extent in the Kushan hilltop temple at Surkh Kotal, which, when excavated between 1952 and 1966, was found to have an inner sanctuary at the top, with a single cella containing a raised square stone platform, flanked by a pillar at each corner.

As mentioned in the previous chapter, the Iranian practice of enclosing the fire was evidently familiar to Jews at the time of the Parthian-era composition of 2 *Maccabees*. The ancient Iranian connection of fire with the sun may be reflected in early references to Parthian-era temples as 'places of Mithra'. A third-century BCE Greek papyrus mentions a 'Mithraion' among the temples in Fayum, Egypt, which may have been established during Ancient Persian rule. The word for a pre-Christian temple in Armenia is *mehean*, from Old Iranian *mithrayana*. One temple, at Pekeric in modern Turkey, is known to have been expressly dedicated to Mithra.[34] It stood until the fourth century CE, when St. Gregory urged the recently converted Armenian king, Tiridates, to destroy it. The current (New Persian) term for a fire temple in Iran – *Dar-i Mihr* – means 'gate or court of Mithra'.

It has been suggested that contact with the Greeks stimulated the development of Zoroastrian image cults in the Seleucid and early Parthian periods. The Parthian word *bagnpat* is attested, which refers to a temple priest, possibly of an image shrine. The title *magush* also occurs, indicating that Parthians continued to use western Zoroastrian terminology from the previous period. References by Isidore of Charax to buildings serviced by Persian priests include a temple sacred to 'Anaitis' at Ecbatana, and one of Greek style at 'Concobar' dedicated to 'Artemis'. A complex unearthed at Kangavar – possibly Isidore's Concobar – was initially thought to be Seleucidera, but is now dated to Sasanian times. So far, no images or temples to Anahita have been positively identified.[35] As the Greek cultural impact waned in the early first century CE, so the Parthians dropped the title 'philhellene' from their silver tetradrachms, and began to reproduce the fire-holder on some of their bronze coinage.[36]

ii. Offerings to Fire and to Water

A Nisa ostracon gives us the oldest title for a priest responsible for tending the fire: *aturshpat* or 'fire master'. In his description of fire-tending by the *magi*, Strabo notes that their mouths were covered by the cheek pieces of their felt hats and that they sang invocations for a long time, while holding tamarisk twigs in their hand. The Persian *Rivayats* state that *barsom* should come from tamarisk or pomegranate tree, 'as is manifest from the Avesta'.[37] A second-century CE relief on a large boulder at Bisutun shows a *magus*, or possibly a ruler (his flowing hair is encircled with a ribboned diadem), pouring oil or incense onto a small fire-holder (Fig. 12). Such ritual activity is iconographically depicted in later Sogdian frescoes and on a Sogdian ossuary, as well as on a possible late Achaemenid seal.[38] It may reflect the ritual offering to fire, referred to in Middle Persian texts as *atash zohr*. According to Strabo, this offering to fire included a small part of the *omentum*, which seems to have been the Parthian equivalent of the fat-offering from sheep referred to in *Videvdad* 18.70.[39] Strabo describes the sacrifice in a manner almost identical to Herodotus, although it remains unclear who killed the animal – the *magus* who oversaw the ritual, or another functionary.

Alongside offerings to fire, there is also evidence of offerings to water by both priests and laity. Strabo refers to this as a sacrifice, remarking that care was taken that none of the blood from the animal would defile the water, although he does not specify what was offered (15.3.14). One section of *Nerangestan* (Ner. 30) indicates that the ritual libation to the waters could be performed as a separate ceremony: another passage states that *any* devout person – man, woman or child, who is able to recite the liturgy (*yasna*) correctly – could perform this *zaothra* (Ner. 22.1–5). The implication is that this ritual was not confined to male priests, but could be offered by anyone, including a layperson, who knew the liturgy by heart.[40] Evidence of a lay offering to the waters has recently been discovered in natural pools in the Chale Ghar cave mines near Veshnaveh, Kashan. These offerings, dating from the third century BCE onwards, include ceramic bowls containing fruit stones, grains, nuts and pomegranate seeds, as well as flasks and pitcher jugs. Such elements suggest the liquid and vegetational elements of an oblation to water, and are consistent with known Zoroastrian ritual offerings relating to the general health and well-being of the land and its inhabitants.

*Fig. 12. Relief depicting an offering to fire (*atash zohr*), Bisutun.*

A rare reference to *haoma* in Greek sources may be found in the writings of Pliny the Elder, who died in the volcanic eruption of Vesuvius in 79 CE. He wrote that the eastern *magi* of his own time were the authorities on 'magic', and that according to Democritus, they used a special herb called *aglaophitis* in order 'to conjure up the gods' (*Natural History* 24.102). The Greek name of the herb means 'shining/bright light', which appears to reflect the Avestan epithets 'bright/light' (*raoca*) and 'sunny' (*xwanwant*) of the plant *haoma* (Y 11.10, Y 9.1).

When Humans will be Happy

In the third century CE, Justin's *Epitome* (which contains much of Pompeius Trogus' earlier *Historiae Philippicae*) records that the Zoroastrians expose their dead, to be torn to pieces by birds and dogs, and then that their bare bones are put in the earth (41.3.5). This echoes Herodotus' description. According to Isidore, the Parthian kings were buried in the necropolis at Nisa, but although this site has been excavated extensively by Russian archeologists and then by an Italian-Turkmeni team, no royal tombs have been found. After the sack of Ctesiphon in 216 CE, the Roman emperor Caracalla is said to have stopped at the Parthian necropolis in Arbela to desecrate the royal tombs and scatter the bones. At Uruk in southern Iraq, several glazed ceramic sarcophagi for Parthian burials have been found, with relief decorations showing how some of the deceased were dressed in jackets and baggy trousers. Fragments of sarcophagus lids from the Parthian period were also found at a site near Susa. Such finds indicate that interment was practiced alongside exposure.

According to Plutarch, the Iranian perception of death was that it was temporary. Plutarch's understanding of the dialectical struggle of Iranian cosmology was that at a time in the future, Areimanios would perish by the very plague and famine that he had inflicted upon the world, and would disappear. At that juncture, the earth would become level and flat, 'and all men will be happy and speak one tongue and live one life under one form of government' (*On Isis and Osiris* 47). This account coheres with the later *Bundahishn*, which narrates that the incursion of Ahriman caused the mountains to be raised up, but that at the end the metals in the mountains will be melted and the earth made flat again (Bd. 34.18).[41]

In the Iranian context, an essential element of the restoration of the material world is that it is rendered 'incorruptible' and 'non-decaying' (Yt 19.89), through eliminating the death-bringing activity of Angra Mainyu. This intimation of a change in the physical properties of the material world also encompasses the human body: the living will be made indestructible, and the dead will arise and live again in this new existence (Yt 19.89–90, 94). Such Iranian ideas of physical resurrection are implicit in Theopompus' reference to the happy state of humanity after the removal of evil, and explicit in his statement, recorded by Diogenes Laertius, that humans 'will come to life again and be immortal' (*Lives of the Philosophers* 1.9).[42]

Eschatological Ripples

It is in the Parthian period that we find the most widespread resonances of the 'vertical split' scenario, which was attributed by Plutarch to the Persians. In a recent article the term 'memetic migration' was coined in reference to reconfigurations of Zoroastrian features across cultural and religious boundaries.[43] Many such 'memetic migrations' can be found between Iranian, Jewish, Gnostic and early Christian eschatology of the Parthian period. In some instances we can adduce the primacy and consistency of a Zoroastrian theme, which then seems to have impacted the formulation of concepts in neighboring religions. In each case of migration of theme (and *meme*), the theological and eschatological resonances differ as each religion develops its own *Heilsgeschichte*.

Jewish texts of this period display a growing emphasis on the struggle between the forces of good and the forces of evil. Such antagonism reflects a time in history when the Seleucid Greeks – particularly Antiochus IV Epiphanes – and then the Romans encroached on the autonomy of the Jewish religious infrastructure.

Throughout this period, the Jews and Parthians maintained positive contacts with each other. Parthian envoys visited Jerusalem early in the first century BCE, and both peoples were equally perturbed by the Roman incursions.[44] In 40 BCE the Parthians conquered Syria and Palestine, installing a pro-Parthian Hasmonean king in place of the Roman ethnarch Hyrcanus II. According to Josephus, the Parthians waited until after the Passover so that pilgrims to Jerusalem could lend their support (*Antiquities* 15.13.4). Such political relations accompanied close cultural interaction, not only in Palestine, but also between Parthians and diaspora Jews in Parthia itself, Babylonia, Syria and throughout Anatolia, particularly the Pontus region.

By the late third century BCE, the Persian concept of *paradeisos* had entered into the Greek-speaking culture of the Jews of Alexandria, to the extent that it was the word of choice for Septuagint translators to use for garden, fruit orchard or vineyard. *Paradeisos* is used in diverse passages where the Hebrew original has 'garden', especially if the idea of wondrous beauty is to be conveyed. Whereas in both Talmudic and modern Hebrew, *pardes* is only an orchard, in the *koine* Greek of the New Testament, the word assumes the sense of humanity's restoration to the Garden of Eden, the original paradise on earth, where the order and structure of God's rule pertains (see, for example, *Luke* 23.43).

It is at this time that novel Jewish expressions of a cosmic division are found in the abundance of references to both angels and demons. The Biblical book of Daniel, compiled in exile and completed around the second century BCE, includes mention of angelic beings and their engagement in the future struggles. For the first time in the Hebrew Bible, these angels are named: Gabriel gives Daniel wisdom and understanding (*Dan.* 8.16, 9.22); and Michael battles against the 'prince of the kingdom' of Persia (*Dan.* 10.13).

The Talmud states that the names of the angels come from 'Babylon' – that is, the place of the exilic community – and it has been suggested that depictions of such beings may have been stimulated by awareness of the named Iranian *yazatas* and *amesha spentas* – especially *Spenta Mainyu* – whose designations incorporate divine qualities. In the Biblical context, however, angels are regarded as servants of God, not as objects of praise and worship.

During the deutero-canonical period, these angels, who were originally conceived as messengers of God, became part of a dualistic division, being identified as either angels of Light and Good, or angels of Darkness and Evil. The book of *Enoch*, which survives only in complete form in the Ge'ez language of the Ethiopian Orthodox Church liturgy, includes angels who come to earth to consort with the daughters of men, then fall into sin and are judged for bringing chaos to the world. *Enoch 83–90*, which was composed some years after the Book of Daniel, includes vivid descriptions of this final judgment, of an eschatological king, and of paradise as an abode of light.[45]

The strongest evidence for an Iranian stimulus to the developing Judaism of this time is the derivation of the name of a demon in the Book of Tobit.[46] The Greek form of the name, 'Asmodaios', comes from the Iranian designation *Aeshma daeva* – the 'demon of wrath': *aeshma* as 'wrath' is one of the vices of daevic beings in the *Gathas* (1.30.6), and is hypostatized as a demonic force in later Avestan texts (Yt 10.8, 19.46). This entity survives in the form 'Ashmedai' in the Jerusalem Talmud, in Rabbinic literature and in the *Zohar*.[47]

The Septuagint translators had no conception of a wholly evil entity, and use *diabolos* to translate Hebrew *satan* in the sense of 'adversary', not as the personification of an evil deity. From around the second century BCE, however, Jewish apocryphal texts such as *Ascensio Isaiae* and *Jubilees* present a world in which Satan, the 'accuser' of Job (1.6), has developed into the 'prince of demons' at the head of named rebel angels, including Belial (Hebrew, 'worthless') and Mastema (Hebrew, 'adversarial'). There appears to be an element of Zoroastrian influence in this development, since the myth of opposing forces struggling against each other until the end of time has no precedent in Jewish tradition.[48] In Jewish ideology, however, Satan and his minions, although adversarial to God, are subordinate to him from whom they derive, unlike Angra Mainyu, who is completely separate from Ahura Mazda.

The Greek *Testament of the Twelve Patriarchs*, an apocalyptic text that may be a Christian redaction of an earlier work, is another example of demonological beliefs circulating in the mid-Parthian period. The discontinuity between apocryphal works and the Hebrew Bible is echoed in other contemporary apocalyptic texts, such as the Dead Sea Scrolls. At this point, there is no evidence among the Romans of the concept of morally evil deities.[49] The question is whether Zoroastrian cosmology was sufficiently developed by this stage to have such a profound impact on first Jewish and then Christian thought, which was born out of, and then grew away from, a Jewish milieu. Plutarch's description suggests that it was.[50]

An evolving savior concept within Judaism appends an almost divine quality during this period, which was to become central in the Christian schema. References in the book of Daniel to 'the one like the son of man' (i.e. 'like a human being'), who appears 'with the clouds of heaven' (*Dan.* 7.13), have drawn comparisons to the Avestan concept of the *saoshyant*. Daniel's 'son of man' ushers in an everlasting rule and a kingdom that will never be destroyed (*Dan.* 7.14). The later use of the term 'son of man' in the Book of *Enoch* was understood to refer to a representative who possessed and dwelt with 'righteousness', and who would inaugurate a new world order. The Hebrew term *maschiach* had been used of Cyrus in this sense in relation to his defeat of the Babylonians and restoration of Jerusalem,[51] and during the protests against Rome in 132–5 CE, the heroic leader Shimon Bar Kochba was also hailed as *maschiach*.[52] That many Jews took refuge in Parthia following the suppression of this rebellion indicates the continued close alliance between the two peoples at this time.[53]

The concept of resurrection of the dead, which is latent in the post-exilic Biblical text of *Isaiah* 25.6–9, is explicitly expressed in the Book of Daniel, the only section of the Hebrew Bible in which the idea is clearly stated (*Dan.* 12.2–3). This passage marks a decisive break with the pre-exilic notion of Sheol, a dull place of shades, where God also reigns. In Daniel's conception, unlike that of the Iranians, the dead are restored to the same life as before – not to a different life. This notion is echoed in a passage in 2 *Maccabees*, which relates that a Jew threw himself on his sword, rather than commit idolatry, crying out that God would in due course give him back his innards (2 *Macc.* 14.37–45). There was no uniform Jewish teaching on resurrection during the deutero-canonical period. Both Josephus and New Testament texts inform us that the doctrine of the resurrection was rejected by the Sadducees.[54] By the time the *Mishnah* was redacted around 200 CE, however, the teaching on resurrection was considered to have originated in Torah (*Sanhedrin* 10.1). Maimonides later commented on this tractate, which today represents the most orthodox expression of Jewish eschatology. Tracing the history of the concept of resurrection in this way enables us to plot the primacy and coherence of its presence within a Zoroastrian cosmological scheme, and its innovation within Jewish, then Gnostic and Christian settings.[55]

Ascents, Aeons and Apocalypses

Other memetic features circulating during the Parthian period, which are consistent with a Zoroastrian eschatological schema, include visions of the afterlife, and 'secret teachings' (*apocalypses*) concerning the mysteries of both the beginning and end times. Although most Zoroastrian accounts of visionary ascents to the eternal lights are found in Middle Persian inscription or text, it has been shown that the concept of a judgment of the soul at death and a journey to a place of light or darkness is present in Young Avestan texts. *Zand-i Wahman Yasn*, a Middle Persian commentary that purportedly refers to a late Avestan *Bahman Yasht* ('Hymn to Vohu Manah'), contains teachings concerning the universal eschaton and a vision prefiguring the fate of the soul at death. It is a developed Zoroastrian apocalyptic work, and since it incorporates some Parthian terms, it is tempting – although perhaps disingenuous – to place its origin in the Parthian period, even though the final form is about the ninth century CE. The text is, however, generally considered to include some Zoroastrian end-time apocalyptic material from pre-Sasanian times.[56] The association of Vohu Manah with the ability of Zarathushtra to converse with and be guided by Ahura Mazda is alluded to in the *Gathas* (2.43.7), and reflected in a Parthian-era Greek reference to Zoroaster receiving teachings from a 'good *daimon* [spiritual entity]' (*Diodorus Siculus* 1.94.2). The motif of Vohu Manah welcoming the soul of the *ashavan* into the abode of Ahura Mazda was also ancient (Vd 19.31–2).

The text of *Zand-i Wahman Yasn* begins with Zarathushtra asking for immortality, upon which Ohrmazd (Ahura Mazda) shows him the 'wisdom of all knowledge'. Zarathushtra then has a vision of the cosmos as a tree with four branches, of gold, silver, steel and 'mixed iron' that relate to four successive Iranian epochs from the creation of the world by Ohrmazd, through the acceptance and growth of the religion, to a progressive descent into the time of conflict, which will end with the millennium of Zarathushtra (ZWY 1.1–11). A similar division occurs in the Middle Persian *Denkard* (Dk 9.8.1–6). As mentioned earlier, the Iranian division of time into successive world ages was familiar to Greek commentators. A fourfold division of ages associated with gold, silver, bronze and then iron also appears in the Hindu *Manusmriti* ('Laws of Manu'), which is generally dated during the Parthian period.[57] Whereas in the Indian context the world eventually becomes so polluted that it is consumed by fire and the whole process begins anew, in the Iranian schema the world is purged once and for always.

The connection of each of the four aeons with a metal is so similar to the division of kingdoms in Daniel's interpretation of Nebuchadnezzar's dream (2.31–3) that much discussion has centered on which text was prior.[58]

Opinions remain divided as to connections between these Zoroastrian and Biblical apocalypses. For some, the common reference to 'mixed iron' indicates a Greek precedent for Daniel, which perhaps influenced the Iranian fourfold schema.[59] The *Zand-i Wahman Yasn* could also have been impacted by the Greek concept, and adapted it prior to its appearance in Daniel.[60]

Daniel's own end-time dream includes four animals, the last of which is a terrifying horned beast, whose rule ends with the arrival of the 'son of man' (7.1–28). The fourth beast has been paralleled with Azi Dahaka, the dragon of ancient Iranian myth, who becomes Zahak in Middle Persian texts.[61] In the Young Avesta it is Azi Dahaka whom Thraetaona kills, with a weapon that is later carried by the *saoshyant* Astvat-ereta.[62] The epithet *verethrajan* ('victorious'), which is given to the *saoshyant*, corresponds to the Vedic *vritrahan* that is used of Indra after he too has slain a dragon. The theme of a beneficial being, defeating a beastly manifestation of evil and bringing in a new world order, is an integral part of Avestan eschatology that predates the existing form of the Book of Daniel.

A fifth-century Achaemenid setting for the initial composition of the story of Daniel is indicated by its Ancient Persian backdrop and the fact that it uses many Iranian loanwords in the imperial Aramaic parts of the text. The story was then further developed during the Seleucid and early Parthian periods.[63] One significant Aramaic loanword, from an Old Avestan word *razar* meaning 'rule' (as in an architectural instrument), appears in the context of Daniel's dream interpretation. There, *raz* is used to convey the notion of the 'mystery' revealed by God about what will be. This same word is used in the Dead Sea Scrolls in reference to the secret knowledge of the eschaton, and occurs frequently in Middle Persian texts in the sense of a 'secret' relating to both the end-time, or to combating evil.[64] In *Denkard*, Yima acquires the 'secret' of defeating the demons, and thus is able to conquer them.[65]

Other Zoroastrian themes may be found in some of the concepts in the Dead Sea Scrolls, particularly the texts known as the *War Rule* (1QM) and the *Community Rule* (1QS), which describe the tension between the Prince of Light and the Spirit (Hebrew *ruah*) of Darkness, named Belial, and between the Spirits of Truth and those of Perversity and Destruction. The *War Rule* describes a great last battle between the Sons of Light and the Sons of Darkness, ending with an ultimate victory of Light and the complete annihilation of the troops of Belial. In the *Damascus Document*, the figure of the Teacher of Righteousness is prominent.

The passage said to display the closest parallels to Zoroastrian motifs is the section of the *Community Rule* that describes the origins of everything according to the planned design of the God of knowledge, including the creation of humanity to rule the world in which the two spirits of truth and falsehood operate. The righteous walk in paths of light, guided by the Prince of Light, and the wicked walk in paths of darkness, corrupted by the Angel of Darkness (1QS 3: 15–24). This document, however, in common with much Gnostic thought of the inter-testamental period, assigns the creation of the two spirits of light and darkness to God. Gnosticism seems to have been a combination of 'the Zoroastrian cosmic struggle between the opposing principles of good and evil with the Greek philosophical concept of the monad'.[66] The resultant worldview informed the subsequent development of Christianity.

Towards the end of the Parthian period, the Iranian prophet, Mani, was born into a baptizing sect in the west of the realm. The spread of Manichaeism within Iran seems to have provided a channel for some of the Gnosticizing tendencies of the second and third centuries CE to radiate back into Zoroastrian thought. Perhaps it was this stimulus that helped to consolidate the importance of *zurvan* (time) in the Sasanian period. In early Manichaean Middle Persian texts, such as the *Shabuhragan*, one of the names for the Father of Greatness, who dwells in the Paradise of Light, is 'Zurvan'. The Manichaean Parthian equivalent does not put *zurvan* in this pre-eminent position, but uses the word elsewhere in the sense of 'old age' or as part of a proper name, *Zarwandad*. This comparison of usage suggests that by the end of the Parthian period, focus on Zurvan as hypostatized Time was more prominent in south-western Iran, among those who spoke Middle Persian, than among those who spoke Parthian.

It is tempting to see further echoes of Zoroastrian notions of judgment in contemporary oracular works. One such memetic text may be a Jewish apocalyptic pseudepigraphon entitled the *Oracle of Hystaspes*, which is mentioned by Justin Martyr (b. c. 100 CE) to support his claim that the world will end in conflagration (1 *Apologia* 20). The original text of *Oracle of Hystaspes* seems to date to the early Common Era, and was popular with Christians in the mid-second century CE. It appears to have been named after Vishtaspa, Zarathushtra's supporter, who is described in the *Gathas* as following the path of good thought to illumination,[67] and whom Middle Persian texts describe as receiving a vision from Ohrmazd explaining the religion.[68]

The *Oracles of Hystaspes* only survives in excerpts, but the frame story is that of Hystaspes (Vishtaspa), 'a very ancient king of the Medes' who had a wonderful dream that was interpreted by a boy who could 'utter divinations'. The dream predicted the tribulations of the last age and the overthrow of all things – including the might of Rome. This apocalypse was probably woven in Asia Minor, either within Roman territory or in Parthia, and seems to emerge from an Iranianized Judaism, which may have adapted material from an earlier Zoroastrian source to bolster resistance to the Greeks and then to the Romans.[69] The various strands – predominantly Jewish, Christian and Zoroastrian – are now impossible to separate, so that it is not possible to reconstruct the Iranian substratum.

Lactantius' reworking of the *Oracle of Hystaspes*, and the exposition of his own apocalyptic schema in his early fourth-century CE *Divine Institutions*, present certain details that echo Middle Persian formulations – particularly in terms of the divine fire that will judge both the wicked and the righteous: the wicked will feel pain, but not be destroyed; the righteous will not be hurt at all. This representation of judgment through an ordeal of fire accords more readily with the Zoroastrian apocalyptic expression in the *Bundahishn* (34.18-19), than with Jewish or Christian eschatologies.[70] Early reference to the *Oracle of Hystaspes* places the development of such apocalyptic material firmly in the Parthian period, rather than in the later Sasanian time.[71]

Many Zoroasters: Wise Men from the East

The late second-century CE Gnostic *Apocryphon of John*, from the Nag Hammadi collection, makes reference to a 'Book of Zoroaster', which is said to describe the angels who preside over many of the passions of human beings. There were many such pseudepigrapha (falsely-attributed writings) circulating throughout the early Roman Empire claiming to be of divine origin, or the work of ancient culture-heroes who were divinely inspired. According to Clement of Alexandria (c. 150–215 CE), the disciples of the Gnostic Prodicos had used some books given under the name of Zoroaster (*Stromates* 15, 69). Later, Plotinus (204–70 CE) recognized that there was confusion between what was 'original' Zoroastrianism and what was later accretion. Plotinus set his disciples Amelius and Porphyry the task of refuting as spurious certain texts, including the revelations (*apocalypses*) attributed to 'Zoroaster' and 'Zostrianos'. The existence of cryptic sayings and extended narrative poems, purportedly authored by Zoroaster, suggested to Porphyry (c. 234–305) that his name was used as a cipher alongside other Eastern sages of ascribed antiquity, in support of the truths of sectarians.

The extant Greek *Zostrianos* text found at Nag Hammadi seems to be early third century CE, and the frame story with its eponymous main character implies a setting in pre-Christian Iran. Zostrianos is a name mentioned by the Christian apologist Arnobius (d. 330 CE) as that of the grandfather or uncle (*nepos*) of 'Zoroaster the Armenian'.[72] This latter figure is the one whom

Clement of Alexandria identified as Er in Plato's *Republic*.

Canonical Christian texts note not only the presence of *magi* in Palestine at a crucial moment in the foundation history of Christianity (*Matthew* 2.1–12), but also Parthian visitors to Jerusalem (*Acts* 2.9). Whether these were actual or symbolic encounters used as a device to show the global reception of the Gospel, what is certain is that from then on Christianity began to expand into Mesopotamia through missionary activity. Christian communities were concentrated in the areas of Adiabene and its capital, Arbela (Irbil), and Osroene, a region in south-eastern Turkey and north-eastern Syria, with its capital, Edessa, on the site of a former Seleucid city. A synod was held in Edessa as early as 197 CE, and it may have been the site of the first purpose-built church that was destroyed by a flood in 201 CE.

The reputed relics of St. Thomas were located at Edessa in the fourth century CE. Eusebius of Caesarea stated that when the disciples were deciding in which parts of the world they would evangelize, the Apostle Thomas was allotted Parthia (*History of the Church* 3.1). This early testimony was extended in Syriac Christian writings to include the Gandharan realm of the Indo-Parthian king, Gondopharnes (r. c. 20–45 CE). Embedded within the early third-century CE *Acts of Thomas*, which for centuries was incorporated into orthodox libraries, is a classic Gnostic myth describing the exile and redemption of the soul. This Syriac text, known as the 'Hymn of the Pearl', appears to have been written in the vicinity of Edessa, sometime in the first century CE under Parthian rule. The soul, malingering in a state of sleepiness 'in Egypt' while on a quest to retrieve the pearl, receives a wake-up letter from the rulers of Parthia: this letter prompts the soul to seize the pearl, to return to its home in the East and to put on once more its robe of glory so that it might take the pearl to the king.

Perhaps one of the closest similarities between such Gnostic narratives and Zoroastrian mythology concerns the geographical setting. The notion of the 'East' as the source of wisdom is most coherently outlined in a fifth-century CE text ascribed to John Chrysostom, but of heterodox origin:[73] beyond the inhabited world to the east, near a wide ocean, on the Mountain of Victory, lies a cave which the Magi visit annually to honor God, until a star appears which leads them to Judaea. After the resurrection of Jesus, the apostle Thomas went to that province and baptized the Magi.

That the Magi of the Christian Gospel tradition were identified as Iranians from the Parthian period seems to be reflected in the mid-sixth century Byzantine mosaic at Ravenna, Italy, in which the 'wise men' from the East bring gifts to the Christ-child. They wear similar pointed hats, Parthian tunics and leggings to those of Xerxes and Mordechai on the synagogue murals at

Dura Europos. It has been suggested that the connection of the Christian Magi with the East may be based on a prevalent Zoroastrian tradition concerning the site of the Parthian fire temple at Kuh-e Khajeh, by the shores of Lake Hamun in the far east of Iran. This is the place where, you may recall, according to Avestan tradition, the *saoshyant* Astvat-ereta would defeat evil and then render the world incorruptible.

The Arsacid Parthians, whose rule had witnessed the dynamic emergence of diverse religious movements from Seleucia to Sistan and beyond, were succeeded, not by the military might of the Romans, but by Persian vassals, the Sasanians, who eventually took the western Parthian base of Ctesiphon in 226 CE. The Sasanians met the challenge presented by the scripture-based proselytism of some of the Near Eastern religions with the commitment to produce a valid sacred text of their own in the form of the Avesta

Chapter IV

Eranshahr: The Sasanian Center of the World

Fig. 13. Investiture of Ardashir I by Ohrmazd, Naqsh-e Rostam.

This rock relief of the investiture of the first Sasanian king, Ardashir I (r. 224–40 CE), depicts both Ahura Mazda and the king on horseback trampling the heads of their respective opponents, Ardavan, the last Parthian king, and Ahriman, as a hypostatized king of evil, whose hair curls like snakes around his head. The imagery symbolizes both material and spiritual victory.

Ahura Mazda, in human form, is the same height as Ardashir. He is identified by the priestly barsom *he holds, by his mural crown, and in an accompanying inscription. In his hand, Ahura Mazda holds the ring of investiture, symbolic of the* xwarrah *(Av.* xwarenah), *which he offers to the monarch, consecrating his rule, and that of the Sasanians. In a bilingual Greek and Middle Persian inscription on Ardashir's horse, the king is acknowledged as 'Mazda-worshipping majesty, king of kings of Iran, whose lineage is from the gods'.[1] The same terminology also appears on Ardashir's coins, and those of subsequent Sasanian kings. The phrase indicates a distinction between Ahura Mazda, who invests the king, and the king himself.*

Eranshahr: Setting the Scene

The powerful representation above (Fig. 13), along with its accompanying inscriptions, tells us that from the outset the Sasanians wanted to create a lasting impression. They also convey much about the way Sasanians wanted to be perceived. Middle Persian inscriptions of Sasanian kings and those of one politically-powerful priest present a perspective on the Zoroastrian religion that takes little account of normative lay practice, but emphasizes the role of priests and monarchs as the key purveyors of religion.

In contrast to the preceding Parthian era, there is a plethora of sources relating to the Sasanians. Alongside rock reliefs and inscriptions dating from their assumption of power from the Parthians in the early third century CE, internal sources include numismatic legends and iconographic representations that also act as expressions of a royal or priestly worldview. These are found on stucco carvings, seals, eating and drinking vessels, and some rare fragments of silk. Middle Persian religious texts were mostly committed to writing in the ninth and tenth centuries, but often reflect Sasanian theology, mores and mythico-history. Much of the extensive Sasanian Middle Persian literature referred to in later Arabic and New Persian works is now lost, however. External sources include Greek, Syriac and Armenian Christian polemical texts, the Babylonian Talmud and Rabbinic commentaries, and later Arabic historiographies.

Regional expressions of Zoroastrianism are attested both within and outside the bounds of *Eranshahr* – the Sasanian name for the realm of the Iranians. Chapter V will explore the form of the religion in Sogdiana and Chorasmia, which remained Zoroastrian until the advent of Islam in the early eighth century CE. In the late fourth century CE, Bishop Basil of Caesarea wrote about the local community of Zoroastrians in Cappadocia as numerous and spread throughout the country.[2] Strabo had earlier referred to the 'tribe of the *magi*' as being large in Cappadocia, where there were 'many sanctuaries of the Persian gods' (15.3.15). Such references to established communities outside the regular boundaries of the Sasanian Empire serve to correct the impression that Zoroastrianism developed solely within the cultural framework of Iran.

The previous chapter mentioned fire temples in Lydia and Armenia, as well as throughout Parthian Iran. For the last 200 years of the Parthian dynasty, Armenia had been in subject status, which was maintained under the Sasanians until the early fifth century CE, although the Roman Empire also exercised power and influence in the region during this period. Armenian Christian historians and apologists provide many details of the Zoroastrian beliefs and customs of both Armenia and Sasanian Iran during the period immediately prior to the conversion of Armenia in 301 CE. Georgia was also a predominantly Zoroastrian country until its conversion to Christianity in the early fourth century. Georgian legend records that in pre-Christian times, the laity would offer sacrifices to their god 'Armazi' (Ahura Mazda) near the 'bridge of the *magi'*, and that at night shepherds would call on Armazi for help.[3] (A Zoroastrian remnant may be found in the use of the title *dastur* for the assistants of self-appointed local priests in the eastern Georgian highlands, and in some of their practices.[4]) These widespread communities, defined in part by their geographic location, exemplify a broader stream of Zoroastrianism, with variant praxes, iconographies and *yazatas*, than is often acknowledged.

The religious entrenchment of some Sasanian monarchs was partly prompted by confrontations with the Byzantines on the western and north-western borders of the empire. This brought not only constant military challenge throughout the Sasanian period, but also the problem of Zoroastrian conversion to the 'Church of the East', firstly in Mesopotamia, where Zoroastrians were not in the majority, but eventually extending across Iran as far as Sogdiana. There were many Christian communities in Iranian territory at the beginning of the Sasanian era, and Bishoprics were founded at Ctesiphon and Gondeshapur towards the end of the third century. Conversions – and martyrdoms – are narrated in Syriac Christian hagiographies, such as that of Mar Giwargis, the grandson of a Zoroastrian *mowbed*, early in the seventh century. The simultaneous spread of Manichaeism followed a similar path along the trade routes throughout the empire. Jewish communities were also well-established in western Iran, and

Rabbinic academies in Mesopotamia – first at Nehardea, then Sura and Pumbeditha – were responsible for generating the Babylonian Talmud during Sasanian times. Although the normative texts of these religious groups construct clear conceptual and behavioral boundaries, and often adopt critical attitudes towards each other, this did not preclude the general population of Eranshahr from a degree of inter-religious interaction.

Given this diversity of religions – many of which were text-based – one can better understand the impetus of the high priest Kerdir's references to 'Mazda-worship' (*mazdesn*) in terms of the fundamental religion of the Sasanians. Questions relating to the superiority of one belief system over another were now added to those ultimate questions about the origins, purpose and meaning of life. The challenge of the religiously 'Other' led to an organizational restructuring in terms of the development of both clerical and ritual institutions, as well as intellectual defense mechanisms. As the dynasty progressed, the Zoroastrian priesthood expanded its authority and prestige, and endowed fire temples became wealthy and powerful places. Increasing control by the priesthood is reflected in attempts to eliminate religious heterodoxy, and to combat proselytism from other faiths.

During this period of consolidation of priestly power, Zoroastrian rituals and texts became standardized and codified, including the *Yasna* liturgy and the Avestan corpus, but there is also archeological and textual evidence for continuity of local shrine worship and domestic praxis by the laity, supported by lived Zoroastrianism in both Iran and India in subsequent centuries.

What is particularly interesting about the inscriptions of Kerdir, and, in fact, of every Sasanian inscription, is that there is no mention of Zarathushtra. Ahura Mazda, not Zarathushtra, is the focus of faith. The question is raised, then, as to whether the religion had yet acquired the fixed form of 'orthodox Zoroastrianism', as defined by later Middle Persian texts. The Middle Persian word often translated as 'orthodox' is *poryotkesh*, which literally means the 'first [early, or foremost] teaching'. It has been argued that it was not until early Islamic times that a small group of Zoroastrian priests created their own 'standardized Zoroastrianism', as represented in Middle Persian books. Such systematization did not develop from a vacuum, but from a particular priestly perspective. The 'Zoroastrianism' of Sasanian times must have been much broader than that which can be assumed from either Sasanian official inscriptions or Middle Persian textual assertions, while retaining a general nucleus of some of the emblematic themes expressed in the 'Avestan world-view' of earlier times.

Preserving the Avesta

The sense of safeguarding and nurturing an ancient tradition dating back to the earliest time of the religion is present in Middle Persian accounts of the transmission of the Avesta. The document form of the *Denkard* narrative concerning the collection of the Avestan texts dates to the time of Khosrow I (531–78 CE), although its final written form is three to four centuries later. *Denkard* records that after the Arsacid king Valakhsh had ordered the preservation of every part of the Avesta and *zand* that had survived the incursion of Alexander, then Ardashir I (the first Sasanian king) commanded Tosar, a teacher priest (*herbad*)[5] and spiritual leader (*menog sardar*), to bring the scattered teachings of the faith to the court. From this collection, Tosar is said to have compiled a canon of authoritative works representing 'the whole teaching of the Mazda-worshipping religion'.

The account in *Denkard* continues that Shapur I (c. 240–72 CE) encouraged the collection of various writings 'from the religion' which had been dispersed to India, the Byzantine Empire and other lands, and 'considered them with the Avesta'.[6] The list of texts collected included medicine, astronomy, geography, physics, logic and other arts and sciences, implying that at this juncture the canon of the Avesta was expanded to incorporate much material that was non-Iranian. This narrative suggests that the original Avestan teachings were perceived as the microcosm, within which everything needful to answer life's big questions and to lead a purposeful life were contained. All other materials that fitted with this perspective were considered as part of the same vision.

Although the *Denkard* narrative reflects a late Sasanian tradition, there is a reference in one of Kerdir's late third-century inscriptions to 'revelation in the *nask*'. *Nask*, meaning 'bundle', is the term used later to refer to the 21 *nask* recension of the Avesta that is said to have taken place in Shapur II's time (309–79 CE), under the high priest Adurbad-i Mahraspandan. The *nask* mentioned by Kerdir may include *Videvdad*, since similar eschatological passages are found in both texts.[7] The *Kephalaia*, a Manichaean Coptic text describing the life of Mani (contemporary with Kerdir), states that Zarathushtra's teachings were inferior to those of Jesus, Buddha and Mani himself, since Zarathushtra's disciples did not commit his teachings to writing until after his death. From this time on, the Sasanians were galvanized to preserve and present the Avesta and its *zand* as authoritative scripture in the manner of other religious traditions.

Shapur II was a strong king who brought stability to the region during his long rule, controlling the intrusion of various external elements such as the nomadic tribes to the east and the spread of Christianity to the west. Evidence for a great persecution under Shapur II and Adurbad is found in the Syriac Christian *Acts of the Martyrs*, which details the martyrdom of 29 Christians in 341 CE, shortly after the Byzantine emperor Constantine was baptized by Eusebius of Nicomedia. Many Middle Persian books, including the *Denkard*, claim authority for their teachings by tracing them back to Adurbad, who is said to have proved the authenticity of his own edition and exegesis of the Avesta by submitting himself to the ordeal of having molten brass poured onto his chest, from which he emerged unscathed. Adurbad is, therefore, regarded as the epitome of 'orthodoxy' and is referred to in the texts as *Zarathushtrotem*, the 'most like Zarathushtra'.

The motivation for a final edition of the Avesta during this time may relate to Constantine's conversion, but it is thought that in fact the Avesta was not finally redacted until the sixth or seventh century CE in the specially invented Avestan alphabet called *den dabirih* – the 'writing of the religion'. Basil of Caesarea's claim, towards the end of Shapur II's reign, that the Zoroastrians in Cappadocia did not use books or teach doctrine, but that their religion was passed on from father to son, is consistent with a long tradition of oral transmission.

The script in which the *Denkard* and other Middle Persian books are written derived from the imperial Aramaic of the Achaemenids, but the language must have been developing for some centuries beforehand. These texts, particularly *Denkard*, claim to be summaries of the various books of the Avesta. Their exegesis (*zand*) of Avestan texts remains an invaluable source of information about the rituals and customs of the Zoroastrians before, during and after the Sasanian period, although it is often difficult to know when to date such material. The attribution of *zand* as an authoritative commentary on the Avesta dating back to Zarathushtra is in keeping with the rise in authority of the priesthood (*Her.* 2.5).

Early Sasanian references allude, however, to the emergence of different schools of thought. In Kerdir's inscriptions, for example, the term *zandik*, 'interpreters', is used pejoratively in the sense of 'revisionist', implying that there were several alternate readings, some of which were heterodox. The Muslim historian Mas'udi noted that *zandik* (Arabic, *zindiq*) is an expression first used during the time of Mani (d. c. 276 CE), to denote those who based their teaching on the *zand* alone, rather than on the entirety of Avesta plus Zand. This confirmation of both the existence and abuse of exegetical works on the Avesta in the early Sasanian period occurs at the same time that Christian ecumenical councils were attempting to distinguish heterodoxies – including the so-called 'Gnostic Gospels' – from that which was orthodox and canonical.

Eranshahr as the Center of the Mazda-Worshipping World

The Sasanians present themselves as continuing the good rule of their ancestors, but make no explicit reference to the Achaemenids. Just as the Arsacids had apparently traced their ancestry through *Artaxsaça* – one 'ruling through *Asha*' – so the name had also been reflected among the Persid *fratarakas*, and appears again with the Persian Sasanians as 'Ardashir'. In the romantic account of the Middle Persian *Karnamag-i Ardashir-i Pabagan* ('Account of the Deeds of Ardashir, son of Pabag': KAP), Ardashir is described as 'Ardashir the Kayanid...from the stock of Sasan, family of king Darius'.[8] His rule was thus seen to be legitimized from two royal lines – that of the mythical Kayanian dynasty and that of the historical Persians through Darius III, who is also referred to as an ancestor of the Sasanians in *Denkard*.

The Sasanians appear to have retained some memory of their Ancient Persian ancestors through a similar oral narrative tradition to the Parthians, and through repetition of names and iconographic themes. Their sacred historiography begins, however, with the Pishdadians (the mythical first rulers of Iran) and the Kayanians, as it does in the *Bundahishn* (Bd. 35), reflecting the earlier Avesta.[9] It is this narrative that is incorporated into the *Shah Nameh*.

The Sasanians identified Iran as the place where the 'good religion' (MP *weh den*) predominated. As seen on Ardashir's investiture relief above, for Sasanian monarchs it was all about the *xwarrah*, the divine fortune or glory, which was brought to the king, and then to the land and its inhabitants through the bestowal of power by Ohrmazd. The 'Deeds of Ardashir' begins with an exciting story of his midnight escape from the court of the last Parthian king, Ardavan. As Ardavan and his soldiers chase after the runaway – who has made off with much of Ardavan's treasure as well as a favorite concubine – an enormous ram is seen racing after Ardashir's horse. Ardavan's religious advisors suggest that this ram embodies the *xwarrah* of the ancient Iranian kings, which is leaving Ardavan and the Parthians behind and seeking to consecrate a new regime.[10]

The image of a ram appears on Sasanian stucco work and personal seals as a symbol of the *xwarrah*. The *xwarrah* is also indicated in various motifs on the crowns of Sasanian monarchs, such as a bird with a pearl in its beak. The significance of the diadem of rule as the repository of *xwarrah* is evidenced on the Sasanian inscription of Narseh (293–302 CE) at Paikuli, which tells of the punishment of one Wahnam, who had been 'driven by Ahriman and the *devs*' to place the crown on the head of a false ruler. Wahnam's punishment was to be bound and brought to Narseh on a maimed donkey, and then killed.[11]

The boar is also a ubiquitous motif, emblematic of victory and protection for the one who possesses *xwarrah*. It is said to be a representation of the *yazata* of victory, Verethragna. Such use of zoomorphic imagery could support the theory that the Sasanians intentionally replaced anthropomorphic representations of the *yazatas*, although this is not consistent. The ram, boar and '*senmurv*' (the *saena meregha* of Avestan mythology) are recurrent motifs in plastic arts from Sasanian times onwards, and are found on silk cloth from western China through Sogdiana to Byzantium. Similar images of the boar were painted prominently on the ceilings of the caves next to the great Buddhas at Bamiyan, dated around the sixth century CE. The use of such motifs within a Buddhist context will be discussed later.

According to a later Arabic account by Tha'alibi, the first throne address of the newly-crowned king began with praise and thanks to Ahura Mazda for bestowing kingship. Those kings who commissioned only a single rock relief

– Bahram I at Bishapur and Narseh at Naqsh-e Rostam – chose the theme of divine investiture. Such illustrations and a few Middle Persian inscriptions provide almost the only contemporary internal information we have concerning that Sasanian institution.

The first Sasanian kings, Ardashir I and Shapur I, combined their claims to the throne with intensive religious propaganda. Early Sasanian gold and silver coins depicting the king on the front, and a blazing fire in a fire-holder on the reverse (Fig. 14), represent an intertwining of state and religion that is expressed in the often-quoted statement from the Middle Persian *Letter of Tosar*: 'For church and state were born of one womb joined together, and never to be sundered.'[12] The *Letter of Tosar* dates to the sixth century CE in its final form and presents a picture of Sasanian hierarchy that from the beginning strove to impose uniformity and subordination to central, divinely-conferred authority throughout the empire. Emphasis is on the primacy of the clergy as 'the first estate' under the king, and the maintenance of correct ritual. This unity of purpose is also symbolized in the early coin imagery of the fire-holder supported by a royal throne, which is similar to that of the Ancient Persians (see Fig. 14).

Fig. 14. Silver coin of Ardashir I, inscribed 'Fire of Ardashir'.

The notion of such a 'religiocracy', in which church and state depend upon each other to survive and thrive, is reiterated in Zoroastrian texts from the Islamic era, in early Arab historiographies, and also in *Shah Nameh*. Right at the end of the national epic, after the last Sasanian king Yazdegird III has been treacherously killed, a Zoroastrian priest declares that 'kingship and religious teaching are two gems set in the same ring'. This reflects a perceived ideal state, but historical reality was more complex.

The Shape of the World

The incursions of scripture-based religions such as Christianity and Manichaeism may have also stimulated the development of an articulated cosmological system within Zoroastrian priestly circles. The Armenian Christian patriarch, Elisaeus Vardapet, elucidates an exchange of theological arguments between the Armenian Christians and Sasanian Zoroastrians that occurred when Yazdegird II (438–57 CE) attempted to re-impose

Zoroastrianism upon Armenia. Elisaeus provides a clear summary of the Zoroastrian cosmological division, as stated in an edict of 449 CE by Mihr Narseh, chief minister (*wuzurg framadar*) of Yazdegird II. This Zoroastrian apologetic was intended to persuade the Armenians to return to their earlier religion, suggesting that the Sasanians still regarded the Armenians as apostates, but the edict was met with uproar from the Armenian Christian ruling families.

Mihr Narseh begins by claiming that anyone who does not follow the religion of Mazda-worship is 'deaf, blind and deceived by the *dev* of Ahriman'. He states the binary opposition of the two forces: Ohrmazd created humans, bringing them happiness as well as 'glory, honour, health, beauty, eloquence and length of days'; in contrast, Ahriman brought pain, sickness and death, all misery, evil and murderous wars.[13] The Christian teaching that both good and evil come from the Creator was abhorrent to Mihr Narseh, who ridiculed the idea that the author of all that is good would become jealous and create death 'just for a fig picked from a tree'. Mihr Narseh also provides a Zoroastrian dismissal of the Christian notion that God could be crucified, die, be buried and rise again. Other documents inform us that Christians were castigated by Zoroastrians on religious grounds because they buried their dead, and believed in asceticism and monasticism. On their part, Christians derided Zoroastrians for their reverence of the natural elements, their near-kin marriages and their purity laws, particularly their exposure of the dead.

Elisaeus' account indicates that at least by the mid-fifth century CE, there was a clearly formulated 'official' Zoroastrian response to the various theological challenges posed by Christianity. Mihr Narseh's edict seems to have been as much motivated by a political clampdown as by religious revival, however, since prohibitions against observance of the Sabbath were enforced on the Jews at the same time. The Armeno-Sasanian war followed shortly thereafter, in 451 CE, in which the Armenians were defeated, and many deported to Iran. Yazdegird II is considered a stalwart defender of the religion in Middle Persian texts.

A fully developed cosmology outlining the creative activity of Ahura Mazda is articulated in the later Middle Persian texts, particularly *Bundahishn* ('Creation'), the *Wizidagiha-i Zadspram* ('Selections of Zadspram') and parts of *Denkard*. These texts contain the entire cosmic event from start to end, in which Ohrmazd generates the conceptual and corporeal worlds in order to trap and eventually eliminate Ahriman. Not only is the moral purpose of creation clear, but the course of history becomes visualized as part of an orderly, predetermined program, in which human participation is a vital part. The scheme unfolds in three periods of time, similar to those alluded to in previous chapters:

1. 0–6000: The Time of Creation: *Bundahishn*

Year 0: Ohrmazd and Ahriman exist outside of time and space 0–3000: Ohrmazd creates the *menog* (conceptual) world over a period of 3,000 years, including the *amesha spentas* and *yazatas*. This conceptual world is invisible and intangible, the world of thought: it is a prototype for the corporeal (*getig*) world.

3000–6000:

3000: Ahriman awakes and rushes to the light. Ohrmazd fixes a spatial and temporal limit for the battle to take place within the created world lasting 9,000 years, to which Ahriman in his ignorance agrees. Ohrmazd recites the powerful 21-word *Ahuna Vairya* prayer, and Ahriman slumps back into unconsciousness for 3,000 years, during which time Ohrmazd establishes the *getig* world – sky, water, earth, plant, beneficent animal and human – within which all activity takes place, including the battle between good and evil.

2. 6000–12000: The Time of Mixture of Good and Evil: *Gumezishn*

6000: On Ohrmazd day of Farvardin month (the spring equinox) at noon, as the sun stands in mid-heaven, Ahriman invades the world through a hole pierced in the sky, starting time and bringing shadow and darkness as the sun and moon begin to move. Ahriman punctures the disk of the earth causing upheaval and the formation of the mountains; he pollutes the water with salt, and the fire with smoke and darkness; he withers the plant, kills the first-created bull, and sickens primal man with greed, want, pain, hunger, disease, vice, lethargy and neglect, before bringing death. To counter the good *menog* and *getig* creations of Ohrmazd, Ahriman shapes miscreations 'from the substance of darkness which was his own self' (Bd. 1.47), letting loose both noxious creatures and toxic emotions and thoughts. The seeds of plants, animals and men are saved and purified by the *amesha spentas* and their respective helpful *yazatas*, and returned to the material world where they thrive and increase.

6000–9000: The Pishdadian kings rule, including Yima's golden age of 900 years, which ends when Yima moves to his *var*. The evil Zahak comes to power, but is eventually overthrown by the good Feridun, who chains him in Mt. Demavand.

8970: Zarathushtra is born.

9000–12000: The Kayanian kings rule. Zarathushtra's advent is no historical accident. He marks the turning point of history, the beginning of the end of evil and the moment of final resolution. Zarathushtra's revelation at age 30, followed by the conversion of Kavi Vishtaspa, places the struggle between Ohrmazd and Ahriman on a new plane. An initial time of goodness is followed by slow degeneration, as people forget Zarathushtra's teaching.

9970: The first *saoshyant*, Ushedar (Av. *Uxshyat.ereta*: 'one who makes *asha* increase'), is born from a virgin impregnated with the seed of Zarathushtra, preserved in Lake Kansaoya. He promulgates the religion (*den*), just as Zarathushtra had.

10000: When Ushedar reaches age 30, the sun stands still for ten days in the noontide position, and creation flourishes for three years. Then the terrible winter of Ahriman occurs and the earth is re-peopled from Yima's *var*.

10970: The second *saoshyant*, Ushedarmah (Av. *Uxshyat-nemah*: 'one who makes reverence increase'), is born, again of Zarathushtra's seed.

11000: The sun stands still for 20 days, and creation flourishes for six years. People become vegetarian and drink only water. Zahak re-awakes, but the hero Keresaspa kills him.

Towards the end of the twelfth millennium,[14] the third and final *saoshyant*, Astvat-ereta, is born from Zarathushtra's seed. For ten years before his arrival people will not eat, but will not die.

The activity of *frashegird* – 'the making wonderful or perfect' – begins with the resurrection of the dead, the reuniting of the soul with the body and the judgment of the whole person, which involves walking through molten metal, representing one's own deeds: for the *ashavan* it will be like walking through warm milk, but for the *dregvant* it will be molten metal. The *saoshyant* performs the final sacrifice of the bull Hadayans, and prepares the white *hom* of immortality for all to drink so that death will be eliminated once and for all. Ahriman and the *devs* are rendered powerless. The *devs* are destroyed by their good counterparts, Ahriman is flung back through the hole in the sky into darkness as Ohrmazd chants the *kusti* prayer of exorcism, and the hole is sealed up with molten metal.

3. 12000: The Time of Separation and Resolution: *Wizarishn*

The resolution at *frashegird* marks the end of history, the end of time, which stops as the sun comes to rest in its noontime position at the spring equinox. The rule or kingdom (*xshathra*) of Ohrmazd, the all good, all-knowing and all-powerful, is established for ever.

Concepts of Time

From this narrative, it is easy to see that the concept of time as both boundless and limited is a significant feature of the developed cosmological scheme. It is often thought that by the Sasanian era, *zurvan* (time) had become the focus of a mainstream religious movement within Zoroastrianism. Manichaean Middle Persian use of the name *Zurvan*, for the first creative principle (synonymous with the 'Father of Greatness'), suggests a hypostatizing of the Avestan concept *zruwan akarana* – 'boundless time'. The elevation of *zurvan* to pre-eminence is reported in Greek, Syriac and Armenian sources from the fourth century CE onwards. In Basil of Caesarea's letter to Epiphanius, he notes that the Zoroastrians of Cappadocia trace their descent from 'a certain Zarnouas'. Zarnouas is usually taken to be a distorted form of 'Zurvan', as the source of all things.

Eznik of Kolb, a fifth-century CE Armenian translator and apologist, in his polemic *Against the Religion of the Persians*, depicts adherence to Zurvan as a mainstream Persian sect.

As reconstructed through such sources, the creation myth had been expanded to place Zurvan as the first principle from whose sacrifice emerged first the good Ohrmazd and then, through his doubt, the evil Ahriman. Mihr Narseh's statement to the Armenians appears to reject any emphasis on Zurvan as supreme god, and Middle Persian texts contain no allusion to an organized system of belief centered on Zurvan. The notion of the 'twinning' of Ohrmazd and Ahriman as brothers from one womb is firmly rejected as a false teaching in the *Denkard*.

Agathias, in his sixth-century CE description of Persian religion, maintained that they held two first principles: 'one good source of all that is best in creation, the other opposite in both respects…the bad, destructive one'.[15] It seems most likely that focus on *zurvan* as the first principle was part of a variant cosmology that co-existed alongside other heterodoxies at the time, all of which are more clearly identified and addressed in Middle Persian texts. Unlike these other heterodox approaches, 'Zurvanite' cosmogony and the predestined role of time were not considered to fall outside the realm of Mazda worship.

Heterodoxies

Extant Middle Persian writings in book form date to the late Sasanian and early Islamic period. Many of these relate directly to matters of theology. One such text, the *Shkand Gumanig Wizar* ('The Doubt-Dispelling Exposition'), contains lengthy sections refuting the beliefs of non-Zoroastrians, which it refers to as *jud denan* – of 'other religion', in contrast to the *weh denan* – 'those of the good religion' of Eran. Apart from *zandik*, another term for those whose teachings were seen as damaging to the religion from within was *ahlomog*, from Avestan *ashemaoga*, the name for a deceptive demon (Vd

5.35, 18.9). It means something like 'deceiver of *asha*' and is usually translated as 'heretic'. Several priests are referred to as *ahlomog* in Middle Persian texts.[16] Those who follow heterodox teachings are called *jud-ristag* – those who go the 'other way' – that is, schismatics.

The context in which *zandik* is used in the late third-century rock inscriptions of Kerdir has led to it often being translated as 'Manichaean', since the cognate term *zindiq* is employed of Manichaeans in medieval Muslim heresiographies. Mani himself is said to have visited the regions of Sind and Baluchistan; to have travelled through Babylonia and Media; and to have spent many years preaching in the regions of Fars and Parthia. Manichaean missionaries visited the Christian communities in Mesopotamia, including Kirkuk in northern Iraq. In each place, the message of Mani was adapted to address the majority faith of the region. In Iran this involved incorporating familiar elements from Zoroastrian cosmology into Manichaean vocabulary, although the eschatology is opposite: for the Manichaeans, *frashegird* is the final destruction, not renovation, of the world.[17]

Upholding the Good Religion

Early Sasanian rock reliefs inscribed in Parthian, Middle Persian and Greek provide the most telling information about Sasanian ethos – at least from the perspective of those whose deeds are described. The longest inscriptions are those of Shapur I on three of the lower sides of the Ka'ba-ye Zardosht at Naqsh-e Rostam (SKZ), and four inscriptions of the priest Kerdir: two at Naqsh-e Rostam; two elsewhere in Fars. The inscription of Narseh at Paikuli in southern Iraq is also important in terms of its promulgation of the division between the order, peace, health and good government of the divinely-elected king of Eranshahr, and the deception, sorcery and evil actions, of the enemies of the king.

Shapur I's inscription describes his various victories against Rome, and claims that his successes are due to the help of Ahura Mazda and the *yazatas*, whose instrument (*dastgerd*) he is.[18] It is with Shapur I that the title of the king expands to incorporate *Aneran*; that is, all the regions beyond the border of Eranshahr that he had conquered. Armenia and the Caucasus region were both accounted as part of Iran in SKZ. Shapur emphasizes his close relationship with the *yazatas* as a legitimation of his royal power, presenting himself as a strong king, during whose reign religious institutions were strengthened throughout the empire. He also exercised tolerance towards the other religious traditions of the realm, including Manichaeism, which has led some to question Shapur's 'orthodoxy'.

An extant Manichaean text, the *Shahbuhragan*, was presented by Mani to

Shapur sometime after his coronation, and Mani was granted the right to teach his faith throughout the empire. Two of the king's brothers, Peroz and Mihrshah, converted. It seems that at this stage, the Zoroastrian priesthood had not yet developed into a fully-fledged hierarchical institution, and that the religion itself had not been defined in an exclusivist manner that would preclude tolerance of other perspectives. Shapur's dedication of fires, support of fire temples and collection of Avestan materials all point, however, to his commitment to Mazda worship.

Religious Experts

Kerdir was a Zoroastrian priest and an important member of the Sasanian establishment. His career spanned the reigns of six Sasanian monarchs. The developing power of the priesthood within the Sasanian court can be mapped by Kerdir's trajectory from *herbad* under Ardashir, to *mowbed* and *herbad* under Shapur I, to *mowbed of Ohrmazd* under Hormizd I (272–3 CE), a title which he retained under Hormizd's brother Bahram I and Bahram II. Under Bahram II, Kerdir reached the apogee of his power and influence (Fig. 15).

Kerdir's own hieratic role is reflected in his particular appreciation of the state of contentment and prosperity of the priesthood. He states that his achievements involved not only the elevation of worship of Ohrmazd and the *yazdan*, but also that of the Mazda-worshipping religion and its priests.

In three of his inscriptions, Kerdir describes how, during the rule of Shapur I and his successors, he had founded a large number of *Wahram* fire temples and religious institutions throughout the empire, including the areas that Shapur had conquered from the Romans. Basil of Caesarea's allusion to the veneration of fire by the *magi* in Cappadocia supports this claim. *Wahram* derives from *verethragna* – 'victory' – and refers to principal fires established in key localities. The most elaborate fire temple in India and Iran today is known as an *Atash Bahram*, or 'victory fire'. It was during the Sasanian period that the fire temple became more closely integrated into Zoroastrian worship.

Fig. 15. Kerdir, Naqsh-e Rajab.

In the inscription on the Ka'ba-ye Zardosht, Kerdir describes the effect of his promulgation of the worship of Ahura Mazda and the *yazatas* throughout the empire as bringing contentment to water, fire and cattle, and as driving out the evil forces, embodied in Ahriman and the *devs*. He later claims to have eradicated worship of the *devs* and to have destroyed their abodes. It is not known where or what these places were. Some suggest that they included Achaemenid and Arsacid temples containing statues of the *yazatas* such as Anahita, but it is more likely that the reference is to Buddha images or those of Hindu deities, given Kerdir's claim to have suppressed both traditions.[19] This could also refer to the suppression of non-Mazda-worshipping Iranian sects, similar to Xerxes' destruction of *daivadana* several centuries earlier.

After the death of Shapur I, under Bahram I, Kerdir takes the credit for ridding Iran of all sects that were seen to be making incursions into the Zoroastrian fold, including Judaism, different denominations of Christianity, Manichaeism, 'baptizers' (usually presumed to be Mandaeans), Buddhists and Brahmins (Hindus). Although Zoroastrian writings remain silent concerning the existence and work of Kerdir, he is excoriated in Manichaean texts. Kerdir's name last appears on Narseh's inscription at Paikuli, which is the last royal inscription in Parthian. Under Narseh (293–302 CE), persecution of religious minorities decreased, as focus returned to the conflict with Rome.

Many titles appear for the first time with Kerdir; these include 'the chief priest and judge of all the empire' (*hamshahr mowbed ud dadwar*) and 'master of ceremony' (*aiwenbed*). Religious officials were referred to as *dastwar*, a title with the general meaning of 'one who has power', but used in Middle Persian texts in reference to a *dastwar-i den agah*, a 'high ranking theologian'. Numerous seals, seal impressions and bullae preserve the name and rank of priests, attesting to the size of the religious body in Sasanian Iran, as well as to its importance for the state bureaucracy. The *mow* or *mogh* (from OP *magu-*) was the lowest rank of priesthood that functioned in various capacities in the districts, cities, villages and temples. This generic term is hardly found in Middle Persian books, however, where specific titles are preferred.[20]

The office of *mowbed* ('head priest') increased in importance as the empire developed. *Mowbed* seals for fire temples, sub-districts and cities indicate that large numbers were involved in the administrative aspects of the empire, particularly over legal and economic matters. Others were scholar-priests and teachers. Syriac and Armenian Christian sources indicate that *mowbeds* also had great control in the provinces. The *Letter of Tosar*'s description of the role of the *mowbed* and his fellow priests in organizing the king's investiture seems to reflect later Sasanian practice. In this account, the *mowbed*, *herbads* and nobles of the realm accompanied the prince to the throne, where he was seated. The *mowbed* then placed the crown on the king's head, asking him if he accepted the kingship from Ahura Mazda.[21]

Although there are no Sasanian seals for a *mowbedan mowbed* ('priest of priests' – that is, high priest), the title is alluded to in a fourth-century CE Syriac reference to a 'head of the *mowbeds*' (*resha de maupate*). Descriptions in *Shah Nameh* and later Islamic texts indicate that, by the time of Bahram V (420–38 CE), the king was crowned by the high priest. The fact that the title mirrors that of the *shahan shah* ('king of kings') denotes that, by this time, the high priest had assumed some of the sanctified power of the early Sasanian kings. According to the Muslim historian, Tabari (838–923 CE) the high priest was in charge of the regalia and royal appurtenances of the later Sasanian monarchs.

Wisdom Literature

Adurbad-i Mahraspandan, *mowbed* under Shapur II, is said to have composed many *andarz* sayings. *Andarz*, or 'wisdom literature', is a Middle Persian genre that has survived better than others. It is intended to teach proper behavior based on the imperative of good thoughts, good words and good deeds. Wisdom literature had been popular since the Parthian period, such as the 800-word riddle-poem the *Draxt-i Asurig*, in which a tree and a goat argue as to which is most useful to humanity. Pithy legends on seals are also considered to be wisdom sayings reflecting the mores of Sasanian society. The maxim on one Sasanian seal, depicting a *padan*-wearing *mowbed* standing before a fire-holder, reads: 'That which derives from right is good for the gods.' Another seal has a maxim that can be read, 'Do good, do not fear evil!' In other words, if you do good, you will have no need to fear either doing evil, or having evil directed against you. An important source of *andarz* attributed to Adurbad is the *Chidag Andarz-i Poryotkeshan* – the 'Wise Precepts of the First Sages'. Both this text and *Denkard* Book 6 contain many maxims relating to the belief and behavior of the faithful. Here are some examples:[22]

'One should be a person who does not complain, who is patient, diligent and confident in doing good works.' (Dk 6.29)

'From knowledge of religion arises consideration of the *manthra*

From consideration of the *manthra* arises increase of religious vocation and praise of the *yazatas*

From increase in religious vocation and praise of the *yazatas* comes the elimination of deception (*druj*) in the world

From the elimination of deception comes immortality, *frashegird* and resurrection.' (Dk 6.C75)

'Religion is the (right) measure...

In every thing, being free from defect is the (right) measure...

This is the (right) measure: good thoughts, good speech, good deeds.' (Dk 6.39–40)

This concept of holding to the 'right measure' (MP *payman*) is expressed in terms of neither excess of evil, nor deficit of good, but as the constant choice to detach oneself from evil and to be united with good (Dk 6.38, 42, 43). In this manner, one counterbalances the negative impact of evil.

The Laity

A few Middle Persian sources also refer to the lives of lay Zoroastrians in the late Sasanian period. The 'Book of a Thousand Legal Decisions' (*Madayan-i Hazar Dadestan*: MHD) was probably written just before the fall of the Sasanians, in the early seventh century CE, but contains judgments from the previous century and earlier. It has been compared with the early sixth-century CE Roman law code of the Byzantine emperor, Justinian. MHD introduces case histories and ensuing legal decisions that relate to family law, particularly to marriage and marital property. It is a valuable source of information about the legal rights, responsibilities and status of upper-class women. The decisions reflect the practice of allowing Sasanian women (as widows or heirs) to manage the family estate, a feature of Iranian life that was noted earlier in Achaemenid times, and that is also considered permissible in the *Herbedestan*. A daughter could also inherit the family- or hearth-fire from her father, but upon marriage would hand over responsibility for it to her husband.

Another important surviving book is a work of religious instruction addressed to the laity, entitled the 'Judgments of the Spirit of Wisdom' (*Dadestan-i Menog-i Xrad*: MX). This text refers to the moral principles that should direct the lay Zoroastrian's life, including basic observances of 'good work', such as prayer, wearing the *sudreh* and *kusti*, venerating the *yazatas*, celebrating the *gahanbars* (seasonal festivals) and religious rites, but not venerating idols or *devs*, nor burying the dead.[23] 'Good deeds' also include caring for the earth, water and fire, as well as helping the poor.

Agathias had picked up on this notion when he described the Persian reverence for water in using it only to drink and to water the land. He also writes of a great lay festival called the 'Removal of Evil', in which the laity kill vast numbers of snakes and other wild creatures in order to please the good spirit and to vex Ahriman (*Histories* 2.25).[24]

The eschatological elements of *Menog-i Xrad* mostly reiterate those of the Young Avesta, but the crossing-over is depicted as a bridge, which widens for the safe passage of the souls of the male and female *ashavan*, who are accompanied by Sraosha into the endless lights, where they receive spring butter (MX 1.123–57). In contrast, hell is a place of both extreme cold 'like the coldest ice and snow', and extreme heat 'like a burning fire' (MX 6.27). The Middle Persian word for hell *dushox* probably derives from an Avestan *daoshahwa*, meaning 'bad existence'.[25]

Resistance to outside proselytism on the part of Mazda-worshippers is found in Basil of Caesarea's complaint about the obduracy of those in his diocese, who continue to worship there according to the ways of their ancestors, and who had come originally to Cappadocia from 'Babylon'. These Zoroastrians had 'peculiar customs' of their own, including 'raving' after unlawful marriages and believing in 'fire as God'. These are all criticisms leveled at Sasanian Zoroastrians in Syriac and Byzantine Christian texts, which, despite the hostile bias, denote the continuity of near-kin (*xwedodah*) marriage, which is also encouraged by Kerdir.

Endowed Fires

Shapur's long inscription states that he endowed five 'named fires' (*pad nam adur*) for himself, his queen and his three sons. Shapur's mention of offerings of lamb, bread and wine to the *yazatas* for the souls of members of the royal family is similar to those granted by Cambyses and subsequent Persian kings at Cyrus' tomb. On the reverse of some of Shapur's coins is a fire-holder with two attendants. This representation and the accompanying inscription, reading 'fire of Shapur', suggest the personal fire that was instituted upon his accession to the throne following Parthian custom. Endowments of fires may also have begun during the Parthian period.

The reverse of coins of many Sasanian rulers depicts a *yazata* offering the ring of power to the monarch, who stands on the other side of a fire-holder, often interpreted as the personal fire of the king. A column at Bishapur is inscribed with the phrase 'in the 24th year of the fire of Shapur'. According to the Roman historian Ammianus Marcellinus (fourth century) and the Armenian, Sebeos (seventh century), the Sasanian regnal fire was on a portable holder. Small, almost hour-glass shaped, fire-holders are depicted on some coins, and an example of such a fire-holder has been found in Shapur's palace complex at Bishapur (Fig. 16). This is similar in form to that depicted on a Sogdian Zoroastrian funerary monument from northern China.

Fig. 16. Sasanian fire-holder from Bishapur.

Four smaller rock-cut fire bowls in outcrops at Pasargadae itself appear to date to the late Sasanian era. They are all located near a single flat rock on which are carved five Middle Persian inscriptions, denoting that the stone was a place of exposure of the dead. The deepest fire bowl is about 26 cm deep, the most shallow about 6 cm, signifying that these fires were not constantly burning. Other rock-cut fire bowls from the late Sasanian period have been found above the grotto at Taq-e Bostan, and to the left of the ledge next to Darius I's relief at Bisutun.[26]

Two large fire-holders (*atashdan*), carved from one solid pedestal of rock at Naqsh-e Rostam, provide further evidence of the cult of fire from Sasanian times. These edifices are thought to be in the style of those at Pasargadae. They have deep rectangular fire bowls and stand at the southern end of the cliff into which the tombs of the four Achaemenid kings are cut. Underneath some of the tombs are bas-reliefs of Sasanian kings, and on the top of the cliffs are several exposure platforms. Another independently-standing square *atashdan* carved *in situ* has been discovered at Kuh-i Shahrak, in the Abarj region to the south of what is now a Muslim *imamzadeh*.[27]

All three fire-holders are similar in shape to the *chahartaq*, the square, four-arched structure surmounted by a free-standing dome, which became a common form of open-fire temple in Sasanian times. Over 40 examples remain of Sasanian fire sanctuaries built on the *chahartaq* plan, including one in Tblisi, Georgia, which is the most northern location yet discovered. Some of the less important fires, located in smaller towns and villages, are probably those referred to as *Aduran* fires in Kerdir's KKZ inscription.

Reference to the Sasanian king Yazdegird I (399–420 CE) worshipping fire 'in a particular house' comes from the fifth-century Syriac hagiography of Mar Maruta. Agathias notes that fire is considered to be sacred and a focus of reverence for the *magi*, who keep it burning in special holy buildings which are set apart (*Histories* 2.25). Another fifth-century Syriac account, by Theodoret, tells how a zealous Christian priest, Mar Abda, destroyed a fire sanctuary (*pyreion*), and then brought about his own execution by rejecting Yazdegird's request to rebuild the sanctuary.

Apart from inscriptional references to dynastic fires, *Wahram* fires and *Aduran* fires, there is also textual mention of the three great ancient fires. KAP records that Ardashir went to the threshold of the sacred fire Farrobay, 'which is meritorious', and solicited spiritual gifts from it. Bahram V (420–38 CE) is remembered in the *Shah Nameh* as much for his offerings to the fire temple at Adur Gushnasp as for his victories against the Hephthalites. According to Tabari, Bahram gave the precious stones from the crowns of the defeated king and his queen to the temple. Mas'udi records that, after coronation, Sasanian kings would undertake a pilgrimage on foot to Adur Gushnasp, where they made vows and brought precious gifts for its upkeep, endowing both land and servants.

Hearth fires also continued as the loci of domestic praxis. Elisaeus records that the Sasanian rulers of Armenia demanded that each household should produce a certain measure of ash to prove that there was a sacred fire burning inside.[28] In the spring of 2009, I discovered that the practice of moving fire from the domestic hearth to a communal place of worship still occurs in the predominantly Zoroastrian village of Cham, where there is no longer a resident *mowbed*. One of the Zoroastrian villagers carried the burning embers from her hearth fire across the street to light the lamp under the ancient cypress tree outside the fire temple.

Archeological evidence has not turned up a fire temple that could definitely be identified as one of Kerdir's *Wahram* fires, but Zoroastrian oral tradition maintains that at least one such fire has been kept burning since Sasanian times. In the city of Yazd, the *Atash Bahram* building constructed in the mid-twentieth century houses a fire believed to have been rescued during the Arab incursion in the early seventh century, and to have been kept alight in private homes until it was incorporated into the previous *atashkadeh* in about 1870.

Reverence to the Waters

Writing in the early Sasanian era, the Neoplatonist Porphyry (c. 232–305 CE) related that Persians conducted religious rites dedicated to the world and to 'nymphs' in both natural and man-made caves, 'on account of the water which trickles, or is diffused in caverns'.[29]

In the flood-pools of cave mines near Veshnaveh in Kashan, offerings discovered extend from the Parthian into the Sasanian period. Materials from Sasanian times include glass phials and bowls, beads of metal, glass and precious stones, along with finger rings, earrings, hair and clothing ornamentation of gold, silver, bronze and semi-precious stones. These objects consist almost entirely of female accessories, and imply an act of offering relating specifically to women, or perhaps to a female *yazata*. The fact that the entrance to the mines is through a narrow opening indicates that this was a site for lay oblation, rather than priestly, since it was not a place that a ritually clean Zoroastrian priest would enter. The deliberate placement of the offerings in the cave pools and the careful covering of groups of objects suggests a managed ritual, but one unlikely to have been undertaken by priests. Numerous other cave sanctuaries within Iran attest to the ubiquity of lay activity at such sites.

Zoroastrian worship at a natural water source on a rocky hill continues in Iran today, most notably at Pir-e Sabz shrine, to the north-east of Yazd. The name of the shrine derives from the greenness of the foliage growing around the sanctuary. Both Pir-e Sabz and the Zoroastrian shrine of Pir-e Banu Pars, also in Yazd province, are associated with legends about Sasanian princesses said to be daughters of Yazdegird III (632–51 CE), the last Zoroastrian king. Fleeing from the Arab invaders, these princesses took refuge behind rock walls that miraculously opened up when they prayed to Ahura Mazda. According to legend, the princess associated with Pir-e Sabz was entitled Hayat Banu ('Lady of Life') or Nik Banu ('Good Lady'). The title *banu*, meaning 'lady', was used for the female *yazata* Anahita during this period, as evidenced in the Paikuli inscription, where she is called *aredvi sura banu*. Such shrine legends may indicate an earlier cult of devotion to Anahita.

Sasanian dynastic connection with Anahita, who becomes Anahid in Middle Persian, is evidenced from the fact that Shapur's daughter was called Adur-Anahid, and that Kerdir claims to be warden over the fires of 'Anahid-Ardashir' and 'Anahid the Lady at Istakhr', near Persepolis.[30] Anahid was apparently revered as a patron deity of the Sasanian dynasty, and it is assumed that the temple dedicated to her at Istakhr was the site of several coronations, such as that of Yazdegird III. Her close association with investiture is also determined through iconography, such as that of Narseh at Naqsh-e Rostam, where the king receives the ring from a female figure, usually identified as Anahita in keeping with the inscription at Paikuli, where Narseh's rule is said to have been conferred by Ohrmazd and Anahid, and all the *yazatas*. The figure in Narseh's investiture wears a mural crown with stepped crenellation. It has been suggested that a prototype for such imagery may be found in the crenellated crown and floral wreath worn by Esther on the synagogue mural at Dura Europos. The synagogue was dedicated in 244/5 CE during the reign of Shapur I, and we know from Middle Persian graffiti that Sasanian Zoroastrians visited there a decade later.[31]

In the great arch at Taq-e Bostan in Kermanshah, Khosrow II (590–628 CE) is depicted receiving a ring of investiture from a figure on each side, which may be identified as Ohrmazd and Anahid respectively. The crowned female to the king's right holds out the ring in her right hand, while pouring water from a ewer held in her left hand, suggesting the increase and benefit that Anahita bestows (see Fig. 18).

A purpose-built aniconic shrine to the waters from earlier Sasanian times is located within Shapur I's palace complex at Bishapur. It is built in similar style to Seleucid/Parthian era temples at Hatra, and was originally thought to be a fire temple, but is now known as the 'Anahita temple'. The temple cella, which is below ground level, is connected to the nearby river by a deep well and channels control the flow of water, so that it enters the precinct one way and floods the lower section, and then drains out by another exit. Perhaps the to-and-fro motion was intended to emulate the cosmic currents, or the pouring back and forth of the waters in the *Yasna* ceremony? Further information is needed, however, to unlock the mysteries of worship at this sanctuary.

The Festival Calendar

The Sasanians continued to use the Zoroastrian calendar established under the Achaemenids, but with some modifications, such as the religious dedications to the *Gathas* of the five epagomenal days and a reconciliation of the practice of celebrating each festival twice, five days apart. The merging of the pairs of festivals into a single six-day observance seems to have taken place under Hormizd I (272–3 CE). Kerdir's accounts of paying out of his own pocket for religious services at fire temples to celebrate the seasonal feasts is in keeping with an attempt to create a uniform festival calendar.

As time progressed, the 365-day calendar had moved out of synchrony with the natural year, so that at the beginning of the Sasanian period, Farvardin fell in the late summer. So, around 500 CE, the calendar was again adjusted to recalibrate *Nav Ruz* with the spring equinox and place all the other festivals in their original seasonal settings. The use of the name *gahanig* or *gahanbar* ('time of the *Gathas*') for the five days before *Nav Ruz* was also applied to the other five seasonal festivals, which were then also celebrated over five, not six days. The sixth *gahanbar*, the festival for the *fravashis* at the end of the year, remained at ten days, however. The festival, a kind of All Souls celebration, was known originally as *Hamaspathmaedaya*, when the souls of the dead were thought to come and visit their terrestrial dwelling-place. This came to be known as *Fravardigan*, later *Farvardigan*.

Most of the information we have concerning the celebration of festivals in Sasanian times is recorded by non-Zoroastrians in late- or post-Sasanian times. For instance, the *Syriac Acts of Persian Martyrs* refers to a celebration of the feast of *Fravardigan* in 518 CE by priests and laity in an Iranian province. The festival began with an act of offering, and was followed by a communal banquet and gift giving. Such banquets were solemn events, shared in the presence of Haurvatat and Ameretat.[32] The Middle Persian *Sur i Saxwan*, or 'Dinner Speech', is a model for a speech offered at a grand Sasanian banquet, beginning with benedictory prayers to all the *yazatas*, and an acknowledgment of Ohrmazd as the creator, guardian and preserver of all the creatures and creation. The text indicates that the food was consecrated in a *dron* ceremony similar to that, which still forms part of the Zoroastrian liturgy (*Yasna*), as well as other rituals. *Dron*, meaning 'portion', is flat, unleavened bread, first consecrated by the priests, then offered to the laity.[33]

Silverware designed for such banquets became the mobile propaganda of the dynasty, spreading Sasanian splendor around the empire and its neighbors, and promoting Zoroastrianism as a state ideology. The most prominent motif on silver dishes was of the king hunting, repeating the Achaemenid theme of the monarch's defeat of secular or spiritual enemies in animal form. The courtly banquet attended by those of rank and state was another common depiction. It was a custom for the Sasanian monarch to present a cup and a flowering branch to guests. Several Sasanian bowls show a high-ranking man or woman clasping a flower in the hand, perhaps denoting this gift, which may symbolically represent Haurvatat (water) and Ameretat (plant).

A ninth-century Arabic text records the fact that the Jewish exilarch presented a gift of 4,000 *dirhems* to the Sasanian king on the Persian feast of *Nav Ruz*. *Nav Ruz* is mentioned in the Jerusalem Talmud as one of the 'Median' feasts, and, by the seventh-century Armenian Bishop Gregory Arsharuni, as the 'feast day of Ohrmazd'.[34] The *Shah Nameh* refers to Sasanian monarchs from Ardashir I onwards, celebrating both *Nav Ruz* and the winter festival of fire, *Sadeh*. Shirin, Khosrow II's Aramaean Christian wife, is said to have donated funds for both festivals.

The seven elements of the modern-day Iranian *Haft Sin* (seven 's') table, set out to welcome *Nav Ruz,* are in keeping with Arabic accounts of the festival at the Persian court, based on Zoroastrian texts describing the seven kinds of seed, the seven grains, and the seven branches of trees considered to be auspicious at this time of year.[35]

The Babylonian Talmud refers to *Nausard* as a festival distinct from *Nav Ruz*. This form of *Nav Sal*, or 'New Year', is echoed in Armenian *Navasard* and Sogdian *Nausard*. It appears to have been celebrated on the sixth day of *Fravardigan*, which is the day of Haurvatat (*Ruz Khordad*), now known as *Khordad Sal*, and sometimes the 'Greater Nav Ruz'. When Biruni reported that the Persians splashed each other on *Nav Ruz*, he appears to have been referring to this 'day of the waters'. In the fourteenth-century Persian version of Tabari's commentary on the *Qur'an*, this custom is explained as symbolizing good will and meaning *zanda bashiya* – 'May you live [long]!'.[36]

Sadeh came to be celebrated on the 100th day before the *Greater Nav Ruz*. Biruni reports that, at this time, the Persians made great fires, worshipped God and assembled together to eat and make merry, and to banish the cold of winter. According to Biruni, the Persians would throw perfume and rosewater into the rivers on the 19th day of the 12th month (*Farvardin Ruz, Spandarmad Mah*), the day called 'the *Nav Ruz* of the rivers and running waters'. This custom is echoed in a later celebration by Mughal kings and courtiers at Tirgan, the midsummer festival dedicated to Tishtrya, which they referred to as the 'Festival of Rosewater' (*Eid-e-Gulabi*) or 'Spraying of Water' (*Ab-Pashi*). A famous painting attributed to Govardhan records the Mughal emperor Jahangir taking part in this event around 1614 CE. After conversion to Christianity at the beginning of the fourth century CE, Armenians retained the tradition of throwing water at each other on the Feast of the Transfiguration, *Vardavar*, held 14 weeks after Easter. Parthian *vard,* meaning 'rose', had entered Armenian as a loanword.[37] Armenians attribute this ritual of splashing water to an earlier 'goddess' worship.

Both *Tirgan* and *Mihragan* were Iranian festivals identified in the Babylonian Talmud. *Mihragan* was retained in the Armenian calendar as 'Mehekan'. It is referred to by Biruni as a day on which fairs were held, and in *Shah Nameh* as one of the feast days supported by donations from Shirin. Biruni also mentions that some Persians preferred *Mihragan* to *Nav Ruz*, since they considered the former festival, which takes place at the beginning of autumn, to be 'a sign of resurrection and the end of the world'; a premonition of the perfection of all things that grow.[38]

Death and the Afterlife

The Sasanian Middle Persian inscriptions on the stone slab at Pasargadae are hard to decipher, but the word *dakhma* has been read on one. Such evidence, alongside the exposure platforms above the cliffs at Naqsh-e Rostam and a dearth of ossuaries, leads to the assumption that the Sasanians mostly disposed of the dead through exposure. A graffito on the rock at Pasargadae includes the phrase 'May paradise (*vahisht*) be the highest reward.'[39] This phrase is still used by Iranian Zoroastrians today – in its New Persian form *behesht* – to refer to the blissful afterlife.

During the Sasanian period, eschatological ideas relating to individual afterlife were apparently the subject of much pondering and debate. Kerdir regarded the matter as significant enough to be mentioned in his late third-century inscriptions at Sar Mashhad and Naqsh-e Rostam. These two texts include an account of Kerdir's vision of the afterworld, following his request to the *yazatas* to see the fate of his soul before his own death. The text is fragmentary and there are many words that are disputed. Some passages seem to have parallels in *Videvdad* 19, and it could be that the inscription was motivated by a desire to counter some of the mythology and visionary activity of Mani.

Kerdir achieves his vision through religious 'services' and 'prayers to the *yazatas*'. He sees his own likeness (*hangirb*) encounter a woman from the East, who is the most beautiful ever seen. They hold hands and walk together to the East on a bright path, and meet a prince on a golden throne, before whom there are scales, presumably of judgment. The two continue and meet another prince on a throne, who holds something in his hands, and they are told by the *lysyks* (mediums?) that this object has become a terrible, deep, bottomless, place, full of snakes, lizards and other vermin.[40] They come to a bridge, which becomes wider than it is long, and another prince appears from across the bridge to lead them over. As they progress towards the East, they pass through one luminous palace and see another palace on high, to which they ascend into the radiance of Verethragna. The likeness of Kerdir takes bread, meat and wine, and then distributes some to others.

This vision reassures Kerdir that his own place will be in the eternal lights as a true Mazda-worshipper. The golden throne echoes that on which Vohu Manah sits in *Videvdad* 19.31, or that of the noble worshippers in the *yasht* to Vayu (Yt 15.7, 11). The description of the soul crossing the bridge coheres with both Young Avestan texts and later Middle Persian descriptions. In *Dadestan-i Denig*, the bridge widens for the *ashavan*, but narrows to a razor edge for the *dregvant*. The fact that there is no mention of an end-time resurrection in Kerdir's inscriptions suggests that this Iranian theme, alluded to in the late Achaemenid period in both Young Avestan and Greek accounts, may only have become prominent again in the late Sasanian period or afterwards, when an end of Zoroastrian rule was in sight or had already occurred.

That much of this imagery of the fate of the soul – particularly the crossing of a bridge – was widespread among Zoroastrians during the late Sasanian period is evidenced in its depiction on Sogdian funerary monuments from northern China (see Chapter V). The Middle Persian *Zand-i Wahman Yasn* (ZWY) continues this theme with a description of Zarathushtra's vision of the afterlife that occurs when he protests against the necessity of his own death for a second time, and is given the 'water of the wisdom of all knowledge to drink' by Ahura Mazda. During seven days and nights of sleep, Zarathushtra sees souls in both the worst and best existence.[41] There are some parallels between this aspect of ZWY and the soul journey of Isaiah in the second part of the deutero-canonical *Ascension of Isaiah*. The Middle Persian *Arda Wiraz Namag* (AWN) also presents the story of a vision of souls in situations of punishment or reward. Although the final date of AWN is probably the ninth or tenth century, it contains many of the themes found in Kerdir's inscription.

AWN is set in the time of persecution following the incursion of Alexander. *Mowbeds* gathered in the precincts of the Adur Farrobay temple question whether their prayers, rituals and purifications were effective means of securing 'relief for the soul'. They chose a lay *ashavan*, named Wiraz, to answer that question, and gave him three cups of wine and the *mang* of Vishtaspa to drink.[42] Wiraz's vision lasted seven days, during which time the priests and his seven sisters, who 'knew the religion by heart', kept the fire alight, burnt incense and 'recited the Avesta and Zand of the religious ritual'. After seven days, Wiraz awoke and told of all that he had seen after he had met his own religious insight (*den*) in the form of a maiden, and had crossed the Chinvat bridge with the assistance of Srosh, Mihr and Rashnu, among other *yazatas*. Wiraz returns with assurances that the good will be rewarded, but the wicked will be punished.

The description of hell takes up four-fifths of the text. It is inhabited by Ahriman, the *devs*, and those sinners who have polluted water, fire and earth with dead matter, who have engaged in illicit sexual activities, or who have otherwise misbehaved morally or ritually, or have accrued sins of omission. Hell is a dark, scary, foul-smelling place, crowded with the souls of the wicked, who each feel totally alone. New Persian and Gujarati translations of AWN often included illustrations of the torments of hell.[43]

It is thought that aspects of this text may underlie Dante's *Divine Comedy*, such as the concepts of purgatory and ice as a punishment. AWN presents a state of being in which the scales of judgment are exactly balanced (*hammistagan*) between good and evil. It is a place of motionlessness, where the only change is mild atmospheric variations between hot and cold. The extremes of severe cold and heat which confront the inhabitants of hell in both AWN and MX were not known in thirteenth-century Christian thought, but may perhaps be reflected in the frozen lake of Dante's ninth circle of hell.[44]

In connection with judgment, it is relevant to revisit the role of Mithra, whose image, as a chariot-riding solar deity, is found on several Sasanian seals. On a late fourth- or early fifth-century Sasanian seal (now lost), from the eastern provinces, Mithra emerges directly above Mt. Hara at dawn, as described in the *Mihr Yasht* (Yt 10.13). The seal inscription is translated as 'perfect friendship', referring to the alliance existing between the *ashavan* and Mithra.[45]

A graphic depiction of Mithra, as narrated in the *Mihr Yasht*, has been found above the 37-m. Buddha niche at Bamiyan in Afghanistan. There, a fresco dating back to the sixth century CE was sketched by the French archeologist and architect André Godard in the 1920s. The scene contains a solar deity soaring into heaven on a two-wheeled yellow-painted chariot pulled by four white-winged horses, accompanied by two winged attendants and a winged driver. The solar deity wears a Central Asian kaftan and felt boots. His hand is on his sword, and he has a nimbus and ribbons flowing from both shoulders, like a Sasanian king. Although this could be a representation of Surya, the Indian solar divinity, it is more readily identified as Mithra, who is described in his hymn as one who is mounted on a beautiful wagon made of gold, pulled by four white horses 'who fly' (Yt 10.125).[46]

The winged driver in the chariot is probably Ashi, the Zoroastrian *yazata* of recompense, who guides the chariot of Mithra (Yt 10.68). Above Mithra, wind deities with scarves in their hands could represent Vayu, the wind *yazata* who aids Mithra (Yt 10.9, 21). One of the winged accompanying figures may be a Hellenized portrayal of Arshtat, *yazata* of justice, who is a companion of

Mithra. But the figures could also depict Rashnu and Chista, the two *yazatas* who are said to 'fly on the right side and left side' of Mithra respectively (Yt 10.126). If so, their images are on the wrong side, as Rashnu is a male *yazata* of justice and Chista the female *yazata* of religious insight.

Next to the chariot are what seem to be Iranicized *kinnaras*, who are bearded and wearing round caps.[47] Similar figures appear on ossuaries from Samarkand and Sogdian funerary reliefs from northern China.[48]

Why does a Zoroastrian *yazata* appear in such an evidently Buddhist context as Bamiyan, which by then was part of a Sasanian vassal state? The *Mihr Yasht*, along with other Young Avestan texts, is thought to have developed within the Afghanistan/Sistan region, and its vivid imagery could have remained familiar until this late Kushan period. Had there been a fusion and confusion of the Iranian Mithra with the Buddhist Maitreya, the future Buddha, who in Gandharan representation of this period is depicted as a Central Asian? Or is this a case of the cross-identification of Mithra's 'qualities of solarity and uncovering of truth' with those of the Buddha,[49] which may echo the earlier Buddha-Mazda connection at Kara Tepe?

The Last Kings

Towards the end of the Sasanian period, the representation of the king enthroned, seen in an earlier relief of Shapur II at Bishapur, emerged as a new theme on silverware. A silver bowl in the Hermitage collection is thought to show either Khosrow I (531–79 CE) or his father Kawad I (488–96, 498–531), seated on the throne in the form of a banqueting couch. This became a model representation of kingship for Byzantine art. Below, the king is shown in a typical scene using the 'Parthian shot' to hunt wild rams.

In the late fifth century CE, a revolutionary movement arose from within Zoroastrianism that, although thoroughly quashed, contained seeds of social reform that was to reappear in later periods in the guise of Iranian nationalist revolts against the Abbasids. 'Mazdakism' takes its name from an eponymous founder, Mazdak, said to have been a Zoroastrian priest under Kawad I, who persuaded the king to introduce reforms that raised the ire of the priesthood. Although it was critical of established Zoroastrianism, Mazdakism did not seek to destroy or abjure the religion, but rather to change it from within, claiming to represent the true religion of Zoroaster rather than a new faith. It seems probable that there were many such reform movements within Zoroastrianism towards the end of the Sasanian period.

Most of what is known of Mazdakism comes from much later polemical sources, which tell us that these internal changes involved egalitarianism in terms of sharing wealth and property, including women. Kawad's implementation of such 'communist' principles brought about a land redistribution that diminished the power of both the priestly and upper classes, and benefitted the lower classes in both Iran and the client states to the west. This quickly led to the imprisonment of Kawad, who, when reinstated in 499 CE, created the priestly office of 'Protector of the Poor and Judge'. The word for 'poor' is *driyoshan*, a cognate of the Gathic word *drigu* encountered earlier. The title suggests a conscious return to an original Avestan ethic that is reiterated in *andarz*, reminding individuals to perform meritorious acts:

'When acts of offering, *gahanbars*, and acts of charity to good people diminish, there is increase of evil government, pain for corn plants, bad husbandry, diminution of the fertility of the land and bad rains.' (Dk 6.C82).[50]

Khosrow I, who followed Kawad I, is recognized as one of the most powerful Sasanian monarchs. His epithet *Anoshirvan* means 'immortal Soul'. In the *Denkard*, Khosrow I is said to have not only dispelled heresy, but to have encouraged all to discern that which was heterodoxy from the true Mazda-worshipping religion so that 'the wise can locate it in the world through deliberation'. Khosrow proclaims that discussion alone cannot produce the beneficence (*abzonig*) or effective teaching that comes through nurturing pure thoughts, words and deeds, the good inspiration (*weh menog*), and the worship of the *yazatas* through the beneficial word. It is the *mowbeds* of Ohrmazd who reveal the vision of the *menog* world and its manifestation in the *getig* world.[51]

Not only is Khosrow accredited with putting down irreligion and supporting the Zoroastrian priesthood, but he also welcomed a wave of anti-Byzantine dissidents of various persuasions who sought refuge in Iran. These included Greek philosophers, who came to the Persian court after the closing of the Neoplatonic academy in Athens by order of Justinian I in 529 CE. Agathias records that among the philosophers were the scholarch, Damascius, and his colleague Simplicius,[52] whose commentary on Aristotle's *Physics* survives. These Neoplatonic philosophers, although only staying in the Iranian capital for a couple of years, remained within the Sasanian territories – probably in Harran (Carrhae) – and left profound impressions on ensuing Middle Persian texts. Damascius provided a report, supposedly based on Aristotle's student, Eudemios, that the *magi* call the entirety of that which is primal and transcendental, 'place or time'.[53] This comment echoes the emphasis on both place and time in the cosmology of the *Bundahishn*. A passage in *Denkard* Book 4 relating to the importance of maintaining an ethical and physical balance (*payman*) during the time of Mixture – neither deficiency of good action, nor excess of impassioned reaction – acknowledges commonalities between the Iranian and Greek understanding of the elements and the humors, particularly with regard to the Aristotelian concept of the Mean.[54] The connection between the two perspectives seems to have come full circle, with ancient Greek and Iranian philosophies finding common ground once more. Indeed, *Denkard* 4 claims that the introduction of such Greek themes into Zoroastrian writings was a restoration of lost Avestan material.[55]

Agathias notes that Khosrow I was much admired both at home and by the Byzantines for his knowledge of works of Greek philosophy (*Histories* 11.28.1–2), suggesting Khosrow's self-promotion as a Platonic-type philosopher king. Admiration for the intelligent and tolerant rule of Khosrow continued into the Islamic period, when the later form of his name *Kisra* became synonymous with the ideal ruler.[56]

By the time of Hormizd IV (579–90), the increasing acknowledgement of Christianity and other religious and philosophical systems in the empire is reflected in a saying attributed to the king by Tabari: 'A throne has four legs, and the two inner legs cannot support it without the two outer ones. The religion of the *magi* likewise cannot stand without opposition.'[57] The passage continues with the admonition to perform good works so that those of other faiths may be drawn to the good religion.

The late Sasanian mystique of kingship is perhaps most evident in the monumental sculptures created by Khosrow II (590–628 CE) at Taq-e Bostan, in the late sixth/early seventh century. The scenes in the arch illustrate the monarch hunting within a paradisiacal setting. The *xwarrah* is figuratively shown as a nimbus around the king's head. On each side of the arch, protective spirits hold out the ring of power. Khosrow II's epithet was *Parviz* ('Victorious'), and his coins promote the idea of Iran as a place of increase and benefit (*abzon*), but his monument at Taq-e Bostan is the last flowering of Sasanian Zoroastrian iconography.

According to *Shah Nameh*, Khosrow II's favorite wife was the Christian Shirin. At Khosrow's death, Ferdowsi describes how Shirin donated all her wealth to the fire temple for the sake of his soul. After Khosrow Parviz, several monarchs reigned in quick succession. One of these was his daughter, Buran, eulogized by Tabari as a queen who made her people happy. Tabari notes that on the day of her coronation, Buran pledged to encourage pious conduct and justice, and that 'she treated her subjects well, spreading justice, minting coins and repairing stone and wooden bridges. She excused people from payment of outstanding taxes and wrote open letters to them in which she explained how she wished to do well by them.'[58] Buran is also said to have concluded a peace treaty with the Byzantine emperor, Heraclius.

It is around this point that Arab armies began to make incursions into the empire, and in 651 CE Yazdegird III died as a fugitive. But that was not the end of Mazda-worship in Iran. Its survival was not entirely tied to the royal *xwarrah*, and many of its beliefs and practices were sustained by Zoroastrian communities throughout 'Eran and Aneran', and by those who emigrated to India. Remnants of the religion are also found in many pan-Iranian customs and celebrations, such as *Nav Ruz*, and are alluded to in the poetry of Sufi mystics and other literary works, not least the great Iranian epic poem, the *Shah Nameh*.

Yazdegird III's sons fled east to China, where they remained. The heir apparent, Peroz, along with many Sasanian nobles, was granted refuge by the Tang dynasty, which recognized him as the rightful king of Iran. He ruled a Persian satellite state in the Zarang region between 658 and 663 CE, but died in the Chinese capital in 679 CE, where his royal status is acknowledged on his statue standing outside the Tang emperor's tomb. Both Sasanian and Sogdian Zoroastrian merchants had been traveling to China for centuries, along trade paths established during the Parthian period, but it is not until the seventh century that Chinese records describe the construction of fire temples in the northern Chinese cities of Langzhou, Chang'An and Loyang. This movement of Zoroastrians towards China will be explored in the next chapter, along with the particular expression of the religion in Central Asia.

Chapter V

The Zoroastrians of Central Asia

'rtm wx wxshtmysht'y
ashem vohu vahishtem asti
wsht'y wsht''y'shtwxm'
ushta asti ushta ahmai
yt wrt'y'xwsht'y rtm
hyat ashai vahishtai ashem

The Sogdian *Ashem Vohu*[1]

Central Asia is a geo-political area to the north-east of Iran that has, in the last few decades, produced a wealth of material relating to its early eastern-Iranian-speaking peoples, whose religion was predominantly Zoroastrian, and whose contribution to both the material and ideological culture of the trade routes from north to south and east to west was substantial.

Iranian speakers were established in the Central Asian steppes before they moved onto the plateau of what we now know as Iran. *Videvdad* 1 mentions Sogdiana, Chorasmia, Bactria, Margiana, Aria (western Afghanistan) and Arachosia (southern Afghanistan) as lands fashioned for the Iranians by Ahura Mazda after '*Airyana Vaejah*' – the Aryan expanse. Other lands referred to indicate that Iranians were present throughout the whole of what we now know as Afghanistan and northern Pakistan. These regions are also identified as Achaemenid satrapies in cuneiform inscriptions beginning with that at Bisutun, and in Herodotus' *Histories* (3.90–4, 7.61–96). Iranian elements among the Kamboja during Ashoka's time, in Kushan Buddhist iconography, and in later Khotanese Buddhist terminology, have been discussed earlier, providing some insight into Zoroastrian remnants in the regions of Bactria and Gandhara, and then into India and western China.

This chapter will concentrate largely on the Sogdians and Chorasmians, who, under Achaemenid hegemony, adopted the Aramaic script, which the former used in various forms in successive centuries and locations. This literary legacy now forms the basis for much of what we know of the religious background of the Sogdians. Very little Chorasmian text remains, but the fact that *remazd* was preserved in Chorasmian as the word for 'sun' – in keeping with Khotanese *urmaysde* and modern Sanglechi *ormozd* – indicates an eastern Iranian appreciation of Ahura Mazda as a divinity of light and growth. Sogdians and Bactrians preserve a version of the name of Mithra for the sun.[2] It is possible that the Bactrians also used Aramaic until it was displaced by Greek after the arrival of Alexander. Bactrian influence has been uncovered in some of the phrases in early Sogdian letters.[3] It is the archeological finds in Sogdiana (mostly southern Uzbekistan and western Tajikistan) and Chorasmia (north-western Uzbekistan and the autonomous region of Karakalpakstan) that provide us with the most fascinating picture of the beliefs and practices of the Iranians in the region. In Djarkutan, southern Uzbekistan, two ceramic 'proto-ossuaries' have been found dating back to around 1500 BCE, which may support the theory that Central Asia was one of the earliest locales for Zoroastrianism, although the function of these containers is debatable.

Sogdian merchants and missionaries traveled vast distances, and inscriptional, textual and illustrative sources from as far apart as north-west Pakistan, Xinjiang and northern China support much of the evidence from Sogdiana proper. Trading had existed between China and Egypt through present-day Afghanistan since the second millennium BCE, but under the Achaemenids more stable trade routes were established. An inscribed list of sources for the materials used to build Darius' palace complex at Susa shows that many of the raw materials were supplied by satrapies in the north-east of the empire: *Yaka* timber, probably Indian rosewood, came from Gandhara; ivory from Arachosia and India; gold from Bactria; lapis lazuli and carnelian from Sogdiana; turquoise from Chorasmia. Central Asian involvement in trade along what is commonly – although erroneously – referred to as 'The Silk Road' began several hundred years before the Sasanians came to power, and continued for a couple of centuries after their wane.

After Alexander's pursuit of Darius III to Bactria and his siege of the 'Sogdian Rock' in around 327/8 BCE, Sogdiana became part of the Greek Bactrian satrapy, and was then briefly incorporated into the seceded Greco-Bactrian kingdom before becoming an independent state, subject to the frequent incursions of nomadic Scythian groups from the steppes. From the mid-second century CE onwards, Sogdiana became a midpoint on the trading routes: a place where merchants who had crossed westwards from China met those who had come north from India, and those who had traveled east from Iran or Syria. Later, Sasanian sea routes vied with Sogdian overland routes to participate in lucrative trade transactions from China to the Mediterranean.

Chorasmia had remained independent during the Seleucid and Parthian periods, but came under Sasanian rule at the time of Bahram II.

Although Sogdiana fell beyond the boundaries of both Parthian and Sasanian hegemony, its culture and religion remained Iranian and closely related to that of its imperial Iranian neighbors. The majority of Iranian speakers in both Chorasmia and Sogdiana continued to practice their ancient faith, Zoroastrianism, which had taken root in Central Asia prior to its arrival on the Iranian plateau with the Ancient Persians. According to a legend preserved in the *Shahrestaniha-i Eranshahr,* Zarathushtra himself brought the religion to Samarkand, where Vishtaspa ordered the teachings to be written down and deposited in the fire temple.[4] Although many Central Asian expressions of the religion are similar to those found in contemporary or later Iranian contexts, other aspects diverge considerably and provide new perspectives of the development of the religion, which, it could be argued, are equally as representative of an 'authentic Zoroastrianism' as the material from Iran.

Let the Dead Speak: Dakhmas and Bone Boxes

In Karakalpakstan, at Shilpiq Kala, a hilltop fortress towers over the Oxus River valley. It was built in the early Common Era, with compacted clay carried up from the nearby Oxus River to form a huge wall around a bare mountaintop. This wall is thought to have surrounded a place of exposure. Local legend tells that Zarathushtra began the composition of the Avesta nearby. The site at Shilpiq Kala is so much a part of local lore that it is incorporated into the regional flag of Karakalpakstan, and newly-married couples drive to stand together at the foot of the hill to have their wedding photos taken. It may be the earliest example of an identifiable *dakhma*, and perhaps provides a clue as to how *dakhmas* first came into being. The *Videvdad* has varying accounts regarding the function of a *dakhma*.[5] *Dakhmas* were constructed in the round so that there would be no corners to hold pollution. Excavation has shown that the Shilpiq Kala *dakhma* was used until the seventh or eighth century CE, being repaired several times before it was finally abandoned around the tenth century. Only a few ossuaries were found at Shilpiq and it is thought that perhaps it was a royal *dakhma*, although it is 72 km from the royal residence of Toprak Kala, which was also constructed in the early Common Era.

Until recently, it was thought that, because ossuary-making abruptly stopped in Chorasmia and Sogdiana just after the Arab invasion in the eighth century CE, the practice of exposure had ended as well. In a medieval New Persian text, however, there is a reference to a letter written in the early ninth century by Adurfarrobay Farrokhzadan to the Zoroastrians of Samarkand, in response to their request as to how to dispose of bodies while they constructed a new *dakhma* to replace the old, damaged one. Adurfarrobay's answer was that until the new *dakhma* was complete, they should put the body on a small pile of stone slabs arranged on the surface of one side of the old *dakhma*, and transfer the body to the new *dakhma* when it was finished.[6]

Also in the Karakalpakstan region, to the north-west of Khiva, is another possible location of a hill of exposure. At a site called Mizdahkan, several ossuaries have been found dating between the fifth and eighth centuries. This points to Zoroastrian practice, substantiated by the existence of an ancient fortress on the opposite hill, the foundations of which are thought to date around the fourth century BCE, and which was restored for use between the late Parthian and early Sasanian era. The hill is named Gyaur Kala. 'Gyaur' comes from a term used by Muslims to refer to Zoroastrians. Gyaur Kala seems, then, to have been a Zoroastrian settlement, whose inhabitants used Mizdahkan for their funerary rituals. One of the rectangular ossuaries from Mizdahkan had legs and a pyramid lid, upon which appears to be a bird. The significance of the bird in Central Asian Zoroastrian iconography relating to death will be discussed later in the chapter.

Wei-jie, a Chinese traveler to the region in the first decade of the seventh century CE, noted that there were 'over two thousand households' outside the city walls of Samarkand, 'which specialized in funerary matters', including taking care of dogs. When a person died, these funerary specialists would collect the corpse and place it inside a particular building for the dogs to devour the flesh, then the undertakers would collect and bury the bones, without a special coffin.[7]

We know from over 300 examples, however, that both Chorasmians and Sogdians also used ossuaries – usually ceramic containers – to hold the bones that had been bleached and dried in the sun. These 'bone boxes' were then placed in family tombs, such as the vaulted burial chambers discovered at Panjikant in Tajikistan, or, less commonly, in graves. One of the last Sogdian kings, Devashtich, was executed by the Arab governor on the site of such a Zoroastrian 'bone depository' (Arabic, *nawus*) in early 723 CE.[8] Besides the ossuaries, vessels with food, golden coins and decorated silverware have also been found in the tombs. In Khiva, vaulted tombs dating from the medieval period onwards echo those of the Sogdians. Even today, Muslim Khwarezmians do not inter the body in the earth, which is the more normative practice, but rest it on top of the ground, or on the brick base of the tomb, so that it is possible to stack the tombs one on top of the other.

The use of clay ossuaries to hold the bones of the dead after exposure appears to be a solid example of Zoroastrian practice in this part of Central

Asia. Ossuaries have also been found in Merv, but none from the Bactria-Tokharistan region, nor areas near the Kopet-Dagh mountain range, the Caspian Sea or Ferghana, all of which were places which were also inhabited by Zoroastrians.[9] Iran proper has produced no clear evidence for the use of similar ossuaries. The earliest Central Asian ossuaries date to the fifth century CE, although enthusiastic museum cataloging often dates them earlier.

A stamped clay Sogdian ossuary from Mulla Kurgan (Miyankala), dating back to the seventh century CE, depicts the familiar theme of a fire-holder flanked by priests (see Fig. 17). Both the seated priest and standing attendant are wearing *kusti*s and mouth covers, so as not to pollute the fire, just as Zoroastrian priests still do today. The seated priest (*Zot*) seems to be holding *barsom* bundles, or sticks, to feed the fire in what may be a funerary ritual: perhaps the *afrinagan* ceremony performed on the fourth morning after death, known as the *chaharom*.[10] The colonnaded building with the pitched roof behind the priests may be a fire temple, and the upper scene of two women with plants standing under a crescent and a circle could represent the feminine hypostases of Haurvatat and Ameretat – the two qualities Zoroastrians aspire to in future life. The *padan* (Av. *paitidana*) worn by the priests is unusual, differing from those in Achaemenid iconography, but close to that depicted on a Sasanian priest's seal, now in the Bibliotheque Nationale, Paris. In some parts of Gujarat it was, until recently, a custom for relatives performing the rituals associated with death to cover the entire face with a *padan*.[11] Another seventh-century Sogdian ossuary, found near Bishkek in Kyrgyzstan, shows priests wearing the same type of *padan*, spooning fuel on the fire. The tripod tables illustrated are similar to those still used by Parsis at *Muktad* (*Fravardigan*).

Fig. 17. Ossuary, Mulla Kurgan.

Most of these motifs are familiar from Zoroastrian text, or praxis, relating to Iran. Some ossuaries, however, incorporate iconography that is unfamiliar, although probably based on Avestan concepts. For instance, an ossuary from ancient Samarkand (Afrasiyab) is thought to represent the winged female *fravashis*, who wear the *padan* that is usually associated with priests.

Sogdian Zoroastrianism

By the mid-fifth century CE, Sogdiana consisted of small city-states in the area extending from the Amu Darya (the river Oxus) to the Syr Darya (the river Yaxartes), mostly in the fertile Zerafshan valley. It included the cities of Samarkand, Bukhara, Varakhsha and Panjikant, and extended as far east as Chach (Tashkent). Local rulers came from the nobility, which was not as stratified as in Iran. Similarly, Zoroastrian priests in Sogdiana and elsewhere in Central Asia were not organized into a hierarchy, and did not have the status of their Sasanian peers.[12]

Contemporary onomastic graffiti at several sites along the Karakorum Highway, in the Upper Indus Valley, marks places on the southern trading route where Sogdians from the north exchanged goods with merchants from India, who were mostly Buddhist, as evidenced from the petroglyphs of *stupas* and the Buddha, and Kharoshti and Brahmi inscriptions. Over 500 Sogdian rock inscriptions in Aramaic script, located mostly at Shatial, Chilas, Thor North and Dadam Das, consist mainly of personal names, including Ahuramazdad, Kirdir, Miren, Yima and Farnah, and day names, such as Rashnu, Mir and Tir.[13] Two Middle Persian, two Parthian and about ten Bactrian inscriptions were also found.

1. Fires

Such inscriptions denote that the Sogdians, while retaining some degree of cultural autonomy, adhered nonetheless to a general 'Avestan' worldview. Evidence of the centrality of fire to the worship of the Sogdians is found in illustrations of fire-holders on murals in private homes at Samarkand, Panjikant and in the East Hall of the palace at Varakhsha (Fig. 18). Such paintings seem to be purely 'Zoroastrian', even though in the case of the latter, dated from the eighth century CE, the king depicted, Tughshada, had supposedly accepted Islam. Narshakhi, in his tenth-century *History of Bukhara*, considered that the king continued to practice Zoroastrianism, and it is known that his corpse was disposed of according to the local version of Zoroastrian funerary rites.[14] The royal couple sit on their heels, just as they and their Persian contemporaries would have sat before modern times. There is no evidence for this pose ever being used in a ritual context by Zoroastrians within Iran, but in Parsi fire temples in India, an initial act of offering for worshippers involves kneeling to place sandalwood and monetary gifts on a tray at the doorsill of the inner sanctuary, and touching a finger to the fire ash on the ladle, then to the forehead. This monetary offering is called a 'gift on the ladle' (PGuj. *chamachni ashodad*).

A similar scene from a private house in Panjikant shows worshippers before the same type of portable fire- or incense-holder also making an offering of fuel or incense, or perhaps liquid. Such holders do not contain an ever-burning fire, but a fire kindled for an offering to a *yazata*.[15] A fifth- or sixth-century CE fresco on the shrine wall at Temple II in Panjikant, and murals in private houses showing a fire being carried, support the notion that the hearth fire was used to light smaller fires, which were then carried to the shrine area of a temple or large residence. An actual mudbrick pilaster fire-holder was found set against the wall niche in Temple I, Room 19 at Panjikant, and a smaller ceramic one in the fifth-century site of Er Kurgan in southern Sogdiana.[16] The fire-holder from Panjikant was similar to the Sasanian-era three-stepped stone altar from Kuh-e Khajeh, and was thought perhaps to have held an ever-burning fire, but there are no traces of fire on the painted wall behind it.

There is no solid evidence of any permanent sacred fire in either Sogdian temples or private homes. The domestic shrine area from a private house in ancient Samarkand includes two shallow dishes in the floor for fire or – more probably – incense, and the base of a pitcher to hold water or some other liquid. The form of Zoroastrianism practiced in Sogdiana appears to have included some elements not evidenced in Sasanian Iran, including the range and representation of *yazatas*. In the mural at Varakhsha, the votaries sit in front of a giant figure of a *yazata* identified as Vashagn (Verethragna), who appears to have been the patron *yazata* of the Bukhara Khuda family.

Fig. 18. Varakhsha fresco, Bukhara Museum, Uzbekistan.

2. Mourning Rituals

A fresco from Temple II at Panjikant depicts gods and humans lamenting the death of a young prince or princess (or possibly a divinity). This scene was originally thought to represent the cult of mourning centered on the eastern Iranian hero Siyavush that is recorded by Narshakhi in his *History of Bukhara*. The Iranian story of Siyavush as narrated in *Shah Nameh* is of a young and innocent prince who takes refuge in Turan to escape the wrath of his father, only to be murdered on the order of Afrasiyab. In *Shah Nameh*, Siyavush was said to have founded the citadel at Bukhara, but the Middle Persian *Shahrestaniha-i Eranshahr* states that he founded Samarkand.[17] The way that Islamic historians such as Dinawari, Tabari and Ferdowsi recorded the tragedy divested it of its Zoroastrian aspects, both religious and cultic, but these elements are found in Narshakhi's narrative. Narshakhi relates that the people of Bukhara have many laments about the death of Siyavush, which is known throughout the regions, and that the musicians have made them into songs, which they chant and call 'the weeping of the magi'.[18] Narshakhi also describes the Zoroastrian veneration of the grave of Siyavush in Bukhara, with an offering of a cockerel before dawn on New Year's Day. The Panjikant setting is more reminiscent of the mourning for Furod, Siyavush's son, as described in *Shah Nameh*, rather than that of Siyavush, however.

In the mural, the mourners seem to be beating their heads, or cutting their hair, beards or even their faces. Zoroastrian Middle Persian texts criticize such action by *weh denan*, but evidence of such practice is found in Sogdian Manichaean texts that disparage a funerary ritual called the 'soul service', in which the mourners engage in 'spilling of blood, killing of horses, laceration of faces' and 'weep, tear (their garments), pull out (their hair).'[19] Such ritual lamentation, including beating the chest and head (but not cutting), is depicted on scenes found on a vase from Merv, a chest from Tok-Kala in the north of the Amu Darya delta, and a fresco in one of the palaces at Toprak Kala; the latter shows a mourning scene of women grieving over a sarcophagus. Such mourning rituals seem to have been part of local eastern Iranian custom, possibly borrowed from the nomadic Huns. The practice of cutting the face with knives is recorded at the funeral of Attila the Hun in 453 CE, and both eastern and western Turks mutilated themselves as a ritual act of mourning.[20]

Wei-jie described an annual mourning ritual in Samarkand that occurred for seven days in the seventh month, when over 300 mourners, clad in black and barefoot, would search in the fields for the remains of 'a divine child' who had died, but whose bones had not been recovered.[21] It has been suggested that such bereavement ritual could have influenced the development of the *ta'ziyeh*, the annual Shi'a passion play about the events surrounding the death of Imam Husayn at Karbala. This aspect will be discussed in the following chapter.

The chief divinity in the Panjikant mourning scene is usually identified as the multi-armed Nana.[22] The other divinity, holding a burning torch downwards seems to be female, although the motif is similar to that of the male *cautopates* in Roman Mithraism. A depiction of Mithra has been identified in Temple I at Panjikant. A Sogdian version of the *Vessantara Jataka*, mentions 'Mithra, the Judge of Creation', a term which is absent from the Pali version of the text. This reference alludes to a Sogdian Buddhist understanding of Mithra, which coheres with the late Kushan iconography at Bamiyan, but which seems to be based on a Zoroastrian precedent (cf. Yt 10.92).[23]

The Sogdians created a syncretistic iconography by combining Greek, Sasanian and Indian motifs. Although Nana appears to have been partly assimilated with the Zoroastrian *yazata* of the beneficent earth Spenta Armaiti, a painting in a private house in Panjikant depicts her as a four-armed goddess on a lion, holding the sun and crescent moon in two of her hands. Such imagery retains the celestial elements of the sun and moon associated with the Mesopotamian goddess Ishtar, but also incorporates aspects of the Indian goddess Durga, whose vehicle is a lion. On Kushan coins, Nana rides a lion and was associated with Uma, the wife of Shiva. Sogdian representations of Nana are similar to those of the Khotanese Saka *śśandrāmatā*, that is, Spenta Armaiti.[24]

Nana is one of the most commonly represented divinities in Sogdian frescoes, but other indigenous Sogdian family or community divinities also appear. One of these is Vesh-parkar, the Sogdian form of the *yazata* of the wind, Vayu. The name derives from the Avestan term in *Videvdad* 19.13: *Vaiiush uparo kairiyo* – 'the wind whose activity is in the upper regions'.[25] An illustration of Vesh-parkar from a building in Panjikant has almost an Indian appearance. In the Sogdian translations of Buddhist texts, Vesh-parkar replaces Shiva Mahadeva, who is described as having three faces. The addition of a horn, blown by one of the three heads, marks Vesh-parkar's specific function as an atmospheric *yazata*.[26]

3. Narrative Themes

Excavations at Panjikant have also revealed painted murals portraying traditional Iranian themes, such as *razm o bazm* – 'fighting and feasting' – and animal fables similar to those of the ancient Indian *Panchatantra*. According to the *Shah Nameh*, under Khosrow I, the *Panchatantra* was translated into Middle Persian by Burzoe as *Kalile o Dimne*. It was then translated into Arabic by Ibn Muqaffa (d. 759 CE). Some of the frescoes at Panjikant also show heroic tales. One cycle of narrative friezes is based on the seven exploits (*haft khwan*) of the hero Rostam, who is portrayed wearing his leopard skin and riding his red horse Rakhsh. In one scene he fights the White *Dev*. Rostam seems to have been the most popular heroic figure on the murals at Panjikent, for he appears as a minor character in two more painted epic cycles, which do not relate to any known text.[27]

One wonders if Rakhsh was one of the famous Ferghana horses so prized by the Chinese from the Han period (206 BCE–220 CE)? The Han Chinese initially used these horses to breed battle steeds for the cavalry, so that they could defend themselves against the horse-riding raids of the steppe peoples named Xiongnu.[28] Alongside the military use of the horse came the leisure pursuit of hunting by members of the Chinese aristocracy, and Central Asians were often employed as horse grooms and trainers by the Tang (618–906 CE).[29]

In the mid-seventh century CE, the king of Samarkand, Varkhuman (r. c. 650–70), recognized nominal Tang suzerainty, and Sogdian merchants were able to register as Chinese residents.[30] The presence of Sogdians at the Tang dynasty courts is well documented, as is their tribute offering of 'golden peaches' from Samarkand. Tang sources describe the Sogdians as people engaged in commerce, who are fond of music and wine. On a mural in a residence at Afrasiyab, a local king, who appears to be the sovereign Varkhuman mentioned in a fragmentary inscription on the same wall, is depicted on his throne receiving envoys from many regions, including Turks, Chinese and Koreans. The mural may represent a ritual gift-giving, similar to that carved on the *apadana* at Persepolis a thousand years earlier. A scene on the adjacent southern wall portrays men wearing the *padan*, suggesting that they are Zoroastrian priests. This seems to continue the festival scene, although the Chinese 'History of the Tang' (*Tangshu*) records that one Sogdian ruler from Chach commemorated a funerary ritual in a temple there, and this second mural may represent such a ritual.[31]

4. Religious Motifs

By the eighth century, silk made in Sogdiana was being exported along trade routes to both east and west. Iranian iconography was popular among Chinese and Tibetans, as well as Europeans, particularly animal designs. A brightly-colored woven silk child's jacket, from the period of Tibetan rule in western China (late eighth/early ninth century CE), has a pattern of stylized pairs of ducks in profile within a roundel of pearls, which probably derives from an original Sasanian image, and relates to the representation of the *xwarrah* as a pearl held in the beak of a bird on some Sasanian coins. In the small Belgian town of Huy, a piece of gold-patterned silk with lions in similar pearl medallions was discovered in the last century, adorning the sepulcher of Saint Domitian in Notre Dame Cathedral. A Sogdian inscription determined that this silk cloth had been manufactured in the remote settlement of Zandan, near Bukhara, probably in the eighth century. 'Zandaniji' silk has also been found in other Christian reliquaries in Rome and Paris, as well as in burials in the northern Caucasus.[32]

Three delegates painted on the palace walls at ancient Samarkand wear similar colorful robes, woven with other designs familiar from Sasanian times: ducks holding pearls; the '*senmurv*'; and the boar. The boar, as mentioned previously, symbolized victory for the one who possesses *xwarrah*. It occurs as a motif woven into a silk cloth dating to the late sixth/early seventh century, placed over the face of a deceased local Chinese ruler in a tomb near Turfan in eastern Xinjiang. A Sogdian contract from the Astana graveyard dated 639 CE specifies the sale of a Sogdian girl as a slave to a Chinese man, and the discovery of fragments of a lawsuit brought by Sogdian traders against a Chinese merchant,[33] as well as several Sasanian coins, point to regular exchanges between the two groups, which must have exposed the Chinese to Zoroastrian imagery on clothing or coinage.

Religious Pluralism

Pre-Islamic Sogdian literary relics, mostly on paper, epitomize the religious plurality found on the trade routes between Central Asia, India and China. We know that some Sogdian speakers were Christians, Manichaeans and Buddhists. Following the persecutions instigated under Bahram I by Kerdir in the late third century, Christians and Manichaeans fled eastwards from Iran. These refugees learned Sogdian before continuing further east to the oasis cities of Xinjiang and beyond. The impetus for translating Middle Persian and Parthian Manichaean texts into Sogdian came from the sixth-century missionary, Mar Shad Ohrmizd, who formed an independent Manichaean church in the east that was separate from Baghdad. Sogdian became the principal language for the dissemination of both Manichaeism and so-called 'Nestorian' Christianity to China. By 650 CE, there was a Nestorian Christian archbishop at Samarkand and over 20 bishops further east. A Nestorian church was built in China in 638 CE.[34] Sogdians also provided some of the earliest translations of both Shravakayana and Mahayana Buddhist texts into Chinese.

A wall painting of Buddhist monastics in the fifth- to ninth-century caves at Bezeklik, near Turfan, shows both East Asian and Central Asian adherents, the latter with blue eyes and a red beard. We can surmise that some Sogdians were converts, but it may be that others patronized the translation of texts into Sogdian, or made donations to Buddhist temples, in order to please their Buddhist clients. Although Sogdians were among the chief translators of Buddhist *sutras* into Chinese, and the largest extant corpus of Sogdian texts is Buddhist, no Buddhist texts were found in Sogdiana proper, nor have any stupas and monasteries been discovered. The Buddhist complexes at Ajina-Tepe, south of Dushanbe, and at Kara Tepe (near Termez) were originally part of the Kushan kingdom. According to Sasanian graffiti found at Kara Tepe, the monastery was plundered by the Persians in the fourth century, under Shapur II. There is little evidence, then, that Buddhism took firm root in Sogdiana, although some parallels with Kushan iconography, a few references in documents from Mt. Mug, and Narshakhi's mention of a *botkhaneh* ('house of idols') in Bukhara, may indicate small groups of Buddhists.[35] In the seventh century, according to the Chinese Buddhist monk Xuan Zang, the people of Samarkand rejected Buddhism and demanded from the neighboring states a reverence for the Sogdian gods and 'scriptures'.[36]

Sogdian Zoroastrians in Xinjiang

Although Indian and Bactrian traders were initially more prominent on the eastern trading routes established in the early centuries of the Common Era, it was the Sogdians who made the most significant contribution to the transmission of both goods and ideas to the region. By the early fourth century CE, the Sogdians had developed a network of agents who lived in sizeable communities at staging posts along the 1,500-mile route, between their homeland and northern China, that passed through what is now known as Xinjiang province. From this time on, Sogdian manuscripts are found throughout Xinjiang that is, roughly between Kashgar and Dunhuang, as well as in Kyrgyzstan and Bugut in Mongolia. Sogdians settled in Toyok in the Turfan area, in Hami in the north, Khotan in the south and Dunhuang at the convergence of routes in the east, as well as in the Chinese cities of Chang'An (modern Xian), Loyang and Yangzhou (see Map 2). A range of written and visual texts attest to both the ubiquity of the Sogdian language across the region, as well as to the extensive relocation of the Sogdians themselves. Sogdian became a lingua franca of these trade routes. Sogdians involved in the network of trade and commerce included merchants, artisans, hotel owners and food sellers; and also people of faith whose iconography and ideology traversed both cultural and religious boundaries.

A range of material discoveries has emerged from Dunhuang, providing information about Zoroastrian Sogdian traders, much of which is only just being evaluated. In 1907, a postbag was found in the ruins of a Han-era watchtower, not far from Dunhuang. The bag contained several letters in Old Sogdian Aramaic script, dating back to the early fourth century CE. These letters were written on rag paper, with the name and location of the recipient on the outside. They provide a glimpse into the lives of Sogdian merchants and their families, who were already well established in the region.

One letter is from a merchant's wife, named Miwnay, to her mother Chatis. Miwnay and her husband, Nanaidhat, had moved from Samarkand to Dunhuang, where Nanaidhat had apparently got into debt and gone away to another town. To make ends meet, Miwnay had become a servant in a Chinese household. In the letter, she grumbles: 'I live wretchedly, without clothing, without money.' She complains that she has petitioned various members of the Sogdian community, including a relative named Artivan, to give her a loan so that she may return home or go and look for her husband. But no help has been forthcoming, so she has had to rely on charity from the temple priest, who had offered to give her a camel and a man to accompany her should she decide to leave.[37]

Sadly, the letters never arrived. It seems probable that they were confiscated by Chinese soldiers at a time when Chinese control this far west was being threatened. These letters tell us that, although she had control over her husband's affairs in Dunhuang, Miwnay had little fiscal autonomy. The reference to a temple priest (*bagnpat*) indicates that at this early stage the Sogdian Zoroastrian community of Dunhuang was sufficiently large to have a place of worship and a serving priest. In fact, an eighth-century Tang Chinese source describes a Zoroastrian (*xian*)[38] temple on the eastern edge of Dunhuang, which had a courtyard and a main hall with a religious painting and 20 niches.[39] Later Chinese documents from Dunhuang indicate that this temple flourished into the early tenth century. This is our latest evidence for the continuity of Sogdian Zoroastrian practice in the region.

A building with niches was found in the second–fourth century CE High Palace at Toprak Kala in Chorasmia. Could this have been a model for the temple described at Dunhuang? There are Chinese records of other such temples established in the Sogdian settlements of Toyok and Hami in the Tarim Basin by the seventh century CE. Other texts mention that these local governments provided material support to Sogdians for annual offerings 'to the gods' (*saixian*), presumably Zoroastrian *yazatas*, in an apparent reference to ceremonies of blessing such as *afrinagan* or seasonal festivals (*gahanbars*) such as *Fravardigan*, which were also celebrated by the Chorasmians and Sasanians.[40]

Although many aspects of the Sogdian form of Zoroastrianism do not fit comfortably with what is known of the religion as practiced in Sasanian Iran, these disparate elements cannot all be dismissed as belonging to pre-Zoroastrian Iranian belief, or to 'foreign' religions. It has been shown that fire retained its emblematic centrality for Sogdians, and further confirmation of an ancient and authentic 'Zoroastrian core' to the religious expression of these eastern Iranians is also found in a small fragment of a Sogdian manuscript, discovered among 40,000 other texts in the 'library cave' at Dunhuang. This cave contained books and manuscripts dating between the early fifth and early eleventh centuries CE, when the cave was sealed up, probably under threat from either the Tanguts or from the Karakhanids, the Muslims who had taken Khotan. One of these manuscript fragments turned out to contain the oldest surviving Zoroastrian text. The main part of the document is written in normal Sogdian of the eighth or ninth century CE, but resembles an Avestan text in both style and phraseology. It describes 'the perfect, righteous Zarathushtra' meeting an unnamed 'excellent supreme god' (*Adbag*), who dwelt in 'the fragrant paradise in good thought'. Zarathushtra addresses this supreme being as 'beneficent law-maker, [and] justly-deciding judge'.[41] This passage could be Manichaean, but it is preceded by a text that is *wholly* Zoroastrian in content (Fig. 19).

Fig. 19. The Sogdian Ashem Vohu.

When the manuscript was discovered, the first two lines of the text were thought to make no sense, until they were recognized as a Sogdian version of the *Ashem Vohu* – one of the ancient cardinal prayers of the religion. It seems that the prayer had been transmitted orally, and was perhaps recorded phonetically by someone who did not understand its meaning. The text is not in the standard Avestan of the Sasanian period, nor a Sogdian translation, but includes some characteristic Sogdian elements that retain archaic Old Iranian forms. For example, the Avestan *ashem* is not replaced by the Sogdian equivalent, but by *-rtm*, representing a form identical to Old Persian *rtam*.[42] This information points to the Sogdian preservation and oral transmission of the prayer from Achaemenid times or earlier, in which case it belongs to an oral tradition independent of the Sasanian recension of the Avesta. The Sogdian manuscript predates surviving Avestan manuscripts from Iran and India by over 300 years.

The existence of both a fire temple and an oral transmission of sacred text at Dunhuang testifies to the existence and endurance of the faith outside the Iranian plateau, and to the continued importance of the earliest prayers and practices of the religion. The occurrence of a Sogdian theophoric name 'Avyaman' or 'Avyamanyu' seems to be a comparative form of an Avestan term '*vahyah- manyu-*' ('the better spirit'), which is not found in any extant Avestan text, but is preserved in the Sogdian loanword. A similar case can be made for the Sogdian word for the devil, '*Shimnu*', as the equivalent of an unattested Avestan '*ashyah- manyu-*' ('worse spirit').[43]

Fragments of secular works found at Dunhuang indicate a similarity in reading material between the Sogdians there and those whose houses were adorned with frescoes in Panjikant. For example, another Sogdian manuscript written in the distinctive handwriting of the Zoroastrian *Ashem Vohu* fragment, and probably by the same scribe, contains a story about Rostam. The episode narrated here does not occur in the *Shah Nameh*, but may come from an east-Iranian cycle.[44]

Sogdian Zoroastrians in China

Dunhuang is the gateway into China proper, where a number of Zoroastrian temples were built in the early Tang period, including one that was restored in Chang'An in 631 CE.[45] This indicates that there were Zoroastrian *magi* in China at that time who had arrived with either Persian or Sogdian traders. A short time later, the Sasanians sought Chinese aid against the Arab incursion, which was refused, but Peroz, son of Yazdegird III, was granted the protection of the Tang court. Chinese texts refer to the presence of Sogdians in Xinjiang in the fifth century, then in China proper.[46] Under the Tang Chinese, Sogdians retained autonomy in terms of governance and had a designated official administrator named a *sabao*, which derives from a Sogdian term meaning 'caravan leader'.[47] By the seventh century most of the larger northern Chinese towns with a Sogdian population had a *sabao*, whose rank was respected and who also acted in a supervisory capacity over the temple, but it is not known whether he functioned as a priest. Chinese texts refer to the 'head of the Sogdian temple cult' and 'the invoker of the cult', which may refer to the two priests (the *zot* and the *raspi*) required in a Zoroastrian ritual for the performance of the *Yasna*.[48]

Recently, several funerary monuments of wealthy Sogdian merchants from this period have come to light in northern China. In Guyuan in Ningxia province, seventh-century Sogdian graves have inscriptions narrating the migration of a Sogdian family from the town of Kesh, modern Shahr-i Sabz in Uzbekistan. Two older men of the family had acted as administrative officials (*sabao*) for the community. Intricately decorated stone funerary couches have also been found, which were made for Sogdian merchants, who lived and died in China in the sixth century CE. These mortuary beds depict specifically Zoroastrian scenes, which demonstrate that, although the surrounding culture of the deceased was Chinese, the predominant religious expression was of Sogdian Zoroastrianism. On one panel of such a couch, the Zoroastrian faith of the merchant is indicated in several motifs: the priest wears the *padan* to prevent him from polluting the fire, which is in a fire vase similar to those depicted on later Sasanian coins, and discovered at Bishapur and Takht-e Suleiman; nearby is a pedestal tray holding round objects, which could be pomegranates or other foods; the dog facing the fire could illustrate the ancient ritual of *sagdid* – the viewing of the deceased by a dog. In front of the priest appears to be the edge of the Chinvat bridge, with the rump of a departing camel (see Fig. 20 overleaf). One of the two women in the background holds a set of clothes, perhaps to give away, along with the food that has been blessed.[49] Such action is part of the *chaharom* ceremony, performed on the fourth morning after death. The act of cutting, which the mourners appear to engage in, may reflect the same eastern Iranian cult of mourning shown on the murals at Panjikant.

In Xian in 2003, a tomb containing the sarcophagus of another Sogdian *sabao*, named Wirkak (Chinese *Shi*), was found. A bilingual Chinese and Sogdian inscription tells us that Wirkak had lived a long life – from 495–579 CE – and that his wife had died only a month later and was buried next to him. On the door to the sarcophagus is a rather odd birdman figure, which, at first glance, doesn't seem to relate to anything Zoroastrian (see Fig. 21). But a closer look shows that the human component is a priest, wearing the mouth cover and tending a fire, directing the *barsom* towards a tray with vessels. The tray is typical of an 'outer' liturgy, such as the *chaharom*.

Fig. 20. Panel from a Sogdian funerary couch.

In the previous chapter we noted a similar *kinnara*-type image on the ceiling fresco at Bamiyan, and it is reminiscent of the image on an ossuary recently found at Samarkand.[50] The bird aspect may relate to an Avestan association with Sraosha. In *Videvdad* 18.14–15, the cockerel is identified with Sraosha, the *yazata* who was the first to tie the *barsom*, to make an offering to Ahura Mazda and to sing the *Gathas*.[51] According to Avestan eschatology, the soul of the dead person remains within the world for three days (Vd 19.28), during which time it is under the protection of Sraosha, who is conceived of as a protector of the soul (Y 57.25). Ceremonies are performed for the good of the soul of the deceased throughout this time. At dawn on the fourth morning, the soul is judged by Mithra the Judge, assisted by Rashnu, the *yazata* of justice, and Sraosha. Then it makes its way towards the Chinvat bridge (Vd 19.29). In Zoroastrian eschatology, the just Sraosha is the only *yazata* to accompany the soul on its journey across the bridge (MX 2.124). It could be that the priest's role at death is equated here with that of Sraosha.

Fig. 21. Bird-priest, Wirkak's sarcophagus.

That connection is reiterated on panels from Wirkak's funerary monument, where Zoroastrian priests with *padan* are shown at the entrance to the bridge, where the fate of the soul in the next life is decided (see Fig. 22). The two Zoroastrian priests are not on the bridge, but appear to have solemnized the *chaharom* ceremony and so to have sent the souls on their way forwards. The panel shows a crowd of departed souls led by the deceased Wirkak and his wife, crossing the Chinvat bridge that is guarded by two dogs (cf. Vd 19.30). The souls have passed the test of the bridge, and are no longer in danger of falling towards the two monsters in the turbulent waters below. These images correspond to Avestan texts concerning the judgment of the soul, although in such texts the soul crosses the bridge alone and the bridge is straight, not curved.

Fig. 22. Drawing of East Wall of Wirkak's sarcophagus.

Above is Vesh-parkar, the wind. In Middle Persian eschatology, *Good Vayu* is described as not only accompanying the soul to the bridge with Sraosha (MX 2.115), but as taking it 'by the hand' and bringing it into 'his own place' – the atmosphere above High Hara (Bd 30.23). The whole scene could be said to illustrate the paradise 'at the level of the sun' (Bd 30.26).[52] The winged woman who welcomes Wirkak and his wife with her left hand, and who holds the *kusti* in her right hand, may be the 'woman-shape' in the wind, who shows the *ashavan* the way to paradise.[53] Animals also cross the bridge, and the fact that one of them is a camel laden with wares reflects the particular concerns of a Sogdian merchant. The various animals recall a statement in the *Anthology of Zadspram* (30.57) about the beneficent creatures (*gospand*) of paradise.[54]

Other scenes on the funerary couches could also illustrate paradise. In the

Gathas, the best existence is described as 'the house of song'. On one of the couches, the deceased merchant and his wife are shown banqueting, whilst listening to musicians and watching both Chinese and Sogdian dancers. This activity would also have been part of their earthly experience. Among the Central Asian performers at the Tang court in Chang'An were the 'leaping' and 'whirling' dancers from Samarkand, Kesh and Tashkent, who would dance on a small carpet.

The funerary beds themselves would have been in line with Zoroastrian practice of keeping the corpse away from water and earth, prior to the collection of bones in a decorated ceramic ossuary, such as described earlier. There was no inner or outer coffin: just the base, platform for the body and upright panels enclosing the bed on three sides, which suggests that they functioned like an ossuary. Although ossuaries have been found as far east as the Sogdian communities in Xinjiang, none have yet been found in China proper.[55]

In 845 CE, the Tang emperor Wu Zong, worried by the rise of Buddhism within China, withdrew recognition of all 'foreign religions' including Zoroastrianism, in order to implement indigenous Taoism. Despite this proscription, evidence remains of the continued construction of fire temples in China into the thirteenth century.[56] After the suppression of several uprisings in Samarkand and elsewhere in the Sogdian homeland, Islam had quickly become the dominant religion there, although Narshakhi maintained that many continued to practice Zoroastrianism in secret.[57] In the late ninth century, however, the Samanids, an aristocratic Persian family from Bactria, became powerful in northeastern Iran (c. 875–999 CE). The Samanids had converted from Zoroastrianism, and claimed descent from Bahram Chubin and therefore from the ancient house of Mihran. They were largely tolerant of divergent religions, although an edict by one of the early Samanids that the local Zoroastrians should build a mosque on the site of the palace at Varakhsha was met with defiance. With the rise in mosque construction, so the fire temples decreased, although a few survived in the villages and in Bukhara into the tenth century.[58] At that time, Narshakhi reports that the Bukharan Zoroastrians would stone Muslim locals who tried to persuade them to attend the mosque.[59]

The Samanids encouraged an Iranian renaissance in the towns of Samarkand and Bukhara, and the earliest writings in New Persian flourished, preserving the rich religious and mythico-historical narrative that was one of the hallmarks of the Sogdian Zoroastrian contribution to eastern Iranian culture, and thence to Iranian culture at large. Ferdowsi began his composition of *Shah Nameh* under Samanid patronage, and in medieval times he was regarded as a co-religionist by Zoroastrians, for whom his poetic accounts of the frequent delivery of Iran from the clutches of the enemy resonated with hope for a future resurgence.

Chapter VI

Gabr-Mahalle: Zoroastrians in Islamic Iran

'I, Mardanfarrokh-i Ohrmazddad, composed this treatise.... And, from childhood on, I have always used my mind to seek and examine the truth... And to this treatise...I have given the title 'Doubt-dispelling Exposition', because it is very suitable for new learners to dispel their doubts about the understanding of the truth and the soundness of the Good Religion, in contrast with the misery of the opponents.'

Shkand Gumanig Wizar[1]

The fall of the Sasanian dynasty to the Arab Muslims occurred for many reasons, which have been evaluated at length by historians.[2] The demise followed a time of external struggle with Byzantines on the west and Hephthalites in the east, and internal turmoil in which there were at least eight contenders for the throne in the four years following Khosrow Parviz's assassination in 628 CE. Yazdegird III assumed the throne in 632 CE when he was quite young. His death in 651 CE, and the capitulation of Merv, the Sasanian stronghold in the east, marked the end of Zoroastrian rule in Iran. Later attempts to restore the dynasty were unsuccessful, and both Peroz and Wahram, Yazdegird III's sons, died in China, as did Khosrow, Wahram's son, after an unsuccessful bid to recapture Iran aided by the Turks.[3] In Iran, Zoroastrians maintained key bureaucratic positions for several generations, however, and their cultural and religious heritage had a lasting impact on the development of Islam in the region and beyond. Numerically minor, but vibrant, Zoroastrian communities survive in Iran, and act as an axial link between the past development of the religion and its modern expressions and exponents.

Keeping the Fires Burning: Until the Mongols

As the Arab armies moved into Iran, defeating the Sasanian warriors and war elephants at Qadisiya, then besieging and taking the capital city of Ctesiphon in 637 CE, and routing the Persians at Nihavand in 642 CE, so they levied a tribute from the local population and confiscated the properties of fire temples. In many cases, the amount was less than the taxation that had been demanded by the Sasanians to fund their war coffers. Initially, there seems to have been little motive for the Zoroastrians to convert, although after the defeat at Qadisiya, many Persian soldiers, realizing the hopelessness of the Sasanian position, joined the Muslim armies as *mawali* – that is, nonArab Muslims.[4] Conversion at this point seems to have been for economic, political or military reasons, rather than religious conviction, and there is no evidence of frequent desertion from Zoroastrianism, nor of active proselytism; indeed, Umar, the caliph who had succeeded Abu Bakr in 634 CE, had moved to restrict Islam to Arabs.

Muslim tradition concerning one early Zoroastrian convert, Salman-i Farsi, claims that he was the warden of a sacred fire, who took interest in Christianity before becoming a revered companion of the Prophet Mohammed, prior to the expansion of the Arab armies into the Fertile Crescent. Zoroastrian texts do not mention Salman, but Muslim sources credit him with showing the Arab army how to dig defense trenches and with translating part of the *Qur'an* into Persian during Mohammed's lifetime. Salman himself is said to have made few converts from among his former co-religionists.

As long as Yazdegird III lived, there was strong local resistance to the Arabs, which took some time to subdue. This is particularly true of Fars province and its capital Istakhr. Al-Baladhuri, a Persian Muslim historian, wrote about the conquest of Fars, which took place in 643–9 CE, noting that Darabgird was surrendered by a Zoroastrian *herbad*, who was in charge of the city. The *Shah Nameh* recounts Yazdegird III's betrayal and murder in Merv in a moving narrative that echoes Arrian's Greek account of the slaying of the last Achaemenid king, Darius III, by his kinsmen in Bactria. The overthrow of the Sasanian Empire did not result in the immediate Islamization of the Iranians. Evidence shows that, in many places, Zoroastrians chose to pay tribute to Muslim overlords rather than convert. Fire temples were, for the most part, protected as belonging to these communities, although one fire known as Adur Farrobay, near Darabgird, was demolished at the orders of the Umayyad governor of Iraq. Some of the embers had been hidden by the *mobeds*, however, and the fire was rekindled elsewhere.[5] Such 'rescue' of the fire became a common trope for Zoroastrian resistance to Muslim assault.

It was in the Arabs' interest to retain the existing and well-functioning government of the Sasanians, and to that end leading Zoroastrian families were encouraged to keep their positions of authority until at least the eighth century, when the Umayyads (661–744 CE) began to exclude non-Muslims from the administration of rule. Conversion became more general at this juncture, although discrimination against converts also ensued. Zoroastrians were frequently victims of political conflict, and this was a difficult period for them, particularly in Fars and Khorasan. The north-east of Iran continued to be a center of foment and uprising into the Abbasid period (c. 750–1258 CE), and several popular revolutionary movements there incorporated Persian nationalist elements, mixing both Zoroastrian and Islamic religious beliefs and motives. Some of these movements were labeled 'Mazdakite' by Muslim historians, such as that led by Sinbad 'the Magian' in Nishapur, who seems to have had a mainly Zoroastrian following. Sinbad was slain by an Abbasid general in 755 CE.

Both *Bundahishn* and *Zand-i Wahman Yasn* refer to an uprising by a group called the *Khorramden* that occurred in 816–37 CE. In Persian, the term literally means 'the happy religion', although the name is often derived from Khurrama, the wife of Mazdak, who is said to have continued his teachings after his death. In the *Bundahishn*, the Khorramden are identified as Persians who were anti-Arab in sentiment. According to both Middle Persian texts and the New Persian *Zardosht Nameh*, members of the group wore red and were considered heretical by the Zoroastrian priests. Their alliance with the Byzantines and their mutilation of Abbasid prisoners after the battle of Zibatrah in Azerbaijan were regarded as apocalyptic premonitions of the end-time.[6] Ninth-century redactions of Zoroastrian oracular texts such as *Zand-i Wahman Yasn* interpreted such turmoil as the presage of a future restoration of the religion. Although these rebellions against the Abbasids were mainly socially and politically motivated, rather than battles over religion, their charismatic leaders seem to have proclaimed an admixture of Zoroastrian beliefs as a means of stirring support against the Abbasids.[7]

The Khorramden movement was suppressed by a ruler from Ustrushana (Sogdiana) named Afshin, and in 838 CE its leader, Babak, was killed before Caliph al-Mu'tasim at Samarra. In the same year, Afshin supported the prince of Tabaristan, named Maziyar, against the Taherid governor of Khorasan. Maziyar's immediate precursors had retained their Zoroastrian faith and continued to strike Middle Persian coinage, and Afshin was accused of being sympathetic to 'Magian' (Zoroastrian) beliefs and practices. Accounts of Afshin's trial record accusations that he read 'Magian' books, and was not circumcised – in other words, that he had not actually converted from Zoroastrianism to Islam.[8]

The suppression of these uprisings led to a further decline in the religion, so that sometime in the tenth century CE the chief priest Adurbad-i Emedan bemoaned: 'Iranian rule has come to an end in the country of Iran.'[9] The late sixteenth-century narrative, *Qesse-ye Sanjan*, claims to describe a migration of Zoroastrians from the port of Hormuz to India in the late Umayyad or early Abbasid period. From this time on, Zoroastrians became a religious minority in the cities and surrounds, but it was not until around 1300 CE that Islam took firm control over both urban and rural Iranian society, effectively endorsing the subaltern status of Zoroastrians for centuries to come.[10]

Further marginalization and decline of Zoroastrians occurred not only through political and economic control, but also subordination of the religion itself. As *dhimmi* ('protected' minority), Zoroastrians paid the *jizya*, or poll tax, until the late nineteenth century CE. This system of taxation is thought to have derived from a Sasanian model. The *jizya* exempted those who paid it from forced labor and military service, but they were not to proselytize, not to intermarry with Muslim women unless they converted, not to wear the same clothes as Muslims, nor to sound any call to worship that could be heard by Muslims. They were also prohibited from building new places of worship, carrying weapons and riding horses. Muslims were privileged in matters of inheritance, which provided a material stimulus for conversion to Islam. Conversion theoretically brought release from the *jizya*, and social equality with Arabs, in contrast to the strict class division of the Sasanians. The majority of *mawalis* were Iranian craftsmen, to whom Ali, the son-in-law of the Prophet Mohammed, had given his support. In practice, however, only converts who were administrators or soldiers were exempt from the *jizya*.[11] This meant that the ruling upper class was more likely to convert than farmers. Although Middle Persian texts allow a contrite convert to return to Zoroastrianism, apostasy from Islam could result in the death penalty, entailing that the *mawali* resumption of their earlier faith could only occur in secret.[12]

The Zoroastrian religion itself was regarded rather ambiguously in Muslim legal and historical texts: some defined it as *ahl-e kitab* ('of the book'), although not quite as authoritative as that of Christianity or Judaism, and others as heretical.[13] In the early years of Muslim rule, Zoroastrians, unlike Christians and Jews, were not allowed into mosques for this reason. The treatment of Zoroastrians varied according to the caliph or governor of the time. During the first few centuries of Islam in Iran, Zoroastrians continued to keep the faith in large numbers in the less strategically important cities such as Yazd and Kerman, Jibal (the region around Hamadan), a few areas of Azerbaijan and the isolated Caspian provinces, as well as Sistan and Khorasan.

At the end of the ninth century, the Abbasids moved their capital to Baghdad, and oversight of the Zoroastrians was undertaken by the *hudenan peshobay* – 'the leader of those of the Good Religion'. These *hudenan peshobays*, such as Adurfarrobay Farroxzadan, who served under caliph al-Ma'mun (r. 813–33), retained positions of authority over the religious affairs of the Zoroastrians, which they exercised under the eye of the caliphate in Baghdad. During this period many fire temples were demolished or turned into mosques, such as the temple of Adur-Anahid at Istakhr, where Kerdir had served as priest.[14] In 861 CE, the Abbasid caliph Mutawakkil is said to have cut down a great cypress tree at Kashmar that, according to *Shah Nameh*, had been planted by Zarathushtra himself. As the numbers of *mobeds* waned, and the Sasanian ruling families converted, often to maintain their elite lifestyle, so the regular laity found themselves without access to educated religious leaders to guide them. Conversion to Islam accelerated in the cities, but was more gradual in the rural areas.[15]

On conversion, Zoroastrians would have stopped wearing the *sudreh* and *kusti* and attending the fire temple, and modified their daily life in terms of dress, diet and domestic praxis. But many Zoroastrian beliefs and practices had close parallels in Islam, so that the two religions may not initially have been seen to be at odds, and the process of conversion made easier. Perhaps the most obvious similarity is the practice of praying five times a day,[16] although the Zoroastrian custom of facing the sun or the fire was replaced by the Muslim injunction to face Makkah.

Preserving the Religion

Ninth- and tenth-century Zoroastrian books reflect an attempt to preserve and intellectually defend the religion as its numbers and authority declined. One, the 'Wisdom of the Ancient Teachers' (*Chidag Andarz-i Poryotkeshan*), attempts to address all those questions about origin, purpose and the end of life, in a first person catechism, which exhorts the Mazda-worshipper to have no doubt concerning the good religion. Such surviving texts that record and codify Zoroastrian beliefs mostly originated with a few priestly families from Fars province, and include the *Dadestan-i Denig*, *Denkard* and *Bundahishn*.

Adurfarrobay Farroxzadan is thought to have redacted the *Denkard* in Baghdad, where a *Denkard* colophon from the early eleventh century was discovered. *Denkard* assigns the normative traditions of Mazda worship to the 21 *nasks* ('bundles') of the Avesta, three-quarters of which had been lost after the Arab conquest.[17] The *Denkard* notes that the division into 21 *nasks* echoes the 21 words of the Avestan holy prayer, the *Ahuna Vairya*.[18] Other Middle Persian texts claim their authority as deriving 'in the religion' (MP *pad den*, *andar den*). They do provide insight into the Sasanian understanding of the Avesta, but are not always helpful in their exegesis of the Avesta itself. Some of the theological and legal problems raised by encounters with Islam are addressed by Adurfarrobay in his polemical *Gizistag Abalesh* ('the accursed Abu 'l-Layth'). This is an account of a debate between a *zandik* – in this case a Zoroastrian convert to Islam – and Adurfarrobay, which was held in the Baghdad court of Caliph Ma'mun. The *Dadestan-i Denig* ('Religious Decisions') baldly states that to abandon the good religion deserves death, and that such apostasy leads to 'the worst existence' (Dd 41.3, 5).[19] Anyone who was able to prevent the apostasy of a co-religionist would be guaranteed a wide path to the best existence (Dd 42.2). One of the ways to help the good religion endure and to thwart the *divs* was through the practice of tying the *kusti* and reciting the accompanying prayers (Dd 38).[20]

The 'Doubt-Dispelling Exposition' (*Shkand Gumanig Wizar*), an apologetic treatise by the scholar Mardanfarrokh-i Ohrmazdad, expounds a Zoroastrian perspective against the theologies and mythologies of Judaism and Christianity, and also addresses some of the teachings of the *Qur'an*, particularly those promoted by the Mu'tazilite school of thought.[21] Other texts allude to Islam using the terms *ag-den* or *wattar-den*, in reference to a person of 'bad' or 'evil' religion. Such wicked persons face two possible endings: either they will 'not arrive in the end' – that is, they will not return to the bodily state after the final ordeal; or they will pass through the molten metal and be cleansed of their sins (PRDd 36.4, 48.70).[22] As the internal scrutiny of Zoroastrian theology, particularly that relating to apocalyptic teaching, continued, so Baghdad became both a stimulus for and a factor in the ensuing discourse.

Early Arabic historiographies provide much information about Zoroastrians in Iran, in particular those of Tabari, Mas'udi, Narshakhi and Biruni. They used the Arabic term *al-majus* in a broad sense to refer to all Zoroastrians, rather than just the priestly class, similar to the use of the term *magi* in some of the later Greek texts. Many learned Muslim writers were Persian by birth, such as Al-Balkhi (850–934 CE) and the tenth-century Istakhri. The former was a scientist and geographer, who wrote that the Zoroastrians of Fars had preserved their customs and their religious books, and that each town or village had its own fire temple where rituals were performed. This depiction is supported by other accounts, particularly concerning the use of fire temples, and descriptions of Zoroastrians as 'fire-worshippers' (NP *atashparastan*).

In the same year that Al-Balkhi died, the Persian Shi'ite Buyid dynasty (934–1055 CE) began its rise to power, based in Shiraz. The Buyids continued many Sasanian customs and practices, such as the celebration of *Nav Ruz*.[23] They not only protected the rights of Zoroastrians in Shiraz to the extent that they did not have to wear the distinctive clothing marking them as non-Muslim, but they also promoted Zoroastrians within the bureaucracy of Fars. One Zoroastrian official named Khorshid, who was the governor of Kazerun, defended his co-religionists against the proselytizing of a local Sufi

Sheikh, whom the Buyid ruler then called to Shiraz and censured.[24]

Buyid support for the ancient Zoroastrian festivals encouraged their continued celebration across Iran, and contemporary Islamic historians, including Mas'udi (896–956 CE) and Biruni (973–1048 CE), describe the persistence of the Persian festival calendar, mentioning *Nav Ruz* at the spring equinox, the mid-winter festival of *Sadeh*, the six seasonal festivals (*gahanbars*), rituals relating to water at Tirgan in mid-summer and *Mihragan* in the fall. For each of the festivals, Biruni narrates an Iranian legend. In the case of *Mihragan*, he relates the story of Feridun's defeat and imprisonment of the evil Zahak, who is chained within Mt. Demavand (Yt 19.36–7).

Although Zoroastrianism declined in Fars, it continued in the central part of Iran, particularly in villages along the desert such as Nain, Yazd and Kerman. The latter two have retained Zoroastrian communities to the present day, and remain centers of the textile industry, particularly carpet weaving. As Muslim settlements spread throughout rural Iran, particularly during Seljuk rule (1037–1194 CE), Zoroastrians became a religious minority, encountering increasing intolerance and relinquishing control of most socio-economic interaction.[25] They seem to have met no systematic persecution, however, until the Mongol invasion of the early thirteenth century inflicted wholesale massacres in some towns, such as Nishapur in Khorasan, leading to general devastation and the destruction of the internal economic structure of the country. In Georgia, however, the survival of Zoroastrianism until the arrival of the Timurids in the late fourteenth century may be indicated in accounts of a rebellion against Timur Lang led by Gudarz, who is identified as a Zoroastrian.[26]

Continuities

From both the Muslim and Zoroastrian viewpoint, 'outsiders' were considered to be sources of ritual pollution and measures were taken on each side to avoid contact. Middle Persian texts specify that sexual contact between a Mazda-worshipper and a non-Mazda-worshipper brought loss of ritual purity. Such injunctions were crucial in the *mobeds'* attempts to counter conversion or intermarriage. Zoroastrian purity laws were to have a particular effect on inter-religious relations with Muslims, whose own purity regulations developed along similar lines, although were less rigid in terms of codes relating to menstruation. The *Rivayats* (letters to co-religionists in India) in the fifteenth–eighteenth centuries show that Zoroastrians in Iran continued to insist on the physical separation of women in menses from the other members of the household, and from the 'good creatures and creations of Ohrmazd' as advocated in the *Videvdad*.[27] This developed into segregation in a small cell-like building, where women in menses would retire until their purification with *nirang* (consecrated bull's urine), and reintegration into communal prayer and domestic life.[28]

Both religions stipulated that it was unlawful to visit bathhouses run by or frequented by the other, reiterating on the part of the Zoroastrians the notion that the waters must be kept pure, and on the part of the Muslims the concept that impurity (Arabic *najes*) could be carried through water. Zoroastrian concern with the purity of the other elements of creation finds some echoes in Islamic practices, such as the 'clean' disposal of hair-trimming, collected teeth and pared nails, but one of the reasons that Zoroastrian artisans and craftsmen converted to Islam as *mawalis* in significant numbers was that their jobs had constantly kept them in a state of pollution through contact with fire and water. Such restrictions were not part of the Islamic worldview.

Reverence for the fire and the waters remained central to Zoroastrian worship in Iran, particularly in private prayers and devotions. Although the laity had less access to a learned priesthood and to ritual centered on the fire temple, domestic praxis was not as adversely impacted, and many acts of regeneration, such as those mentioned at the beginning of this book, continued to take place in the home, where women took an increasing responsibility for the perpetuation of the religion. The home was a place where the religion could be upheld despite the upheavals outside. Ritual observance helped to keep the house a safe refuge against evil in all its forms.[29]

It remains common practice for Iranian Zoroastrian women to perform an offering to the waters (*ab zohr*) without the presence of a *mobed*. The women pour their libation into streams or the village well, while reciting some of their daily Avestan prayers. The offering may be undertaken in fulfillment of a vow, or for the well-being of a member of the family. This stand-alone lay ritual seems to be a domestic mirroring of the priestly *ab zohr*, performed at the conclusion of the *Yasna*.

One ancient domestic celebration that was a purely female occasion still takes place among Zoroastrian women in Yazd during the midsummer festival of *Tirgan*, when the *chak-o-duleh* ('pot of fate') ritual is performed to dispel drought and disease, and to bring good fortune and well-being to the home and the wider community. The women of the household place a small personal object of non-porous material, such as a bead, ring or bracelet, into a ceramic jar (*kuzeh*) or large pot (*duleh*), which is full of water. The water is covered with a cloth and placed under a myrtle or pomegranate tree for the night, creating a temporary cave-like or womb-like environment. The next afternoon, the women sit together and a young unmarried girl gradually retrieves each object from the water, as the older women recite verses of poetry relating to the future of its owner.[30]

The fact that this practice has an Armenian Christian parallel seems to indicate its origin in an earlier Zoroastrian ritual dating back to Sasanian times. On the eve of Ascension Day (*Hambartsum*), young Armenian girls place *hawrot-mawrot* flowers or other greenery in a bowl filled with water, before immersing personal items and covering it with a cloth. The bowl may be blessed by a priest before being left outside overnight. The following day, the girls enact a similar ritual to that of the Zoroastrians. The name *hawrot-mawrot* derives from the Iranian Haurvatat and Ameretat, and the ritual has the same purpose as the *chak-o-duleh*.[31]

Some of the theological differences between the Zoroastrians and Muslims were cause for concern in both communities. Although both religions believed in a supreme creator God, they differed as to their understanding of the source of evil. In his treatise, Mardanfarrokh refers to Ohrmazd as the single Creator of the universe and everything good that is in it.[32] To counter the argument as to why Ohrmazd did not prevent the existence of evil, Mardanfarrokh states that the omnipotence and omniscience of the Creator relate only to that which is possible, not that which is impossible. Since good and evil are absolute principles that cannot be changed and are mutually exclusive, the only possible resolution of the essential antagonism between the two must take place within the purpose-built *menog* and *getig* worlds, where time and space are confined.

This notion of 'two principles' was perceived as being at odds with the Islamic concept of *tawhid*, the unity or oneness of God. Rumi (1207–73 CE), in his *Fihi ma Fihi* ('Discourses'), remarks that it is this Zoroastrian teaching that good and evil come from separate sources which leads to debate with Muslims, for whom good and evil cannot be separate, since there is only one God, not two pre-existent forces. From Rumi's perspective, the co-existence and inseparability of good and evil, knowledge and ignorance, is necessary to propel humans towards God.[33] From the Zoroastrian perspective, ultimate wisdom is of a completely different nature than ignorance, just as absolute good is completely other than evil. Debate regarding the origin of evil and the omnipotence of Ahura Mazda continues to play out not only in inter-religious discourse, but also in internal interpretations of the Zoroastrian religion.[34]

A curious New Persian text dated around the thirteenth century CE, which is wholly Zoroastrian in composition, but which incorporates a belief in *zaman* (time) as a first principle preceding Ohrmazd and Ahriman, was apparently perpetuated among Iranian Zoroastrians without remark. The name of this text, *Ulama-i Islam* ('the sages of Islam'), is confusingly also given to another dogmatic treatise: both are appended to the 1932 edition of *Persian Rivayats*.[35] *Ulama-i Islam I*, which is only found in its complete form attached to the *Rivayats*, is an apologetic in defense of Zoroastrian beliefs and principles against Islam. *Ulama-i Islam II* was initially published separately, and seems to be the elaboration of an earlier treatise on Zoroastrian doctrine, particularly concerning cosmology. It has been used to explore the continuity of some form of Zurvanism through the middle ages. In *Ulama-i Islam II*, although Zaman ('Time') is the source of Ohrmazd and Ahriman, they are not 'twinned' in any way, nor referred to as Zaman's 'sons', and the emergence of evil as the product of Zaman's moral wavering is censored in some places, but not others. The circulation of this text indicates that, for many later Zoroastrians, elevation of undifferentiated time was accepted as a natural corollary to the postulated co-existence of Ohrmazd and Ahriman before limited time began. *Ulama-i Islam II* also affirms that Zoroastrian theological discussion of the later period had retained a focus on the source of good and evil, and the rationale for human ethical conduct.

The Zoroastrian concept that the thoughts, words and actions of the individual meet the soul of the deceased prior to judgment seems to have had a profound impact on Sanai (d. c. 1131) and Rumi, for they both expressed the idea that every thought would be made visible on the day of judgment, and that 'death will meet each human like a mirror, which shows either a beautiful or an ugly face according to their good or evil deeds'.[36]

Many such themes relating to Zoroastrianism became central metaphors in Persian mystical poetry. Gurgani's eleventh-century *Vis and Ramin*, which hearkens back nostalgically to the time of pre-Islamic Iran, makes particular mention of the Zoroastrian predilection for the good things in life, including wine-drinking. In the poetry of Sa'di and Hafez, the Zoroastrian tavern owner is transformed into the *pir-e Moghan* – the 'wise man of the Magi' – who aids the floundering seeker, the *rend* (often translated as 'the drunk' or 'the scoundrel'), on the path towards the divine. The Zoroastrian youth who serves the wine is complicit in this spiritual transmutation. Since wine was not permitted for Muslims, one source of revenue for a Zoroastrian was to open a tavern where alcohol was made and served.

Commonalities

As Iran became part of the greater *Dar al-Islam* ('house of Islam'), so an Iranian impact upon the development of the religion occurred. This impact extended into the definition of peoples as either 'faithful' including *mawali*, or *dhimmi*, apparently modeled along the lines of the Zoroastrian's categories distinguishing between *weh den* (the 'good religion') and *jud den* (of 'other religion'). Muslims had no incentive to examine *dhimmi* heritage for elements of religious value, but some Zoroastrian customs were appropriated. For instance, the Sasanian practice of endowing fire temples for the benefit of one's own soul, or that of a deceased member of the family, seems to have impacted the subsequent Islamic establishment of *waqf* ('pious endowment'). Zoroastrians were able to register their own *waqf* with Muslim authorities, which then remained in the legal care of those who administered it. This was one way of circumventing the law of inheritance that bequeathed to a convert to Islam the entire estate of his or her Zoroastrian parents, leaving nothing for non-Muslim siblings. Zoroastrian *waqf*s were maintained for generations, being most commonly used to fund *gahanbar*s and a meal for the whole community, including the sick and house-bound.[37] Then, as now, food was shared with needy Muslims waiting outside the house where the *gahanbar* was held.

The Avestan concept of *xwarenah* (NP *farr*) continues in the *Shah Nameh*, as well as in Shi'a thought, where a tenth-century Iranian narrative that Ali's son Husayn had married Yazdegird III's daughter introduced the belief that the *farr-i izadi* (the 'divine power') rested on the descendants of Ali.[38] That the Prophet Mohammed and his early followers were familiar with elements of the Zoroastrian religion is indicated by the appearance of Zoroastrian, as *al-majus*, alongside Jews, Christians and Sabaeans in *Sura* 22.17 of the *Qur'an*, and of the angels Harut and Marut in *Sura* 2.96.

Although these last two figures are substantially different in function from their Zoroastrian originals, *Haurvatat* and *Ameretat*, their inclusion as angels suggests an awareness of their function within Iranian cosmology. The Zoroastrian 'bridge of accounting' (MP *Chinvad pul*) is echoed in eschatological descriptions in various *hadiths* of the straight path (*as-sirat al-mustaqim*) of *Sura* 1.6, which is said to lead at the time of final judgment to the *pul-e Sirat*, a bridge across hell to paradise that is as sharp as a sword.

Another instance of adaptation of a Zoroastrian end-time motif can be found in the reformulation of *Serosh* (Av. *Sraosha,* 'readiness to listen') as an angelic messenger in New Persian texts, including Ferdowsi's *Shah Nameh*. In later Iranian mystical works, beginning with Suhrawardi in the late twelfth century, the *qutb* (axis pole), who is the highest spiritual guide of the faithful, is considered the 'channel' for *Serosh*. Suhrawardi's work is an amalgamation of Islamic mysticism and metaphysics, Zoroastrian symbolism and Neoplatonist cosmology. It is replete with angels, many of whom have Zoroastrian names and whose aspects derive from Iranian tradition.[39] These angels are conceived of as pure light devoid of matter. Suhrawardi is spoken of as 'the master of the philosophy of illumination' (*Shaykh al-Ishraq*), and the school of thought based on his theories as *Ishraqi* – that is,

'Illuminationist'. This school was to have an impact on Parsi theology in India in the nineteenth century.

Although Ferdowsi (935–1020 CE) reworked many of the stories in the *Shah Nameh* to fit within an Islamicized context, there remain many allusions to Zoroastrian *mythos*, including the narrative of Zarathushtra and elements such as the benevolent winged-creature, named Simurgh (Av. *saena meregha*), in the stories of Zal, Rostam and Isfandiyar. Only remnants of Zoroastrian praxis can be traced in *Shah Nameh*, however. Perhaps the most moving occurs towards the end of the epic, when Yazdegird III takes refuge in a mill in Merv after his army's defeat. Although he has not eaten for some time, he asks the miller to find some *barsom* so that he can pray over the paltry amount of food that the miller has provided, before eating in the requisite silence. It is this request that leads to Yazdegird's recognition and assassination. For many Iranians, Muslim as well as Zoroastrian, *Shah Nameh* remains a primary source not only for their early history, but also for a 'Zoroastrian' worldview, even though its stories and ethos do not always correspond with the Avesta.[40]

Many Zoroastrian 'shrines' became Muslim places of pilgrimage, such as that of Bibi Shahrbanu in Rayy, to which attaches a narrative that echoes stories related to the Zoroastrian sanctuaries of Pir-e Sabz and Pir-e Banu Pars.[41] In the case of the shrine of Bibi Shahrbanu at Rayy, the frame story of the perilous flight of one of Yazdegird III's daughters becomes incorporated into a Shi'a context through a Persian legend, which tells how Shahrbanu was captured during the Muslim invasion and married to the Prophet Muhammed's grandson, Husayn. Shahrbanu was said to have born one son, Ali b. Husayn, the fourth Imam, who died shortly after his birth. When the Sunni Umayyads attacked Husayn and his family at Karbala, Shahrbanu fled on her husband's horse from the pursuing enemy back to Persia and was almost captured near Rayy, when the cliff-face opened to conceal her.[42]

Rites of Mourning and Return

The annual Shi'a commemoration of the death of Husayn at Karbala may also owe some of its elements to prevailing Iranian mythology and praxis. The Sunni siege of Karbala began on the first day of the Muslim month of Muharram in late 680 CE and came to a bloody end on the tenth day, called Ashura. During the Safavid period (1501–1722), a unique type of religious drama evolved that may be termed a 'Passion Play', in that it concerns the enactment or narration of the martyrdom of Imam Husayn and his family at Karbala. This ritual play, known as *ta'ziyeh* ('an expression of mourning'), appears to have an earlier Zoroastrian precedent. The *Ayadgar-i Zareran* narrates the treacherous slaying of Vishtaspa's general, Zarer, by the Chionian Bidarafsh, who pierces him through with a poisonous lance. The account includes a moving threnody by Zarer's young son, Bastur, as he stands by the battered, lifeless body of his father. Bastur volunteers to fight Bidarafsh and avenge his father's death.

The recitation of this text seems to have functioned as a cathartic act of devotion for Zoroastrians, just as the later *ta'ziyeh* eulogies served for Shi'ites. Although the events, outlooks and contexts of the two commemorated events are not the same, the core elements are similar.[43] Some of the ritual actions performed during the congregational meetings and public processions held on Ashura – such as beating the chest or head – may also be compared with those depicted in the eastern Iranian contexts discussed in the previous chapter.

A Flickering Flame: From Mongol Times to the Present

From the early medieval period onwards, Zoroastrians were absent from the Iranian political power structure. As Islam in Iran had become 'Persianized', so Zoroastrians became increasingly isolated, and the depredations they faced under the Mongols served to further marginalize them. The Mongol incursion across Iran was devastating to both the land and its inhabitants. Baghdad was taken by the Mongols in 1258, ending Abbasid rule, and a time of relative calm followed during which European traders began to make the journey through Iran to explore new land routes to Central Asia.

Marco Polo's accounts of his travels in 1271–92, recorded in his 'Description of the World', provide an apt example of the kind of romantic hyperbole which roused the imagination and lust for the wealth of 'the East' throughout Europe. Polo (1254–1324 CE) wrote about Yazd as a splendid city, which was a center of commerce. He considered Persia as the origin of the three Magi who had visited Christ, although his account seems to be a conflation of current Christian legend concerning the Magi and elements of Zoroastrian practice. He explains that the Magi and their followers, who were very numerous in Persia, became 'fire-worshippers' (using the Persian *atashparastan*) after receiving a stone from the Christ-child which they threw down a well, whereupon it was struck by a burning fire from heaven: the Magi then took some of this fire back to their own country and placed it in one of their places of worship, where it is kept perpetually burning and worshipped 'as a god'.

Dastur Dhalla (1875–1956), a high priest of Karachi, described the period from the downfall of the Sasanians to the eighteenth century CE as one of decadence, during which the Iranian Zoroastrian community 'lay steeped in the grossest ignorance and darkness', but nonetheless were able to maintain their superiority in knowledge of their sacred literature over their co-religionists in India.[44] It was because of that perceived superiority of knowledge that the Parsis wrote a series of letters (*Rivayats*) between the fifteenth and eighteenth centuries, asking Zoroastrian communities in Yazd province questions about the calendar, ritual, doctrine and domestic praxis.

The first *Rivayat*, brought from Iran by a layman, Nariman Hoshang, is dated 1478, towards the end of the Timurid period of rule. This was accompanied by a letter, in which the Iranian Zoroastrians note that until then, they had not been aware that there were any followers of Zoroaster in India. The second *Rivayat* of 1481 refers to Nariman Hoshang's earlier visit to Yazd, claiming that he could not speak Persian when he first arrived from Baruch, but quickly learned enough to question the residents. The respondent also says that he is not writing in Middle Persian because Nariman Hoshang had told him that the Mazda-worshipping priests and laity of Gujarat did not know it. Even at this late date, a few Iranian priests evidently knew enough Middle Persian to contemplate writing a doctrinal response in that language, and to exhort the Parsis to learn it.[45] The early *Rivayats* use the terms *herbad* and *dastur* loosely, and it seems that by this time, the term *mobed* was no longer used to refer to someone with administrative power, but to denote a rank higher than a *herbad* and lower than a *dastur*.[46] The Iranians urge the Parsis to send a couple of priests to visit Iran via the land route from Kandahar through Sistan to Yazd. The land route may have been suggested because of Zoroastrian proscriptions about crossing water.

A *Rivayat* dated 1511 confirms the existence of a community of Zoroastrians in Sistan, numbering nearly 3,000. Correspondence between the co-religionists continued until 1778, being arranged in three great collections that show a strong Zoroastrian tradition in Yazd and Kerman, despite the hardships which faced the adherents over the centuries. It is not surprising, however, to find many references to the hope for a future *saoshyant*, known as *Behram Warzawand* ('victorious miracle worker'), who will bring about the renaissance of the religion. A current Iranian belief was that this *saoshyant* would be born in a mythical 'copper city' in the East, either in India or China.[47]

Much of the information in the *Rivayats* is to do with the preoccupation of both Indian and Iranian Zoroastrians living under Muslim rule. Their concerns relate mostly to observation of ritual praxis: the recitation of prayers; the tying of the *kusti*; the consecration and maintenance of a fire; the priestly performance of ceremonies; and purity laws, particularly in relation to interaction with *jud-denan* (who are also called *anairan* or 'non-Iranian') and how to confront 'dead matter' and dispose of a corpse. There is also much general information about marriage contracts, education of children, hagiography of Zarathushtra, and the world myth.[48]

With the introduction of Shi'ism as the official form of Islam under the Safavids, the situation of the Zoroastrians became precarious again. Many Zoroastrians took refuge in the desert, joining existing communities in the regions of Kerman and Yazd, where the *dasturs* of Turkabad and Sharifabad had made contact with Nariman Hoshang in 1477. Under Shah Abbas I (1588–1629) many Zoroastrians were forcibly relocated from Kerman and Yazd to Isfahan, where they worked as labourers, gardeners, and agriculturalists. Under Shah Soltan Hosain in 1699, Zoroastrians were forcibly converted to Islam or martyred, although a few escaped back to Yazd. An early seventeenth-century manuscript in the Dastur Meherjirana Library in Navsari demonstrates an attempt by beleaguered Zoroastrians to deflect Shi'a antagonism: the New Persian *Mino Khirad* claims that Zarathushtra had prophesied the advent of Mohammed, which amazed Imam Ali when he heard about it, causing him to recognize the wisdom of Khosrow Anoshirvan and therefore not destroy the *dakhma* at Ctesiphon as he had intended.[49] The survival of this document attests to the Zoroastrian need to defend their places of ritual from attacks, such as those decreed by Shah Hosain (1694–1722) towards the end of Safavid rule. Many *atashkadehs* were converted to mosques and *dakhmas* were desecrated or demolished.[50]

Since Isfahan was the capital of Safavid Persia, any visitor to the country would pass through it. From the seventeenth century onwards, several European merchants who traveled through Iran described their impressions of the various cultures and religions they met, including that of the Zoroastrians. Although many of the accounts of these Europeans were well informed and sympathetic towards the Zoroastrians, others offered only anecdotal material and descriptions of scenery. Some authors, such as the Capuchin missionary Father Gabriel de Chinon, who wrote in the 1650s, had read classical accounts of the Persians including Herodotus and Quintus Curtius, but also included their own insights into contemporary Zoroastrian practice and belief.

The French merchant Jean Tavernier encountered Zoroastrians in both Iran and India, and sometimes neglected to make a distinction between the two in his accounts. He first met the *gaurs*, or 'ancient Persians who adored fire', in Isfahan in 1647, and spent three months with them in Kerman at the end of 1654 in order to conclude business relating to the purchase of wool.[51] Tavernier says that the *gaurs* numbered more than 10,000 in Kerman, and lived in liberty there. The French words *gaur* and *guèbre* are commonly used by European travelers when referring to the Zoroastrians. It is a rendition of the early New Persian *gabr* and its dialect variant *gawr*, the derivation of which is still disputed. Under the Safavids, *gabr* or *gawr* was the current Muslim term for Iranian Zoroastrians. These terms are generally used in a disparaging or culturally distinguishing manner. The area outside the city wall in which the Zoroastrians lived in Isfahan and Kerman, was known as *gabr-mahalle*, 'the Zoroastrian quarter'. The location of the *gabr-mahalle* outside the city walls often placed the Zoroastrians in a vulnerable situation: during the Afghani attacks of the early eighteenth century, when the city gates of Kerman were shut against the invaders, many unprotected Zoroastrians in the surrounding countryside were killed.[52]

Tavernier's reports from Kerman show the Zoroastrian community there to have been wealthier and more prominent than that of Isfahan. This view is supported by a 1644 inscription in Kerman, commemorating the construction of a fire temple there by a wealthy individual. Tavernier was sufficiently interested in the religion of the *gaurs* to provide a detailed account of their eschatology as he had heard it from priests in Kerman: this coheres mostly with that of Middle Persian texts, including reference to the three successive *saoshyants*. Tavernier also appears to have seen one or more illustrated copies of the *Arda Wiraz Namag*, for he describes books belonging to the Zoroastrian priests, which had small pictures depicting the punishments of hell.[53] The *Rivayats* record that a copy of this text was sent from Persia to the Parsis in India.[54]

Zoroastrian purity regulations were also fascinating to Tavernier, and he describes those relating to pollution resulting from a sin, from contact with death and after the segregation of menses. He writes about Zoroastrian life passage rituals, describing rites relating to death and the *dakhma*, as well as marriage, although he apparently misunderstood the five different types of marriage as detailed in the *Rivayats* to imply that five different wives were allowable to one man. In his record of seasonal festivals, he refers to one day of the year on which all the Zoroastrian women assembled to kill as many frogs in the fields as they could. This acknowledgement that some animals were noxious and some good is in keeping with traditional classification; both Tavernier and De Chinon included cats as 'bad', which coheres with Middle Persian texts.[55]

This binary categorization of domestic animals may have been one of the most noticeable differences between faith practitioners at a local level. For Zoroastrians, the dog remained important, especially due to its part in the death rituals, whereas in Shi'a Islam, the cat was regarded as having mystical, even miraculous qualities. Some Sufi *khanaqahs* – cultural and theological centers – had cats as guardians, in keeping with popular belief that the divine presence (*sakina*) would appear in the form of a white cat.[56] In contrast, there are several *hadiths* that speak of the dog as 'impure' (*najes*), and only to be kept for hunting, herding or protection.

A decade after Tavernier's travelogue, Jean Chardin, another French merchant, who was a jeweler by trade and a Calvinist Christian by conviction, published a very popular account of the *guèbres*, whom he knew were descended from the ancient Persians who had constructed the monuments of Persepolis and its environs. Chardin (1643–1713) subsequently attempted to find a Zoroastrian symbolism in the ancient monuments of Persepolis, Naqsh-e Rostam and Ka'ba-ye Zardosht. He spent much time exploring these ancient sites and insisted that one of his servants should climb up to look inside one of the high tombs at Naqsh-e Rostam. The servant made the difficult climb and nearly died of fright when he disturbed a flock of pigeons nesting there. This was the first recorded entry of one of the tombs. Chardin refers to the winged figure as being of importance to the religion of the *guèbres*, although he was not sure what the emblem signified.

The Zoroastrians are described by Chardin as having 'soft and simple customs, living peacefully the same way of life as their ancestors', and encouraging the cultivation of the land because 'it used to be a godly and meritorious action to plant a tree, reclaim fields for cultivation, turn barren ground into growing fruit'.[57] Chardin states that the Zoroastrians of Isfahan produced the best grapes, which they looked after with more care than the Muslims because they were allowed to drink wine.[58] He describes these descendants of the Ancient Persians as independent and self-sufficient, keeping to themselves as much as possible. Although their women did not wear veils, like Muslim women, Zoroastrian men were apparently not allowed to wear dyed clothing.

European travelers were fascinated by the *dakhma*, and Chardin was no exception. He gives an eyewitness account of some of the rituals surrounding the exposure of the dead and describes their *dakhma*, which was about half a league from Isfahan in an isolated spot. From earliest times, the *dakhma* was located on tops of hills or on elevated ground (Vd 6.44–5), apart from human dwellings, so that no one would overlook them or be polluted by proximity to them (Fig. 23). Chardin notes that there was no door to the *dakhma*, and that the corpse-bearers used ladders to scale the walls and ropes to raise the corpse over the wall. The corpse-bearers are referred to in Zoroastrian texts as *nasa salars* ('bearers of dead matter'), who are in a state of constant pollution due to their profession. They live separately from the community (Vd 13.19) and do not attend the *Atash Bahram* until they have purified themselves with a nine-day ablution and purification ritual, a *bareshnum*. *Videvdad* describes the *bareshnum* as cleansing from pollution by dead matter, and the ritual is expounded in detail in the *Rivayats*.[59]

Fig. 23. Dakhma *at Cham, Yazd province, Iran.*

Chardin's portrayal of the religion of the *guèbres* is explicable in terms of his own Calvinist background. He emphasizes the two principles – the one of light, 'Ormous', and the one of darkness, 'Ariman' – and identifies Ariman as a 'created god', which may reflect a misunderstanding or an interpretation such as is implicit in *Ulama-i Islam II*. Chardin described the prophet of the *guèbres* as the 'chief priest of the Magi', a holy man to whom had been revealed a book from heaven and about whom many stories were told. Chardin identified these Magi with the figures in Matthew's Gospel.

An interesting aspect of Chardin's research was his short-lived attempt to learn Avestan. He discovered that there were 26 books of Zoroastrian scriptures, known as the '*Zend pasend vosta*', that were written in ancient Persian and are still in existence in the Royal Library of the Safavids. Chardin managed to locate a copy of this 'Avesta with *zand*', and identified its contents as: prayers; a fire ritual; praises of 'inferior divinities' (presumably the *yazatas*); and astrological treatises. When he came to learn the script from one of the Zoroastrian priests, he found him to be 'ignorant' and gave up, dismissing the Avesta as being without scriptural authority, nor in keeping with his prior knowledge of the religion from classical or Muslim literary sources.

Such travel narratives remained the most authoritative sources of information about the Zoroastrian religion for Europeans, until the initiative of Anquetil Duperron a century later stimulated a new study of the religion, this time through their texts.

In late Safavid times, Zoroastrians became embroiled in the armed conflicts between the Safavids and the Afghans (1722–5 CE), and then between the Zand dynasty (1750–94) and the Qajars (1794–1825). During this period, many Zoroastrian communities between Sistan and Isfahan were decimated. In 1736, Nader Shah (1688–1747) had come to power in Iran. Given the choice between conversion and death, many Zoroastrians in Kerman were put to the sword and their property plundered and destroyed, including sacred books.[60] The English painter Sir Robert Ker Porter (1777–1842), on a visit to Isfahan in 1821, reported that there were hardly any Zoroastrians left in the city and that *Gabrabad* – the Zoroastrian suburb – was in ruins. When the Danish philologist Niels Ludvig Westergaard (1815–78) visited Iran in 1843 to collect ancient Iranian texts, he wrote to a friend that during his stay in Yazd and Kerman he had come across only a few manuscripts, including the *Yasna, Videvdad, Khordeh Avesta* and part of *Bundahishn*. The rest had been destroyed.[61]

Over the centuries, Zoroastrians in Yazd and Kerman had created a spoken ethnolect known as *Dari*, or *Behdinani*. It is a form of dialect that was intentionally unintelligible to other Persian speakers. Studies of the language indicate its subtlety as part of the survival skills developed by the minority community negotiating with a sometimes-hostile majority. By the mid-nineteenth century, Zoroastrians in Iran had increasingly created a wall, both psychologically and literally, around their private lives, particularly with regard to religious ritual and worship in the fire temple, as well as in the home. The Zoroastrian houses of Yazd built during this later period included specific features, such as a vaulted hall (Dari, *peskem-e mas*) where religious services would take place in the home, and where an area was reserved for commemorating deceased family members with pictures or mementos.[62]

When new fire temples were constructed, the main fire would often be placed to one side, out of sight of the casual visitor, and a false fire-holder put in the center, which was only lit on festive occasions. This relocation discouraged pollution or desecration of the fire by non-Zoroastrians, such as had been inflicted by the governor of Kerman when he spat on the flames of a Zoroastrian fire-holder.[63] Many of the fires in Yazd today retain this plan, including that in Sharifabad. Even those fires that burn in open *ateshkadehs*, such as the *Atash Bahram* in Yazd, can only be viewed by non-Zoroastrians through glass.

During the rule of Karim Khan Zand (r. 1750–79), a Parsi named 'Mulla' Kaus visited Kerman, with a question concerning which dating system to use.[64] He reported back that he found his Iranian co-religionists in dire straits and still paying the same amount of *jizya* tax that had been due in earlier times, despite the decline of the Zoroastrian population. Mulla Kaus took their case to Karim Khan and obtained relief from the excessive tax, but the *jizya* tax was not formally removed until the late nineteenth century, when the Parsis had re-established strong ties with Iran and sought to better the lot of their co-religionists.

In 1854, the newly-founded Society for the Amelioration of the Condition of the Zoroastrians in Persia sent Maneckji Limji Hataria (1813–90) as an emissary to Iran. Maneckji wrote reports back to India describing the miserable situation in Yazd, Kerman and Tehran, and the general ignorance of his co-religionists, particularly the priests' understanding of sacred texts.[65] Available population figures for this period indicate that the number of Zoroastrians in the Yazd and Kerman regions together was well below 10,000. As well as the levying of the *jizya* – a hardship and humiliation in itself – Zoroastrians also suffered constant discrimination from the majority population. Persistent acts of violation included vandalism, physical assault and the rape of Zoroastrian women.[66] The flow of conversions to Islam continued on a voluntary basis, particularly accompanying marriage to a Muslim spouse or to retain employment, but was also partly enforced through abduction of Zoroastrian girls, who were then married to Muslims against their will. These conversions not only undermined the religious standing of the community, but also its economic wealth due to the laws of inheritance, which privileged Muslims.

On behalf of the Amelioration Society, Maneckji coordinated many constructive activities aimed at reducing the material disadvantages of his Iranian co-religionists, providing orphanages, hospitals and a dispensary, as well as schools for boys and girls, which offered both religious instruction and secular knowledge. He sought to regenerate their religious life by funding *jashans*, festivals, weddings and initiations, and by renovating congregational centers, including fire temples, community hall, and *dakhmas* in Yazd and Kerman provinces, and in Rayy, in the suburbs of Tehran.

Maneckji remained in Iran for almost 35 years, marrying a Zoroastrian woman from Kerman. His detailed reports of his work and of the way of life of the Zoroastrian community in Iran include a critique of some of their practices, which he perceived as Islamic accretions, such as polygamy and the ritual slaughter of animals (particularly cows), the fat of which was offered to the fire during the *chaharom* ceremony. A century earlier, De Chinon had reported an animal offered, with alms, for the soul of the deceased on the fourth day. Maneckji provides the first 'insider' look into Zoroastrian life in Iran since the early *Rivayats*, albeit from a Parsi perspective. Glimpses were also supplied by the Cambridge academic, Edward Browne (1862–1926), and the British Anglican missionary, Napier Malcolm. The latter described the particular discrimination of Zoroastrians in Yazd at the end of the nineteenth century: they were not permitted to engage in trade nor to school their children; they had to wear dull-colored clothing; they were discouraged from wearing rings, using umbrellas for shade or spectacles to improve their sight, and had to wear 'peculiarly hideous' shoes.[67]

Maneckji also published books on ancient Iranian mythico-history and Zoroastrianism, including a preface to an 1854 edition of the *Sharestan* and an annotated translation of *Ain-e Hushang* ('The Mirror of Hushang'), a Middle Persian collection that had been translated into New Persian. *Sharestan* was a narrative text produced in seventeenth-century India, which combined Zoroastrian cosmology with Sufism and Hindu philosophy. Maneckji's presence and perspective had a particular impact on the Qajar prince, Jalal-al-Din Mirza, whose *Nameh-ye Khosravan* incorporated Maneckji's *Tarikh-e Parsian* ('History of the Zoroastrians') as an appendix. Mirza's inclusion of Zoroastrian and neo-Zoroastrian themes in his own narrative reflected the rising interest in pre-Islamic narrative.[68]

It was Maneckji who met with British diplomats in Iran, and campaigned to effect a legal change in the Zoroastrian payment of the *jizya*, until eventually a Qajar decree of 1882 permanently released Zoroastrians from the poll tax and gave them an equal status with Muslims in matters of taxation. In 1898 another royal decree officially abolished all discriminations against Zoroastrians, but the law and its implementation were not always in synchrony. These decrees did, however, provide Iranian Zoroastrians with the legitimacy to affirm their own political agenda. This was facilitated by the creation of associations (*anjumans*) in the late nineteenth century that continue to regulate the internal governance of local Zoroastrian communities in terms of both social and religious matters – particularly with regard to the upkeep of fire temples and the training of priests – and also to represent Zoroastrian interests to the Iranian government. The introduction of such a community administration reflects the adjustment in power structure from the traditional leadership of village elders and priests to a more collective effort that could operate within an increasingly urbanized environment, as provincial towns grew and Zoroastrians migrated to Tehran.

The effect of these changes is manifest in the career of the respected community advocate Jamshid Jamshidian (1851–1933), who was born in

Yazd and moved to Borujerd and then to Tehran, where he was elected as the first Zoroastrian representative on the newly-created Iranian parliament (*majles*) of 1906. Jamshidian was succeeded in the second *majles* of 1909 by Kaykhosrow Shahrokh (1875–1940). Such self-representation enhanced Zoroastrian standing throughout Iran, particularly in urban communities, where their mercantile connections and contributions were highly valued. As Iranian Zoroastrians began to prosper, they were able to contribute to their community through philanthropic acts. The family of Mehraban Rostam (known as 'Mehr') was particularly active in this respect, founding new schools and building new fire temples, *dakhmas* and water cisterns. One of Mehr's seven sons, Godarz, constructed a shelter for guests at the mountain shrine of Pir-e Sabz, and also donated land in Yazd on which Christian missionaries constructed a hospital (Fig. 24).[69]

In the first two decades of the twentieth century, Iranians had begun to look to India as a source of inspiration for their own nationalist revival. The Parsis in Bombay were viewed as having preserved a core of pre-Islamic Iranian authenticity, which could be effectively reintroduced into Iran. Not only were Parsi architectural forms, based on ancient Iranian edifices, incorporated into Zoroastrian buildings, particularly fire temples, but the achievements of Parsi women were also vaunted as part of the nationalist advocacy for reform of the position of women.[70] One of the advocates of modern nationalism in Iran, Ibrahim Pour-e Davoud (1886–1968), translated Parsi Gujarati material into Persian, and introduced the study of the Avesta to Iran. Pour-e Davoud had studied in France, Germany and India, and in 1928 published his own Persian translation of the *Gathas*, largely based on the work of the German scholar Christian Bartholomae, and assisted by Dinshaw Irani, the Parsi president of the Iran Society of Bombay, which had supported the work. This translation rejected any connection between the *Gathas* and the later Avestan texts, including the *Yashts*, which Pour-e Davoud also translated, along with the *Khordeh Avesta*.

Fig. 24. Pir-e Sabz shrine and sheltered area for pilgrims, Yazd province, Iran.

Born into a Muslim family, Pour-e Davoud championed Zoroastrianism as one of the earliest monotheistic religions, promoting the image of Zarathushtra as a brave and just Iranian ancestor in his attempt to regenerate the glory and greatness of ancient Persia. In so doing, he engendered an increased respect among liberal Iranian Zoroastrians for their own religion, and a renewed interest in the *Gathas*. Pour-e Davoud's approach set a precedent for subsequent translations, just as the rationalist perspective had encouraged a transformation and simplification of ritual. Urbanization also resulted in the attenuation of many traditional community affiliations and praxes, such as the supplementation or even replacement with natural gas of the dry firewood that had once been noted as such an important element of Zoroastrian rituals concerning the fire. The fire is still 'fed' by the priest, however, with slivers of sandalwood.

The Pahlavi period (1925–79) maintained a political emphasis on the ancient heritage of Iran, which fostered a popular enthusiasm for the mythico-historical past. The officially mandated Iranian solar calendar, implemented by Reza Shah Pahlavi on his accession in 1925, uses ancient Zoroastrian month names. The reckoning of the Zoroastrian calendar from the date of accession of Yazdegird III in 632 CE, designated as AY (*anno Yazdegirdi*), had been in constant use by Zoroastrians in both Iran and India, in conjunction with the Islamic AH (*anno Hijra*) and Christian AD (*anno Domini*) respectively. Reza Shah formally changed the name of the country from 'Persia' back to 'Iran' in 1935 in a conscious reiteration of the past.

As the century progressed, Iranian heritage sites saw a rise in tourism as well as Western academic interest. Archeological digs sponsored by the French until the late nineteenth century, then by American universities, began to uncover much of the ancient history of Iran. The Zoroastrian priesthood, although considerably diminished in numbers through migration to India and relocation to Tehran, developed a stronger structural and mentoring base within Iran, but by the mid-1950s the council of *mobeds* was opened to anyone who could claim descent from a priestly family through either parent, since there were no longer enough practicing priests.[71] In the mid-1960s, Zoroastrians in Iran numbered about 60,000, with the majority living in Tehran.[72] A housing colony for lowto middle-income Zoroastrians had been built by Arbab Rustam Guiv in the late 1950s, with its own *atashkadeh*. Arbab and his wife Morvarid also established Zoroastrian schools in the city, and later donated funds to establish *Dar-i Mihrs* (places of worship) in New York, Toronto and southern California.

A few European and American scholars spent time in Iran in the late 1960s and early 1970s living with and writing about Zoroastrian communities, in both Yazd and Tehran.[73] Parsis began to visit their 'homeland', not only from India and Pakistan, but also from Europe, Australasia and North America. As Zoroastrianism became more widely respected within this new veneration of the past, so fire temples were opened to all faiths, and differentiating signs of faith, such as the ritual washing (*padyab*) prior to entering the *ateshkadeh* precincts and the wearing of the *kusti*, began to be neglected by the laity. *Nirang* was no longer produced or used in rituals of purification, which were gradually dropped altogether.[74] Reform of the system of exposure in the *dakhma* was extended in the mid-1960s, along with the attenuation of other rituals relating to death. This reform had begun with the construction of consecrated Zoroastrian cemeteries (*aramgahs*) in Rayy and Kerman in the mid-1930s, but was probably stimulated by the need to decide whether to replace the *dakhma* in Sharifabad, which had been built in 1863 and had been used for 100 years, at which point, according to tradition, the pollution was considered too great to be contained. A similar situation existed in other locations, such as Yazd and Cham, and the Tehran *anjuman* decided to replace the *dakhma*s with burial in stone at an *aramgah*, in emulation of the rock burials of the Ancient Persians.

Such reconfiguration of rituals, accompanied by a rise in socio-economic standing, placed Zoroastrians more in the cultural mainstream and led to a resurgent sense of identity. The general secularization of Iranian society under the Pahlavis brought more egalitarian treatment of Zoroastrians and other religious minorities, who had been granted a wide framework of judicial rights with the introduction of the Uniform Legal Code in the 1930s and the Family Protection Law of 1967, which was revised in 1975.[75] During this time, 16 schools from primary to secondary level were established for Zoroastrians, which, along with previously-founded schools, provided a Western-type secular education for most Zoroastrian children, girls as well as boys.

The fact that the religion and its adherents had been so enthusiastically promoted in nationalist discourse from the beginning of the twentieth century had led to a positive approach on the part of the majority population, which lasted through the tumultuous time of the revolution. Despite Ayatollah Khomeini's castigation of the Pahlavi regime as seeking to revive Zoroastrianism, Islamic militants refrained from directly targeting the community, although revolutionaries replaced the picture of Asho Zarathushtra in the main Dar-e Mihr in Tehran with a photo of the Ayatollah. This act was seen as a portent of things to come.[76]

Under the Constitution of the Islamic Republic of Iran in 1979, Zoroastrians received the rights of a religious minority (*aqaliat*). The use of this term and the institutionalization of minority communities as inferior was considered by many to be too close to the reintroduction of the discrimination that existed in the medieval period, and they chose to leave the country rather than return to a modern version of *dhimmi* status.[77] Since the revolution, Iranian Zoroastrians have retained a seat on the *majles* and a degree of religious freedom, being legally permitted to perform ceremonies, to take separate religious holidays and to educate according to the tenets of their religion. But their control over religious education has been compromised in that the curriculum has to use a textbook on religion, produced by the Ministry of Education and Training, as part of its course fulfillment, even in the predominantly Zoroastrian-attended schools in Yazd. In the summer of 2009 it was reported that, due to the small number of Zoroastrian girls attending the Anushiravan High School in Tehran, their religious education would now be offered on Fridays, rather than in school time.[78]

Both internal and external pressures often compel the Zoroastrian minority to conform to majority norms, particularly with regard to codes of clothing and social interaction between the genders. The 15 Zoroastrians who died on the front during the Iran–Iraq war of 1980–8 are acknowledged as martyrs in a similar manner to their Muslim compatriots.[79] Although members of an officially recognized religion, their legally subordinate status and the implementation of *dhimmi*-type ordinances creates a continued sense of precariousness, which is compounded by instances of persecution, forced marriage of women to Muslim men, employment discrimination and the revival of the notion that Zoroastrians are *najes*, and therefore not allowed to touch certain daily objects belonging to Muslims, such as food or clothing. The terms *gabr* and *atashparastan* remain as pejoratives.[80]

In 2004, the population of Zoroastrians in Iran was estimated at about 25,000 by the Federation Zoroastrian Associations of North (FEZANA), based on 1996 revised national census figures and input from priests and community leaders. Although this number has fluctuated in official reckoning, it denotes that the Zoroastrian population of Iran is in decline. The low statistic may also reflect an unwillingness on the part of some Zoroastrians to declare their faith openly.[81] Zoroastrian communities persist in traditional neighborhoods in Yazd and Kerman, but numbers in these areas are decreasing as the populace emigrates or moves to Tehran. Community *anjumans* are active in these and other cities, including Isfahan and Shiraz, and support the upkeep of fire temples, celebration of *gahanbars* and *jashans*, festivals such as *Nav Ruz* and *Mihragan*, and rites of passage including initiations, weddings and funerals.

Despite – or perhaps because of – dwindling numbers, there seems to have been a revival of faith among some Zoroastrians, but in a devotional rather than a 'fundamentalist' sense. This takes the form of renewed interest in religious education; regular visits to the fire temple, particularly in Sharifabad and Yazd; and a restoration of the rite of ordination into the priesthood (*nowzut*, equivalent to the Parsi *navar* and *martab*), alongside the initiation of *mobedyars* – laymen from non-priestly families – who train and function as priests.[82] The decline of a full-time hereditary priesthood after the revolution means, however, that most priestly rituals have been modified and simplified – the *Yasna* is no longer performed regularly or in its entirety –often being limited to the first eight sections – and the laity is increasingly responsible for the upkeep of the festival calendar. Women are often in charge of co-ordinating community events, and literally keep the flame burning in oil lamps or candles set in Zoroastrian areas of town, or outside fire temples. 'Pilgrimages' to sacred places, particularly Pir-e Sabz, have increased. During the five-day festival of *Tirgan*, in the middle of summer, visitors stay overnight in the hilltop shelters next to the shrine, and celebrate together with prayer, food, music and dance. The spring water is regarded as having healing powers, and is popularly called *ab-e hayat* ('water of life'). Many will stand under the dripping water, drink it and take bottles of it home with them. Local folklore tells that the waters stop flowing if a woman in menses approaches, but drops faster when groups of pilgrims arrive. Such devotional piety focused on worship at shrines is held in balanced tension with a pragmatic rationalism regarding theology (Fig. 25).

The maxim that is written over the entrance to this fire temple is one that resonates among the Zoroastrian and non-Zoroastrian populace alike: *Pendar-e nik, Goftar-e nik, Kerdar-e nik* – 'Good Thoughts, Good Words, Good Deeds'. Respect for both the antiquity and ethos of the faith may, perhaps, provide the key to its survival in Iran.

Fig. 25. The upper façade of the Atash Bahram in Yazd.

Chapter VII

Parsipanu: Zoroastrianism in India

'In their religion, there are certainly many points of faith which inculcate the purest doctrines of benevolence and very many practice the most extensive charity. Their idea of the supreme being is very definite and they worship with apparent zeal and sincerity.'

William Rogers, *Journal containing Remarks and Observations during a Voyage to India 1817–18.*[1]

A Story

After the defeat and death of Yazdegird III in 651 CE, many Zoroastrians had fled from the Arab Muslim incursions to the mountains of Kohistan, the 'hill country' of southern Khorasan, where they lived for the next century. Eventually, tired of their exile, they wandered towards Hormuz, a port on the Persian Gulf, where they spent another 15 years.

A *dastur* who was also an astrologer advised them to leave for India, and so they set sail, arriving at the island of Diu off the south coast of Gujarat, and staying there for 19 years, until another priest-astrologer among them advised that it was time to leave for the mainland. On the way, they encountered a violent storm, and prayed to Ahura Mazda that, if they landed safely, they would erect an *Atash Bahram* in thanks.

The storm abated, and they landed at a place which they named Sanjan, after a town near Nishapur in Khorasan. The leader of the Zoroastrians asked for asylum for his people from Jadi Rana, the local ruler. The Hindu Rajah replied that he would allow them to settle if the *dastur* explained Zoroastrian beliefs and practices to him, and only if the community accepted certain terms.

The Zoroastrians were then allowed to land and to build their settlement, including the *Atash Bahram*. During the next three hundred years the Parsis spread out from Sanjan to Navsari (named after Sari on the shores of the Caspian), Baruch, Anklesar, and other places in Gujarat.

From Jadi Rana to the Mughals

So goes the foundation story as to how the first Parsis – Zoroastrians from Iran ('Persians') – came to the shores of India. The *Qesse-ye Sanjan* (*Qesse*) is the oldest extant account of this event, written by the Parsi priest Bahman Kaikobad Sanjana, of Navsari, in Persian verse in 1599 CE. According to the author, the story was based on what he had been told by his teacher, Hoshang, and on writings that he had seen. The story contains no dates, which has caused some debate, as has the interpretation of the *Qesse* as a folk chronicle.[2] J.J. Modi was the first to use the *Qesse* data to correlate important events in this early history of the Parsis, but his chronology has been disputed.

Current estimations for the date of immigration deriving from the *Qesse*, and a later *Qesse-ye Zartoshtian-e Hendustan*, range from the mid-seventh to early-tenth century.[3] Parsis tend to favor the date of 916 CE, based on calculations by S.H. Hodiwala.[4] Excavations carried out at Sanjan from 2002–4 by the World Zarathushti Cultural Foundation point to a time of settlement there between early to mid-eighth century CE, but indicate that it had been a trading post during the Sasanian period. Excavation of a *dakhma* indicates that it was probably constructed between the tenth and twelfth centuries CE, and remained in use until the early fifteenth century.

The *Qesse* does not claim that all Persian Zoroastrians fled by sea to India, and so does not preclude the establishment of other early Zoroastrian settlements in India by groups who traveled overland from eastern Iran via trading routes through Central Asia. Although we have no archeological trace of such communities, there had been close links between Iran and northern and western India under the three empires, beginning in the sixth century BCE, when the Achaemenids named the three Indian satrapies: Gandhara, Thatagush (Sattagydia) and Hindush. Although Achaemenid rule over these areas may have been short-lived, the satrapies continue to appear on their reliefs. (The Ancient Persian claim to north-western India partly explains Alexander's eagerness to exert his own right to Gandhara and the Indus Valley.) During the reign of Darius I, Iranians are known to have sailed across the Indian Ocean to Sri Lanka to reconnoiter sea routes and the resources of other countries. A Sanskrit text records that in Sasanian times, mercenaries accompanied by a *magus* had traveled to Sri Lanka to support king Dhatusena (r. 455–73 CE), and that there had been Sasanian military attacks on Sind and the Punjab.[5] The use of Iranian motifs in Kushan iconography and local inscriptions also continued in north Indian numismatics into the sixth century CE.

The strong presence of Zoroastrians in the region of Surat may be due to familiarity with this area from commercial activity during Sasanian times. Persian traders would have visited Baruch, and probably had branch offices and warehouses there. Some might even have relocated there permanently before the advent of Islam in Iran, or decided to do so at the fall of the Sasanian empire. Ceramic finds at Sanjan indicate that these early settlers were, indeed, traders. It can be surmised that, apart from merchants who envisioned better prospects for economic survival and social status in a new land, the other refugee 'boat people' of *Qesse* lore would have included Zoroastrians fleeing from growing religious intolerance and assimilation and from the burden of *jizya*.

That the first act upon settlement in the new land is recorded as the consecration of the sacred fire tells us as much about late sixteenth-century Parsi self-definition as the perceived religiosity of the early Zoroastrian settlers. Tradition has it that this fire came with the original emigrants from Iran and was installed with due ceremony using ritual objects that they had brought with them. It was named '*Iran Shah*', or 'King of Iran', and was located first in Sanjan, then Navsari. This *Atash Bahram* was the only Zoroastrian ever-burning fire in India until the eighteenth century, and most Parsis continued the Iranian practice of saying their prayers before domestic hearth fires or purpose-lit fires (*dadgah*). The original *Atash Bahram* fire was relocated to Udwada, Gujarat, in 1742, where it remains precious to Parsis, emblematic of their close conceptual and cultural connections with Iran. *Iran Shah* also symbolizes the victory of Parsi struggles to preserve the faith, which they had carried with them from Iran to India, and nurtured, like the fire, amid the uncertainties and insecurities that they encountered as a minority group.

The earliest textual evidence we have for a Zoroastrian community in India comes from a late ninth-century CE copper plate found in Kerala, a south-western state. An inscription on the plate concerns a grant made by the local king to a Christian community, and among the signatories of witnesses are several Zoroastrian names, written in cursive Pahlavi.[6] The context implies that at this stage there was a Zoroastrian mercantile community in Kerala. The Zoroastrian scholar Mardanfarrokh claims to have 'wandered for the sake of inquiry' to the 'land of the Hindus' at around this time (SGV 10.43). Subsequent epigraphic testimony dates to the early eleventh century, and was found in the Kanheri Buddhist monastic complex near modern Mumbai. This takes the form of a Middle Persian 'I was here' type of graffiti on the walls of cave 90, providing the Zoroastrian date of 'year 378 of Yazdegird' – that is, 1009 CE. One damaged inscription includes the toponym '*eran*', which suggests that the visitors may have come from Iran – Kanheri was near the port of Thana – but the reading is uncertain.

More Zoroastrians fled to India from Iran under the later Abbasid persecutions, and during the Mongol invasions of the thirteenth century. A fire temple was installed in Baruch around this time, and a brick *dakhma* sometime before 1300. Another *dakhma* was built in 1309, suggesting a growing Zoroastrian community there.[7] Parsis continued and elaborated on the Iranian practice of exposure, and India is now the only country in which Zoroastrians practice the *dakhmenashini* (exposure in the *dakhma*) funerary ritual, although this has been jeopardized by the recent decimation of the South-East Asian vulture population.[8]

In the 1320s a Dominican friar named Jordanus traveled through Gujarat on his way to the Malabar Coast and encountered Parsis, whom he noted as a 'pagan folk', 'who worship fire', neither bury their dead nor burn them, but 'cast them into the midst of a certain roofless tower and there expose them utterly uncovered to the fowls of heaven'.[9] (The descriptive euphemism for these places as 'Towers of Silence' is thought to have been coined by a British colonial official, Sir Robert Murphy, in the 1830s.) Jordanus followed his comments on the death rituals of the Parsis, with a note concerning their theology of two First Principles: the one Evil, the other Good' the one Darkness, the other Light.[10] The fact that he moves straight from a description of the *dakhma* to an allusion to the binary division of the world indicates that he knew of the Zoroastrian connection of death with the work of evil.

Interaction between Iran and India continued at the level of textual transmission. In the late thirteenth century, an Iranian Zoroastrian scribe, Rustam Mihraban, had transcribed manuscripts of *Videvdad* (with MP version) and *Arda Wiraz Namag* for the community in Anklesar, where he lived for some time. The *Videvdad* codex had been brought to India from Sistan by a Parsi priest named Ardashir Bahman, but does not seem to have been used as part of Parsi ritual at this time, although it had been an accepted part of Iranian Zoroastrian observance since the ninth century.[11] Towards the end of the fourteenth century, Rustam's great grand-nephew, Mihraban Kay-Khosrow, was invited to India by a Parsi merchant for the purposes of copying manuscripts. Mihraban visited Thana, Navsari and Cambay to transcribe codices of Middle Persian texts, as well as the *Yasna* and *Videvdad*.[12] Such contacts seem to have been completely forgotten by the Iranian Zoroastrians at the time of the first *Rivayat* of 1478, which expresses their astonishment on discovering co-religionists in India. Once the relationship was re-established, Parsis expected their envoys to Iran to return not only with answers to doctrinal or ritual questions, but also with religious books, such as *Yashts* and the *Visperad* (an extended *Yasna* with *Videvdad*).

The *Qesse* picks up the story of the Parsis again 'seven hundred years' after the arrival of the initial group of Zoroastrians in India, when 'Alf Khan, the general of the Sultan, Mahmud' attacked the region of Sanjan. According to William Rogers' *Journal* account, early nineteenth-century Parsis identified this assailant as 'Mahmood Begra, prince of Ahmadebad', which probably refers to Sultan Mahmud Begada, who did besiege the Gujarati fortress of Champanir in 1484.[13] The *Qesse* narrative continues that the Parsis, under their leader Ardeshir, fought fiercely alongside their Hindu protectors, but were eventually overcome. Sanjan fell and tribute was exacted. The Parsis took the sacred fire *Iran Shah* and fled to the mountains, remaining in hiding for a dozen years, before carrying the fire to Bansda where they stayed for 14 years, until they were able to take it to Navsari and install it there – the traditional date is 1492 – under the care of priests from Sanjan, who tended the fire, and a group of Parsi priests from Navsari, called 'Bhagaria', who performed all other rituals and ceremonies. At this juncture, there were five districts, or *panthaks*, each controlled by a priestly family whose income derived largely from fees collected for the religious services they conducted.[14]

Sultan Mahmud's rebuilt town of Champanir was captured by the Mughal Humayun in 1535 CE, signifying a Persianate Islamic rise to power in India that lasted until the early eighteenth century. In 1579 CE, the Mughal Emperor Akbar summoned the chief *dastur*, Meherji Rana, a learned Bhagaria, from Navsari to Delhi to explain to him the tenets of the Zoroastrian faith. It is said that the emperor was favorably impressed, and bestowed 200 acres of land in Navsari to Dastur Rana. In 1582, Akbar incorporated Zoroastrian motifs into his syncretic cult known as *Din-i Ilahi*, including the use of Zoroastrian calendar names, and the introduction of the veneration of fire and the sun at court. That the Zoroastrian community continued to hold the Mughal emperor's interest is attested by the 1597 court visit of an Iranian *dastur* named Ardashir Nushirvan from Kerman, who helped the emperor to compile a Persian dictionary.[15]

At this time, Navsari was the main center of religious authority. Its first priest had arrived from Sanjan in 1142, and today the priests of Navsari trace their descent from two families who arrived there in the early thirteenth century. Parsi communities in other parts of India would send to Navsari for their priests, and lay families still affiliate themselves with certain *panthakis* (priests descended from one of the five *panthak* families), usually those who are working in the local area.[16] There are three grades of Parsi priest: *dastur* (high priest); *mobed*; and *herbad*. Those who have undergone the first stage of initiation, the *navar*, are known as *herbad*. Those inner rituals conducted in the inner sanctum of the fire temple, such as the *Yasna*, can only be performed by priests who have undergone the second degree of initiation (*martab*).

Apart from two accounts of confrontation in *Qesse*, Parsi lore presents a smooth integration into the local culture of first their Hindu, and then Muslim, neighbors. This transition may have been ameliorated by the fact that the Zoroastrians presented their faith in a manner that would not antagonize the Hindu majority. According to *Qesse*, upon their arrival in Gujarat the *dastur* and his co-religionists drew upon similarities between their own faith and that of the Hindus in order to persuade Jadi Rana to allow them to stay: they speak of their reverence for the sun, moon, water and fire, and above all for the cow; they mention that they wear a sacred girdle, which they tie on with professions of faith; they also note that their women do not look at the sun, sky or moon when menstruating, and are isolated after childbirth. In *Dadestan-i Denig*, the Iranian *hudenan peshobay* Manuschihr (fl. c. 881 CE) also shows awareness of the correspondence between the sacred thread of the Zoroastrians and that of other peoples, presumably the Hindus (Dd 39.19–20).

Many of the similarities are reiterated in an extant collection of 16 Sanskrit *shlokas* (distich verses), which are in an antiquated style that appear to predate the *Qesse* manuscript of Kaikobad. These verses are often attributed to Dastur Neryosangh Dhaval, who is said to date around the twelfth or thirteenth century, but the author may have been a Hindu. The 15 *shlokas* that describe Parsi religion mention in addition the practice of observing silence when eating; women's celebration of marriage with songs and perfumes; distribution of food and clothing to the poor; and the use of the five products of the cow to purify, including urine, which is also a ritual cleansing agent in the Hindu tradition.[17] The recognition of parallels in praxis, particularly with regard to the emphasis on purity and pollution, would have eased relations between Zoroastrians and their Hindu neighbors. This comparative list also indicates the Parsi's own ambiguities with regard to their position in Indian society. There is no mention of Zoroastrian disapproval of asceticism, nor of divergence of doctrine, such as the Avestan demonization of the Hindu deities Indra, Saurva and Nasatya (Vd 10.9, 19.43).

The Parsis did not hold with the Hindu notion that some were born in a more spiritually advanced state to others, nor did they bring a rigid Sasanian social stratification with them. Instead, they adhered to the ancient priest/lay division wherein purity and impurity were strictly defined, but not permanent states. Impurity relating to *nasu* ('dead matter'), such as bodily excretions, was contained through separation and ablution, which often included consecrated bull's urine (*nirang*). In medieval India, Parsi women in menses were apparently secluded in a place known as the *dashtanestan*, but by my grandmother's time in the early twentieth century, there was a designated room in the house, with a metal bed, which was thought to be impervious to the pollution of *nasu*. Many of the elaborate purification rituals to counter the pollution of dead matter – such as the nine-night *barashnum* ceremony – were simplified, or delegated to priests to perform on behalf of lay Parsis.

As in Iran, Parsis practiced endogamy (marriage within the group), perhaps initially because intermarriage was discouraged by both religions. In so doing, they retained a separate status, along the lines of a 'caste', and it was within this framework that Zoroastrianism was both preserved and developed in India. Although they maintained many Sasanian Zoroastrian practices, including disposal of their dead in *dakhmas*, worship at fire temples and many domestic rituals that also continued in Iran, the Parsis had to adapt some of their customs to accommodate the requirements placed on them by the indigenous Hindu community. *Qesse* relates that the Zoroastrian community agreed that their weddings would take place in the evening, their women would wear 'Indian dress' (i.e. a sari), and that they would speak the 'Indian language'. Such customs persist today, although first cousin marriages are practiced by Parsis, contrary to Hindu teaching, and may have been reintroduced after the renewal of contact with Iranian Zoroastrians during the time of the earliest *Rivayats*.[18]

Although the form of the Parsi marriage ceremony is Iranian in origin, the ceremony incorporates some peripheral Hindu elements, such as the marking of the forehead of the bride and groom with red *kumkum* (turmeric powder). Parsi women sing wedding songs throughout the four-day festivities accompanying marriage, one of which, the *Atash nu Git*, was a lay composition dedicated to the founding of the second *Atash Bahram* in India (at Navsari) in 1765, but which then entered into the women's repertoire, being sung while preparing the hearth fire as well as during nuptials.[19]

The Gujarati dialect of the region remains the most common language spoken by Parsis, wherever they live in India, although prayers and religious ceremonies continue to be recited in Avestan. Persian remained the language of literature until the mid-seventeenth century, when Gujarati translations began to be available. The use of English as the principal medium for social interaction did not occur until the mid-nineteenth century. That Middle Persian continued as the literary language of learned Parsi priests until the early middle ages is evidenced by the existence of thirteenth- and fourteenth-century translations of several texts into Sanskrit, including the *Yasna* and *Khordeh Avesta*, the *Menog-i Xrad*, *Shkand Gumanig Vizar* and *Arda Wiraz Namag*. Neryosangh Dhaval was the most prominent Parsi Sanskritist, and copies of some of his translations are extant today. This impetus indicates a working knowledge of Avestan and Pahlavi among at least some of the clergy, although it is uncertain as to why the texts should be translated into Sanskrit.

During subsequent centuries, this high level of education and scholarship seems to have waned, as indicated by the series of communiqués (*rivayats*) sent between the Parsis of Gujarat and the Zoroastrian priests in Iran, requesting information concerning the correct way to conduct rituals and other observances. You may recall that one of the early Iranian respondents stated that he did not reply in Middle Persian because Nariman Hoshang had told him that the Mazda-worshippers of Gujarat did not know the language. In the early nineteenth century, Gujarati translations of Avestan texts, based on Middle Persian, Sanskrit and New Persian versions, were published, as well as inter-linear Gujarati translations of both Avestan and Middle Persian texts.

One of the Parsis mentioned in *Rivayats* from 1668 and 1670 is Ervad Rustam Peshotan Hamjiar (Hormazdyar) of Surat, the first Parsi poet of any note. Hormazdyar produced some of the earliest Parsi literary texts in Gujarati, composing verse translations from the New Persian *Viraf Nameh* ('Story of [Arda] Wiraz'), *Zardosht Nameh* ('Story of Zarathushtra') and *Siavakhsh Nameh* ('Story of Siyavush'). The *Zardosht Nameh* was first published in installments in *Zarathoshti*, a quarterly magazine that ran between 1903 and 1906, and was co-edited by Behramgore T. Anklesaria and Dastur M.N. Dhalla. Behramgore published it as a book in 1932. His father, Ervad Temuras Anklesaria, had previously edited and published the *Siavakhsh Nameh*. It is this latter Anklesaria to whom Mobed Abadan brought the edition of the *Greater Bundahishn* from Yazd in about 1870, which is the core text for modern translations.

The British Arrive

By profession, Parsis were mostly agriculturalists, weavers, artisans and merchants. Their trading acumen was a particular asset when the British East India Company became established in Surat. By the sixteenth century, Surat, one of the main Parsi settlements, had become a commercial port and trading center under the Mughals. European merchants from Portugal, Holland, France and Britain engaged in trade there, developing the city as a major entrepot on the west coast. Many well-known Parsi families of today rose to prominence during this period, particularly the Wadias, who became renowned as ship-builders under contract to the British East India Company (BEIC).

The British crown acquired Bombay from the Portuguese in 1662, with the aim of creating a viable trading port to serve both east and west. Bombay was transferred to BEIC possession in 1668, and Parsis were encouraged to move there with gifts of land. A Parsi contractor had already supplied the manpower and materials to begin the transformation of the swampy land with fishing villages into a thriving port city. A Tower of Silence was erected on the Pedder Road at Malabar Hill in Bombay around 1672–4, and the first *Atash Adaran* was endowed in 1673 in the Fort area of the city. Such attention to the religious needs of the community on the part of wealthy Parsis seems to have provided an incentive for others to move from the Surat region, although for the first hundred years or so, as the city developed, the population was fairly mobile. It was not until the second half of the eighteenth century that a permanent Parsi population of Bombay existed.

In 1750, Lovji Wadia and his brother Sorabji built the first dry dock in Asia there. Lovji's grandson, Nusserwanji Wadia, became the Bombay agent for French commerce, and also established thriving trade relations with clients in the Boston area of America. Nusserwanji was one of the first foreigners to donate items to the new Museum of the Salem East India Marine Society (now part of the Peabody Essex Museum), providing a complete set of 'Parsi dress' in 1803, the same year that his portrait, by a Chinese artist, was also donated. Such international engagement enabled the Wadias to become one of the most influential families in shipbuilding and trade in Bombay, producing many of the ships used in the British wars against Napoleon. One of the Wadia ships, the *HMS Trincomalee*, launched in 1817, is still afloat in the UK, and another, the *HMS Minden*, is thought by some to be the ship from which Francis Scot Key watched the British bombardment of Fort Henry in 1814 and wrote the poem which later became the anthem of the United States, 'The Star Spangled Banner'. The Wadia family constructed one of the first *Atash Bahrams* in Bombay, which was consecrated in 1830.

The urbanization of the Parsis, and the increasing wealth of some individuals, resulted in a rise to social and political prominence during the British period. Since Parsis had no caste barriers to interacting with the British, they quickly became involved in all industries relating to trade, including banking, brokering and revenue collecting. One of my great uncles, Meherji Hormusji Frenchman, was in charge of guarding the trains to and from the British military outpost in Rawalpindi. His granddaughter described in vivid detail how he was stabbed with a poisoned curved dagger by robbers in the course of performing his duty, but fought courageously until he was thrown off the train. He crawled on his hands and knees, 'his intestines hanging out of his stomach', back to the nearest station, surviving for another 13 days until he succumbed to the poison.[20]

Parsi historical narrative is full of such stories, indicating both their loyalty to the ruling regimes of the time and the advantages and disadvantages that such associations could bring. To a certain extent, the Parsis adapted and assimilated to the Indian setting. They not only relinquished the sacrifice of the cow and the consumption of beef, which would have been abhorrent to Hindus, but also gave up pork so as not affront Muslim sensibilities. Henry Lord, Chaplain to the East India Company in Surat from 1625 to 1629, remarked that, in order to give no offence to either of their neighboring religions, the Parsis abstained from eating 'kine- (beef) and hogs-flesh'.[21] My grandmother (Fig. 26), who grew up in a household in Rawalpindi with both Hindu and Muslim servants, complained that as a child, her diet consisted only of chicken or lamb. The prohibition on ritual sacrifice had become so engrained that by the mid-nineteenth century, Maneckji Hataria was shocked to discover that it was still practiced by Zoroastrians in Iran, and he brought pressure to end it. The unique role of the white bull (*varasyo*) and the consecration ceremony (*nirangdin*) of the bull's urine for purificatory purposes indicate the influence of the Indian environment on the development of Zoroastrianism in India.[22]

By the early twentieth century, Parsis had also discontinued the sacrifice of sheep, goats and poultry. At this time the Parsi Vegetarian and Temperance Society was formed in Bombay. Most Parsis abstain from eating any meat for three days after the death of a family member, and some refrain from eating meat, and sometimes also eggs, on the days of the month relating to Vohu Manah (NP *Bahman*) and the *yazatas*, who assist in taking care of the animate world – *Gosh* (*Geush Urvan*), *Mah* (moon) and *Ram* (joy, air). Some give up meat for the whole of the 11th month, which is dedicated to Bahman.

In the centuries since their settlement in India, Parsis have assimilated several 'Hindu' elements into their domestic and communal praxes, such as the application of *kumkum* (red-colored turmeric) for the *tilak* – a ritual mark on the forehead; decoration with colorful chalk patterns on the threshold of a home, business or ceremonial meeting place symbolizing good luck; and the use of coconuts and betel leaves or nuts in ritual. The introduction of such components into Parsi praxis did not, on the whole, challenge the underlying beliefs inherent in the rituals.

Fig. 26. Shereen Khorshid Boga, the author's grandmother.

Challenges to Belief

One controversial question discussed in the Persian *Rivayats* is that of conversion. It is hard to assess the extent to which the Parsis may have admitted non-Zoroastrians into the community prior to the eighteenth century. The emphasis on endogamy tended to preclude proselytism, and the Hindu caste system operated against such assimilation. There is some evidence from the *Rivayats*, however, that prior to the writing down of *Qesse*, Parsis had selectively admitted some 'outsiders', and that this was a matter of debate. The Iranian priests address Parsi concerns about the conversion of household slaves or servants, with the advice that this was permissible as long as no harm would occur either to the religion or to the community, and that the correct initiation ceremonies took place.[23] Parsi scruples appear to have related mostly to purity issues regarding these non-Parsi servants' preparation of food for consumption at religious festivals and ceremonies. The Iranians, on the other hand, understood the question to stem from a concern to bring all humans to the right path of Mazda worship. The *Rivayats* urge the Parsis to permit such converts all of the rights of a Zoroastrian, including deposition in the *dakhma*.

The question of proselytism and conversion looms large for Zoroastrians today, as does the definition of who is a Zoroastrian – and who is a Parsi. Issues of self-definition became more pressing in the late eighteenth century with the influx of Iranian Zoroastrians into India, which increased in the following century until the Second World War. Iranian Zoroastrians who migrated in the modern period were accommodated by the Parsis, but are known as 'Iranis' and constitute a distinct sub-group of Indian Zoroastrianism. Their arrival alerted the Parsis to the plight facing their co-religionists in Iran and it was to help them that the Amelioration Society was founded in 1853, under the auspices of which Maneckji Hataria was sent to Iran.

This is the first example we have of an established Parsi foundation engaging in 'external' charity. Through renewed contact with their co-religionists in Iran, Parsis became more aware of their own Iranian heritage, particularly in terms of its material grandeur and cultural ideology and aesthetic. European travelogue descriptions, which from Chardin's *Travels* of 1711 onwards included engraved illustrations, provided stimulus for the architecture and iconography of many Parsi buildings, both religious and secular. Today's Bombay (Mumbai) has several examples of fire temples (*agiaries*), flanked on the outside with two winged beings modelled on those guarding the gateways of Persepolis (Fig. 27). The Ancient Persian winged figure became in India, as in Iran, a symbol of the Zoroastrian tradition, although the fire in the *afarganyu* is considered to be more religiously emblematic.

As the Parsis relocated to different parts of India, so they constructed fire temples, which were regarded as places of purity and which only admitted Parsis. Although continuing many Iranian practices – such as feeding the fire with dry wood, accompanied by a prayer to fire – the form of worship became more elaborate, with the introduction of sandalwood and priestly etiquette in relation to the fire.[24] In eighteenth-century Bombay, where a Council of Zoroastrian elders (*Punchayat*) had been formed, a particular concern was to keep the community distinct from the surrounding Hindu community. The Punchayat discouraged the laity from visiting Hindu shrines, and rejected Parsi proselytizing or accepting converts into Zoroastrianism.

Fig. 27. Cusrow Baug Agiary, Mumbai.

Another cause of controversy, stimulated by the arrival of Iranian Zoroastrians in the early eighteenth century, was the co-ordination of the ritual calendar, which differed by a month between the Parsis and Iranis. One group of Parsis assumed that the Iranis had held more closely to the original organization of the calendar and adopted the Iranian version, following the responses sent from Yazd in a *Rivayat* of 1743. This is known as the *Qadimi* ('ancient') calendar. Most Parsis, however, disputed the change, and left the calendar as it was. They are called *Rasmi*s (traditionalists) or *Shehenshais*, a word of uncertain origin that could derive from *Shahanshahi*, meaning 'imperial'. Although this was ostensibly a dispute about when was the correct time to observe seasonal festivals, and which days to honor the *yazatas*, it was also an expression of lay frustration with priestly authority.

Over four decades later, Anquetil Duperron, who was taught by Dastur Darab and his nephew Mulla Kaus, both Qadimis, recorded the thrust of this controversy, which by then had resulted in the introduction of some doctrinal changes. The main innovation seems to have been a tendency towards the elevation of Time (*zurvan* or *zaman*), which was implicit in the *Ulama-i Islam* text used by Anquetil to help interpret the Avestan corpus and the *Bundahishn*. Anquetil affirms that the Parsis with whom he conferred maintained the existence of a First Principle as the source of Ahura Mazda and Angra Mainyu, and concludes that this was Zurvan, although these Parsis also claimed to be monotheists. The Qadimis also had an interest in mysticism, and seem to have been drawn to an esoteric work called the *Dasatir*.

So great was the influence of this work that Sir William Jones, Anquetil's British detractor, claimed that the *Dasatir*, not the 'Zend-Avesta', was a genuine work of authority and antiquity. The text of the *Dasatir* ('Ordinances') was alleged to have a 'heavenly' origin, being written down during the reign of Khosrow Parviz. The religious teaching it contained was said to have prevailed in Iran from the time of a primordial prophet named 'Mahabad', until the last of 15 successive prophets, who lived just before the Arab conquest. It appears to contain Neoplatonic ideas consistent with the Ishraqi school. A manuscript of *Dasatir* had been brought back from Iran by Mulla Kaus, and was published in Bombay in 1818 by his son, Mulla Firoze, arousing great interest there. Zoroastrian communities in both Iran and India accepted this work as genuine, and used it to reinterpret the Avesta in the light of the 'hidden' doctrine that it expounded. When Edward Browne visited Iran in 1887–8, he was astonished that the *dastur* and one of the local Zoroastrian leaders both regarded the *Dasatir* as a genuine work, when he knew that it was spurious. The work is now generally regarded as a literary forgery, deriving perhaps from within an Iranian Sufi sect.

The Missionary Challenge

From the early nineteenth century onwards, Zoroastrianism in India was confronted by Christianity. The European challenge came armed with an appropriation of Zoroastrian teleological narrative, first in the form of Thomas Hyde's application of classical Greek and Latin texts to reinterpret the religion as an ethical dualism, then with Chardin's dismissive report of the *guèbres* in both Iran and India. More serious challenges emerged, as texts brought back from India to France by Anquetil Duperron in 1762 began to be translated into European languages – first French, then German, then in the English *Sacred Books of the East* series. They were thus available for criticism by Europeans, but not so readily accessible to the majority of Parsis.

The Parsis also came under direct assault from Christian missionaries, particularly John Wilson, a Church of Scotland minister, who began with a critique of the *Videvdad* in 1833. In 1839, Wilson baptized two Parsis on consecutive days at his Mission School in the Fort area of Bombay. This act sparked outrage among the Parsis, and a court case sponsored by the Bombay Parsi Punchayat (BPP) in an attempt to return one of the boys to his uncle on a writ of *habeas corpus*. The British judge in Bombay asked the boy, Dhanjibai Naoroji, who was not yet of majority age, to decide for himself.[25] Dhanjibai chose to go to Europe with Dr Wilson, where he trained at the Free Church Theological College in Edinburgh before returning to India and settling in Surat.

In 1843, John Wilson published another broadside offensive in the form of a book entitled *The Parsi Religion as contained in the Zand-Avasta and propounded and defended by the Zoroastrians of India and Persia, unfolded, refuted, and contrasted with Christianity*. This text demonstrated that Wilson, who had been appointed as President of the Bombay Branch of the Royal Asiatic Society in 1836, was much better read than some Parsis in terms of translations and exegesis of the Avestan and Pahlavi texts. The *Gathas* and Old Avestan prayers do not appear to have been part of Wilson's reading repertoire, but he was familiar with Burnouf 's French translation of and commentary on the *Yasna*, Anquetil Duperron's French translation of the *Vendidad* (*Videvdad*) and second-hand accounts of the *Bundahishn* and *Denkard*.

That the Parsis were unfamiliar with many of these texts is not remarkable, since they are in languages that were no longer accessible to Zoroastrians in either India or Iran. It is also salient to remember that the prayers recited by both laity and priests in their respective daily and seasonal rituals had been passed down orally from one generation to the next, as had much other religious-mythological material such as the story of the life of Zarathushtra. The Christian emphasis on the authority of sacred text, as revealed and then written, once again challenged Zoroastrians to produce their own authoritative scriptures. This emphasis on the authority of written text was at odds with an understanding of the process of inspiration that came primarily through recitation of *manthras*, patterns of hieratic and domestic praxis, community celebration and the light of human reason.

Despite evidence of Parsi devotion to the one Creator, Wilson attacked Zoroastrian teaching that good and evil were two First Principles, declaring such 'dualism' to be 'both monstrous and supremely unreasonable...a dogma, according to which God is robbed of his essential and peculiar glory'.[26] He accused the Zoroastrians of being polytheistic nature worshippers, and he also attacked the Zoroastrian texts, particularly *Videvdad,* as being 'in style and in substance destitute of all claims to be considered a revelation from God, but...from beginning to end most singularly despicable as a human composition'.[27] Wilson mocked 'the descriptions of Ahriman, Nasush, and their company', of the *Videvdad,* claiming that no one of intelligence could suppose that God was the author or Zoroaster the composer of 'such absurdities'.[28] In Wilson's eyes, the fact that much of the Avesta was missing meant that it could not be 'divinely-inspired'.[29]

The form of Zoroastrianism attacked by Wilson seems, however, to have had little to do with the religion as understood by lay Parsis of the time. One indignant Parsi claimed that what Wilson had written about the *Bundahishn,* in an earlier article in *The Oriental Christian Spectator,* was irrelevant since it is 'not one of our religious books. Nor is it the work of any of our *dasturs...* what is written in the Bundeshne is entirely false, and is far removed from our religion and faith.'[30] Following Wilson's attack, the laity expected the *dasturs* to rise in defense of the Good Religion, and were appalled that the priestly response did not manifest a deeper comprehension of their own theology.

Wilson cited a Gujarati translation of a text known as the *Dabistan,* as if it were an authoritative Zoroastrian work of an esoteric nature. Like the *Dasatir,* the much later *Dabistan* was spurious, based on Ishraqi teachings, which were thought to reflect an ancient Persian creed. *Dabistan* uses 'Zarathushtra' as a generic name for a hierarchical progression of great reformers and law-givers, beginning with the divine Zarathushtra in the *Videvdad,* and ending with the great but mortal man bearing that title, and now lost to history. Given this dimension, it is easier to understand the source of some of Wilson's disparagement. Several decades after the Wilson debacle, Dastur Dhalla maintained that the information in the *Dabistan* derived from the *Dasatir,* and had been written in India in the seventeenth century, based on material gleaned from Zoroastrian mystics in Patna, Kashmir and Lahore.[31]

After summarizing all the works cited by Parsis concerning the life and mission of Zoroaster, including the *Dabistan,* alongside Eastwick's recent translation of the *Zardosht Nameh,* Wilson dismisses them in the following words: 'Every impartial Parsi, even, must arrive at the decision...that there is no evidence that Zoroaster ever uttered a single prophecy, or performed a single miracle. He will also see and admit, that the legends about Zoroaster and his followers, which are now current among Parsis, are a mere tissue of comparatively modern fables and fiction.'[32] Wilson contrasted the 'lack of evidence' of Zoroaster's mission with the divine authority of Christian scripture, and challenged Parsis 'to prove that Zoroaster had a divine commission and that his doctrines were in every respect pure and holy'. They should seek 'to know what evidence he gave that he had ever left the earth, or was brought into close communion with God'.[33]

The Parsis were most concerned about Wilson's attack on what he perceived as their 'dualism' and 'polytheism', and on the credibility of their prophet and his teachings. They initially felt unable to address the charges that he had brought against their religion because both the lay and priestly leadership lacked the linguistic knowledge to counter his exegesis of their own texts. This galvanized some to pursue education in their own religion, and a few Parsi priests and lay leaders went as far as Europe and America for that purpose. One influential figure was Khorshedji Rustamji Cama (1831–1909), whose business frequently took him to Europe and who attended classes relating to Zoroastrianism at several European universities. He studied Avestan and Pahlavi with Friedrich Spiegel at Erlangen University, and later translated some of Spiegel's works into English, as well as those of Adolf Rapp and Johann-Gottlieb Rhode. On his return to Bombay in 1861, Cama started classes in his own house for Parsi priests, whose level of scholarship he found deplorable, and went on to found colleges (*athornan*) to train priests. The priests trained at these colleges produced some important studies of ancient Iranian texts. In 1864, Cama created a society to research into the Zoroastrian religion, and four decades later a society to disseminate Zoroastrianism in Parsi schools.

At the same time, European scholars were crafting their own image of Zarathushtra and the Zoroastrian religion, which continues to impact Zoroastrian self-understanding today. The most significant input in this regard came from Martin Haug, a German philologist, who was professor of Sanskrit at the Government College in Poona from 1859 to 1866. Haug was the first European to produce an academic translation of the *Gathas* (1858–60), which he considered to be the only texts that could be attributed to Zarathushtra – 'untouched by the speculations of later ages' – and therefore to be the only authoritative scriptures.[34] In Haug's view, voiced in lectures and in print, Zarathushtra was the spiritual equal of prophetic figures in other religions, and the teachings in the *Gathas* propounded an ethical monotheism in which Ahura Mazda, as the supreme divinity, gave rise to the two 'spirits' of good and evil.[35] Haug dismissed the concept of theological 'dualism' as a corruption of the purity of Zarathushtra's teaching, introduced by later adherents, along with veneration of the *yazatas* and ritual activities.

This approach addressed many of the criticisms posed both by Wilson and by reformers such as Dadabhai Naoroji (1825–1917) and members of his Rahnumae Mazdayasne Sabha ('Religious Reform Association of Mazda-Worship'), founded in 1851. The latter gave precedence to the *Gathas* and deprecated many of rituals, such as the use of *nirang*, as not befitting the religion. This perspective was to influence subsequent debate between 'reformers' and 'traditionalists' concerning authority and authenticity of text, and theological and cosmological doctrine: in short, the very nature of the religion. To an extent, Haug provided Parsis with the antidote for Wilson's bile, but the distinction between the *Gathas* and the other Zoroastrian texts and traditions brought fragmentation in its wake. Many priests and laity alike were perplexed by this new *Gatha*-only school of thought, which seemed to make much of their daily praxis redundant. Some reformers wanted to jettison the traditional prayers in Avesta, and to replace them with vernacular translations.

Such concerns were taken up by Maneckji Nusserwanji Dhalla (1875–1956), who came from a priestly family in Surat. By 1905, Dhalla had scraped together enough donations to travel to New York and study for a doctorate at Columbia University. His mentor for nearly four years was A.V. Williams Jackson, who held the Chair in Indo-Iranian Studies. Dhalla wrote his dissertation on the *Nyayishn*, the Avestan prayer songs to the *yazatas*. After his initiation as high priest in Karachi, Dastur Dhalla wrote several seminal works on the texts, history and evolution of the religion, in which he combined a rationalist 'reformist' approach with Western exegetical analysis, claiming that an original ethical monotheism revealed to Zarathushtra had been corrupted by polytheism and superstition. Dhalla is sometimes referred to as the 'Protestant *dastur*' because of his use of Western Christian terminology and rationalism, and his distrust of obsolete ritual, but as a high priest his devotion to his religion was also expressed through the ritual performance of the *Yasna* and the recitation of prayers to the *yazatas*, as well as compassionate concern for the welfare of his flock.

Dastur Dhalla's books, teachings and the colloquia he promoted resulted in a dynamic reinvestigation of the religion. His own mix of rational intellectualism and spiritual devotion prefigure the spiritual and intellectual struggles, which resonate among many Zoroastrians today. In his book *Zoroastrian Theology*, published in New York in 1914, Dhalla wrote:

'It seems that we tread a very delicate path when we set aside as non-Zoroastrian all that does not appear in the *Gathas*. Are we sure we are standing on firm ground when we dogmatically assert that the prophet of Iran discarded the pantheon and purposely kept it out of his religion of reform? The Haoma ceremony is indissolubly interwoven in the Yasna ritual from the Avestan period down to the present day...'[36]

Just above this passage, he had written concerning the *yazatas*,

'To think of Zoroastrianism without them is inconceivable. The two cannot be separated.'

In 1906, while Dhalla was studying in New York, two significant events occurred that still impact Parsi self-definition. In that year, an attempt was made to resolve the *Qadimi/Shehenshai* division with the introduction of a new calendar along the lines of the Gregorian calendar. This provoked the formation of a separatist group (*fasli*) who are mostly based in western India. The *Fasli* ('seasonalist') calendar holds *Nav Ruz* on the traditional date of 21 March, and intercalates a day every four years. Three different Parsi calendrical systems remain in operation today, which mostly affect community celebrations regarding the observance of the New Year.

The Shehenshais remain in the vast majority in India, but many Parsis celebrate *Jamshedi Nav Ruz* on 21 March with a visit to the *agiary*, a *jashan* at home or a meal out with the family. This festival is said to date back to Jamshid (Yima), and the retelling of his story as found in *Shah Nameh*, along with some of the elements set out in a special area of the house, recall aspects of the Iranian *Nav Ruz* festival. In parts of the world where both Iranian and Indian Zoroastrians live in the community, both traditions are often celebrated at the spring equinox. The connection of Yima with *Nav Ruz* echoes its eschatological dimension.

Pateti, meaning 'repentance', is the name for the beginning of the Shehenshai New Year, which is celebrated in August over two days, the second day being referred to as *Nav Ruz*. Just before Pateti, the ten days dedicated to the *fravashis* are commemorated with the *Muktad* festival (a parallel to Iranian *Fravardigan*, although the Parsi festival can last 18 days), when families will bring flowers into the home or to the fire temples each morning, and arrange them in vases on a table next to a lit *divo* (oil lamp) or small fire in a portable holder, before reciting the appropriate prayers. In *Farvardin Yasht*, the *fravashis* are associated with the good waters and with plants (Yt 13.147). The flowers represent *ameretat* – 'continuity of life' – and the water in the vases *haurvatat* – 'wholeness' – both qualities that Zoroastrians aspire to in this life and in the future.[37]

The second event of 1906 was to have far-reaching ramifications, not just among Parsis in India, but for all Zoroastrians. A lawsuit filed in the Bombay High Court by the BPP was motivated by the concern that converts could claim access to Parsi benevolent funds and institutions, such as *dharmsalas* (guest houses), *dakhmas* and fire temples. The lawsuit focused on the validity of the BPP trustees and their claim to manage the properties and funds of the

Parsi community. It related to two specific instances of conversion: that of a Rajput woman married to a Parsi, whose *navjote* had been performed, and who wanted to be consigned to the *dakhma* at her death; and that of the French widow of Ratan D. Tata, who had also been initiated. Justices Davar and Beaman ruled that the BPP Trustees were invalidly appointed, and that a scheme for new rules and elections should be devised.

They also issued two separate judgments in the form of *obiter dicta* (learned commentaries) in late 1908, concerning the legal definition of 'Parsi' and 'Zoroastrian'. Justice Davar's more lengthy ruling was accepted by the Parsis as definitive. He determined that a Parsi was the offspring of two Parsi or Irani parents who professed the Zoroastrian religion, or who was the child of a Parsi male by a woman who had been 'properly admitted into the religion'. The non-Parsi wife who converted to Zoroastrianism could not be considered to be a Parsi. Since non-Zoroastrians were not allowed into Parsi fire temples, any ceremony they were invited to, such as a wedding or *navjote*, was (and still is) held in a public place or *baug*. The fire is carried in a fire vase from a nearby fire temple to the *baug*, where it is placed on a cloth demarcating the ritual arena. One wonders if this could be an echo of the practice illustrated in ancient Sogdiana.

Justice Davar's ruling is still held as valid by many today, although others reject the patrilineal definition as unconstitutional. The exclusion of the spouses and children of intermarried Parsi women, on the grounds of patrilineage, remains a cause for tension within the community in India. The Justices also allowed, however, that the Zoroastrian religion 'not only permits, but enjoins conversion'. It is in this spirit that the Association for the Revival of Zoroastrianism (ARZ), in alliance with the Association of Inter-Married Zoroastrians (AIMZ), has created an alternative environment to the Parsi fire temples in Mumbai. The purchase of a meeting hall in 2005 by the ARZ has opened the way for the public performance of *navjotes* and inter-religious wedding ceremonies in a congregational ceremony, rather than in private at home, as they had to date.

'Zoroastrian Theosophy': Ilm-i Khshnoom

The first decade of the twentieth century also saw the beginning of a 'Zoroastrian theosophical' movement in India. Known as *Ilm-i Khshnoom* – the 'knowledge of spiritual satisfaction' – by its adherents, it generated a way of thinking about the religion that was to have an enduring influence even on those who would not have identified themselves as khshnoomists. Theosophy had been introduced to Bombay by Madame Blavatsky and Colonel Olcott in 1879. According to Dastur Dhalla, theosophy subverted the basic principles of the Zoroastrian religion, drawing much of its materials from Hindu and

Buddhist teachings. Parsis were drawn to theosophy in large numbers, however. In 1882, Col. Olcott delivered a lecture to Parsis at Bombay Town Hall entitled 'The Spirit of the Zoroastrian Religion', in which he urged Parsis to preserve their ancient prayers and rituals, and not to abandon their later scriptures as some of his Western peers had argued.

At the beginning of the twentieth century, an esoteric approach was promoted from within Zoroastrianism. A Parsi named Behramshah Shroff claimed that at the age of 18 he had studied for three years under the guidance of holy Zoroastrian sages, who had gone into seclusion in a secret paradisal dwelling place in the mountains of Iran – half a century before the fall of the Sasanians and who were the custodians of the ancient treasures and knowledge of the religion. Shroff is then said to have returned home to Surat, where he remained silent for 30 years before beginning his teaching in 1907.

Khshnoomist precepts include theosophical ideas relating to vegetarianism, reincarnation and the notion of different planes of existence: in this context, *Atash Padshah* (the 'Enthroned Fire') is not just the physical fire in the holder, but a living and conscious entity in tune with the energies of the material world. The fire is said to have a '*yazatic* conscience', divine wisdom and the vibrations of Sraosha surrounding him at all times, so that he receives the beneficial forces of divine energy that help him to reduce the maleficent effects of evil. Fire is the means of communicating the thoughts and prayers of Zoroastrians to Ahura Mazda, and of bestowing blessings from the Creator to the faithful.

Within this framework, the priestly performance of the *Yasna* – which is often interspersed with *Visperad* and *Videvdad* particularly at the seasonal festivals – becomes an act which energizes its various components at a cosmic level through the power of sound, heat and the spiritual purity of the reciter. From the Khshnoomist perspective, both ritual and the recitation of prayers in Avestan are effective means of combating evil, which manifests physically as well as spiritually. New branches of Khsnoomism have emerged in the last three decades, including that represented by the 'Madayasnie Monasterie' founded by Dr Meher Master-Moos, one of the few females in a leadership position in terms of religious discourse.

A general tendency towards esotericism among some Parsis may also be seen in their placement of a picture of the pseudonymous 'Dasturji Kukadaru', a nineteenth-century priest credited with mystical powers and miraculous works, next to the image of Zarathushtra. The picture of Kukadaru was in the *agiary* in Bombay, where a Parsi priest, named Ervad Aibara, officiated. Aibara claimed that the spirit of Kukadaru spoke to his inner self, and told him which prayers to give individuals who came to him for help.[38]

Many Parsis are also attracted to shrines of non-Zoroastrian spiritual masters, including that of Sai Baba in Shirdi. One of Sai Baba's disciples, who took the name 'Meher Baba', was an Irani Zoroastrian from Pune, whose *ashram* is visited by many Parsis. Veneration of spiritual adepts such as Meher Baba, Kukadaru or a living Parsi named 'Jalbhai' at the Aslaji *agiary*, relates to the need for the kind of spiritual support that was provided by the *Dasatir* in the early ninetennth century. So, too, does the cult of Jal Bawa at the Banaji Atash Bahram, Mumbai, which is accompanied by ritual communal prayer (*hambandagi*).[39]

Charity thy Name is Parsi: Parsi thy Name is Charity

One impact of Christian proselytism was a push to create schools owned and operated by Parsis, to ensure that the young would not have to attend the missionary schools. The encounters with Wilson also impressed upon the community as a whole that they needed to be educated not only in their own religion, but in professions that would enable them to take material care of each other. They sought careers in legal, medical, fiscal and scientific fields.

From a situation of very low literacy in the early decades of the nineteenth century, Parsis became educational pioneers for both men and women, supplying funding for both schools and colleges run by Europeans. The Parsi Benevolent Institution, founded by Sir Jamsetjee Jeejeeboy in 1849, pioneered the establishment of 21 schools in as many years. His philanthropy created a model of charitable giving that others sought to emulate. In the 1901 census, the Parsi male literacy rate was almost 88 per cent and that of Parsi females 63 per cent. By the end of the century, Parsi girls such as my grandmother had the option of being educated in English at European missionary schools, or in the vernacular at Parsi schools. The first English-speaking school for Parsi girls began in a private home in 1860, with the intention of providing 'the blessing of an English education upon sound moral principle'. The curriculum was secular, and the school was open to pupils of all religions.[40]

The extension of Parsi secular amenities, such as schools, hospitals and orphanages, to the wider community denotes a larger vision than the preservation of their own community, or the negotiation of status under colonial rule. James Ovington, a missionary to Surat in the late seventeenth century, spoke of the Parsis he met as those who would assist the poor and 'were very ready to provide for the Sustenance and Comfort of such as want it. Their universal kindness, either in employing such as are Needy and able to work, or bestowing a seasonable bounteous Charity to such as are infirm and miserable, leave no Man destitute of Relief.'[41] Such concern reiterates the

ethical concept that advocating for the poor is one of the beneficent acts
expected of the *ashavan*.

The act of bestowing charity on behalf of the soul of a deceased member of
the family remains a central element of Zoroastrian philanthropy. The
fravashi of a righteous person is said to continue to be concerned with the
welfare of those members of its living family who perform meritorious acts
(Y 16.7). A charitable endowment is, therefore, often announced by the
family of the deceased at the ceremony on the fourth day after death. On
subsequent death anniversaries, the family may give food and clothing to the
poor of the community and money to charity. In India, Iran and diaspora,
buildings and charitable foundations are often endowed in memory of a
deceased relative, as are community feasts.

Parsis in Diaspora

Previous chapters described the dissemination of Zoroastrians throughout
various parts of Western and Central Asia and China, and this chapter has
considered the establishment of the religion in India. Trade connections
across the British Empire motivated much resettlement of Parsis from the
mid-eighteenth century onwards, with Britain as an early and favorite
destination. The history of Zoroastrians in the UK is well documented.[42] The
first three Indian Members of Parliament in Britain were all Parsis, each
representing a different party, signifying that no one political party was
particularly associated with Parsi values. Dadabhai Naoroji became the
Liberal MP for Finsbury Central from 1892 to 1895, after a term as President
of the Indian National Congress. He took his oath of office as the first Indian
MP in the British parliament, with his hand on a copy of the *Khordeh Avesta*,
the Zoroastrian prayer book. Naoroji was followed by Sir Muncherji
Bhownagree (1851–1933), who was the Conservative MP for Bethnal Green
North East from 1895 to 1905.

Both Naoroji and Bhownagree were presidents of an association of
Zoroastrians, which was founded in 1861. Its original title was the Religious
Funds of Zoroastrians of Europe (now the Zoroastrian Trust Funds of Europe,
Inc.), and it was set up to manage funds to bury the dead; to establish a place
of prayer; to help impoverished Zoroastrians in Britain and elsewhere in
Europe; to create a library of Zoroastrian publications; and to promote
Zoroastrian scholarship among Zoroastrians and non-Zoroastrian academics.
One of the earliest religious decisions for the Parsis in Britain and in other
diaspora communities was how to dispose of their dead. In 1862, a
Zoroastrian burial section was dedicated at Brookwood Cemetery, about 30
miles south-west of London, where many Zoroastrians from Europe are
buried, including Shapurji Saklatvalla (1874–1936), the Communist MP for

Battersea North from 1922 to 1923 and 1924 to 1929. Freddie Mercury (b. Feridun Bulsara), of the rock group Queen is also interred at Brookwood.

Parsis acting as middlemen in sea trade with China began to settle there in groups from the 1770s, buying a plot of land for a Zoroastrian cemetery in Canton in 1847. This was the first interment site outside British India. By this time, Parsis had also settled in Hong Kong, East Africa, Zanzibar, Sind province (now in Pakistan) and Aden. In each of those places, they constructed fire temples and, in the last two regions, *dakhmas*. When India and Pakistan became separate nations in 1947, some Parsis migrated to Britain or further west, but many stayed put.

After the British left Aden in the late 1960s, Parsis departed too, and it was decided to try to remove the *Adaran*-grade fire elsewhere. By this time, the fires in Shanghai and Zanzibar had been allowed to 'grow cold', but the Parsis were determined that this should not happen again. A specially modified and consecrated Air India Boeing 707, flown by a Parsi crew, brought the fire from Aden to Mumbai in 1976, and the fire was installed in the Adenwalla *agiary* in Lonavala (Maharashtra state), India. Such a determined and ingenious rescue testifies to the continued centrality of fire to Zoroastrian devotional life.

The three grades of consecrated fire are still found in India: the *Atash Dadgah* ('fire in an appointed place') can be looked after by a member of the laity and is the type of fire in most Zoroastrian centers in diaspora; the *Atash Adaran* is found in most fire temples, where it is tended by a priest with simple rituals; and the *Atash Bahram*, which is often referred to as a 'cathedral' fire, and requires elaborate purification rituals. There are eight *Atash Bahrams* in India, all in the north-west (including the *Iran Shah*, which now burns in Udvada[43]), and over a hundred *agiaries* (lesser fire temples) throughout the country, most with *Adaran* fires. Zoroastrians in India may visit their nearest fire temple on a daily basis on their way to or from work, but most attend only for special ceremonies, such as *Khordad Sal* on the sixth day after *Nav Ruz*. The waters of the well in the precincts of the fire temple are also revered, and laity may decorate the well on *Aban Jashan*, the day dedicated to the waters (*Aban*), in the month of *Aban* (the tenth day of the eighth month). This is the day that Parsi lay men and women make their way to the sea, to a flowing river or to the fire temple well, in order to make their own offering to the waters as a source of life and renewal.

The hope of blessing and increase implicit in those offerings to the waters has taken on a new significance in the decades since the late 1960s, as Parsi population numbers began to drop, due to emigration, a low birth rate and intermarriage. Despite an influx of Iranian Zoroastrian refugees after the revolution of 1979, and the introduction of a subsidized fertility program, the number of Zoroastrians continues to fall. Although India remains home to the largest Zoroastrian population in the world – with a count of about 47,000 in Mumbai and around 70,000 in total – the population is aging and the death rate far outnumbers births. This has brought many challenges to Zoroastrians in both India and in diaspora. In a FEZANA Journal, dedicated to the study of Zoroastrian demographics worldwide (Winter, 2004), Firdosh Mehta, the then President of FEZANA, remarked that at the core of the demographics lies the question 'Who is a Zoroastrian?' This question, which relates to both group identity and self-definition, is one that Parsis and Irani Zoroastrians in India have been wrestling with since the legal decisions of the early twentieth century. It is now a question that follows them into diaspora in Europe, North America, Australia, New Zealand and the Gulf States – all parts of the world with several hundred, if not thousands, of Parsi/Irani families.

Chapter VIII

Zoroastrians Present: Revisited

'The greatest value I derive from Zoroastrian teachings is a devotion to the truth, which is more than simply speaking the truth. To me, it is the courage to seek truth by being willing to break from the realms of comfort and to see reality as it is, much like a scientist does. The more I study this, the more I learn that the truth may be uncomfortable, and may make the process of seeking truth difficult. But what I love about the Zoroastrian vision is the faith that this devotion to truth, despite its challenges, proves to be wonderful in the end.'

Neekaan, age 21

This penultimate chapter is intended to provide a more nuanced look at some of the issues raised at the beginning of the book, and also to reiterate that Zoroastrianism, however it may be defined by 'insiders' or 'outsiders', is a lived and living faith, which has never existed in a situation of stasis. While Zoroastrians now are grappling with the fact that numerically the self-destruct button has been pressed, in that the number of deaths exceeds the number of births, the prevailing mood is not one of doom and gloom – nor of outright panic – but, true to the Gathic outlook, one of trust in a positive outcome.

The presence of Zoroastrians in sizeable numbers in the UK (about 5–7,000), North America (15–20,000 in the USA and Canada together), Australia, New Zealand and Pakistan (together, just under 6,000) has meant that their voice is now being heard, not only among those of other ethnic minorities, but also as members of a religion that has had a significant impact on Western history and philosophy. As an ancient and important religion, Zoroastrianism deserves a place in any well-rounded educational curriculum. Zoroastrianism is officially recognized as one of the nine major faiths of the UK, and Zoroastrians are therefore consulted by diverse government committees that require interfaith input. But Zoroastrians find themselves still having to make their case to be recognized as a 'world religion', rather than being acknowledged merely as a minority ethnicity (Parsi or Iranian) who hold to a minority faith. Nowhere is Zoroastrianism classified as a 'main' religion, even in the homelands of Iran and India, where it continues to hold minority status. It remains, therefore, always 'other', despite its increased representation in governmentally-supported or locally-generated interfaith initiatives. I witnessed such outreach in the spring of 2008, when an American tour group visiting the Isfahan fire temple encountered a group of local (Muslim) elementary school teachers learning about Zoroastrianism from the incumbent *mobed*. It is through such initiatives that a Zoroastrian voice is most likely to be heard by the majority, although this voice will not represent any officially stated theological, political or ethnic perspective.

The absence of an authoritative body whose task it is to interpret the religion makes it difficult to determine the 'Zoroastrian position' on many issues. Such was the experience of two acquaintances of mine (one a Parsi), who were working individually in different continents to draw up healthcare directives concerning the 'Zoroastrian approach' to certain bioethical matters. Each was hard-pressed to find a definitive Zoroastrian response to ethical questions relating to organ donation or stem cell research. In each case, the researchers were pointed towards early textual sources promoting action that brings benefit, rather than detriment. The *dasturs* in Mumbai occasionally give pronouncements, such as their public condemnation in 1983 of the initiation in New York of an American with no Zoroastrian birth parent, or their rejection in 1990 of the use of the *dakhma* in the funerals of intermarried women.[1] For Zoroastrians looking to Mumbai as the locus of religious authority, these statements were considered to be helpful interpretations of the religion, and affirmations of the way forward; for others, both the priests and their decrees were viewed as belonging to the old country or regime, and as therefore operating under assumptions that were irrelevant in the new setting.

A Parsi newsletter published in Mumbai alluded to the desire of North American Zoroastrians to have their presence acknowledged in 'an environment that is throbbingly vibrant, but disturbingly different from anything that the Parsi/Irani mind has encountered in the old world'.[2] This rather unsettling image highlights the different needs and demands of Zoroastrians in diaspora. For many migrant Zoroastrians, removal from the supportive community institution of the *anjuman* (the lay council responsible for community affairs) and from a ritual life centered on an *agiary*, or *atashkadeh* (fire temple), has been a strong incentive to study their religion anew. Confronted with new questions concerning self-definition and normative practice, they feel the need to clarify the emotional and intellectual core of their identity.

That Zoroastrians have increasingly assumed a declaratory position regarding their religion has been part of my own experience in both Britain and America. When the North American Interfaith Network (NAIN) was being established in the late 1980s, under the impetus of the non-denominational Temple of Understanding in New York, I served as the honorary Zoroastrian representative, until I could find a local 'insider' who was willing to stand. Formal interfaith activity was only just beginning in the USA, whereas Zoroastrians in London had already been my co-consultants in creating a course component on the religion, which was incorporated into the Inner London Agreed Syllabus on Religious Education of 1984. Such co-opting of both the religion and its adherents by 'outsiders' into a broader sphere of educational and interfaith activity has, in the past two decades, been replaced by direct initiatives from within the Zoroastrian communities. In recent years, Zoroastrians have been prominent at international interfaith gatherings, such as the Parliament of the World's Religions and World Conference of Religions for Peace events.[3]

The 'outsider' dominance of textual translation, scholarship and interpretation of praxis remains, however. This is partly because few Zoroastrians have taken up and expanded upon what Dastur Dhalla's mentor A.V. Williams Jackson referred to as 'the Avesta cause'.[4] To an extent, that 'outsider' perspective with its many implicit biases is inherent in the writing of this book, and I am aware that my own status in this enterprise will be a cause for concern among some Zoroastrians.

Towards the end of the twentieth century, Western scholarship began to be questioned by Zoroastrians as being too 'orientalist', too academically removed from the lived reality, or too biased in terms of introducing theological reconstruction and ritual reform. Members of Zoroastrian Associations now tend to weigh the merits of Western academics based on their perceived positioning within the theological or ritual spectrum, before deciding whether to invite them to participate in events organized by their association or to attend seminars at which they are speaking. In the past decade, however, Zoroastrian individuals (alongside non-Zoroastrians) have helped to fund lectureships in Zoroastrian Studies at the University of London (SOAS), Claremont Graduate University and Stanford University in California. This support for the academic study of the religion in a secular place of learning continues the impetus generated in the mid-nineteenth century. To paraphrase Voltaire, for centuries European scholars and dilettanti have had much to say about Zoroaster and Zoroastrianism, and will, no doubt, continue to have much to say in the future.

Information about the religion and its practitioners has, from the very outset, been largely observed and interpreted through an external lens. The ability to 'see ourselves as others see us' has often been reflected in aspects of Zoroastrian self-definition: just as living in a predominantly Hindu culture impacted Parsi practice and social structure, so living under Islam affected areas of Zoroastrian theology, particularly the understanding of monotheism.

The impact of Islamic concepts upon Zoroastrians in India from the time of the Delhi Sultanate onwards is found in the Parsi reference to focus on the fire in the *agiary* by the Arabic term *'qibla'* (the direction of Makka in Islam). Iranian Zoroastrians, in their turn, looked to the Parsi Amelioration Society for help in revitalizing their religious institutions and in sending their priests to India to train. Now, however, Zoroastrians who are firmly established in Europe and America are re-appropriating their own narrative, addressing the question 'Who is a Zarathushti (Zoroastrian)?' on their own terms. In the past decade, many have chosen to redefine themselves in a way that transcends national and ethnic boundaries, by using the form 'Zarathushti' of themselves, and referring to their religion, not as 'Zoroastrianism' but as 'Zarathushti Din'. Such self-definition is significant in terms of internal discourse, but does not always translate into a public sphere of discourse, where ignorance about the religion remains.

Rather than replicate the work of others, it seems relevant here to focus on a few of the issues that are raised as Zoroastrians redefine their own paradigmatic models within a global context.[5] Just as a century or so ago, Parsi experience in the West had a profound impact on Zoroastrians in India, so the experiences of Zoroastrians in diaspora are now having an influence on communities in India and Iran. This circle of appropriation is a dialectical process, which raises the question of there being a shared human, as well as purely intra-cultural, narrative.

The main text of this book has shown that Zoroastrians have been making connections across geo-political boundaries for several thousand years. In the more recent history of the religion, we saw how a member of the Wadia family in the late nineteenth century acted as a trading agent for both French and American companies. Members of the Wadia family are now located throughout the USA and Canada, as well as in India. Many other Zoroastrians have relocated once or more, across national and continental boundaries: from Iran to Germany to California; from Karachi to Toronto to Melbourne or Auckland; from Mumbai or Zanzibar to London and then to Dubai. Zoroastrians who have emigrated provide economic support for religious institutions in their new location, as well as in the 'old country' of Iran or India. In their new homes, the Iranian and Parsi émigré communities were initially cautious in their interactions with each other. This reticence to integrate as a united Zoroastrian community, particularly in the London metropolitan area, where Parsis had settled for over a century by the time of the Iranian revolution, was ostensibly based on differences of language and cuisine, as well as the divergent festival calendars. The divergences were symptomatic of a deeper division concerning such issues as the authority of an hereditary priesthood in transmitting and interpreting the religion; the significance of patterned ritual; the nature of Ahura Mazda and the nature of evil; the agency of Zarathushtra; the authenticity and canon of sacred text; faith as a matter of birth or belief – or both; and the connected issue of ethnicity in the unfolding of the religion in diaspora.

Despite the correspondence between the two groups as charted in the Persian *Rivayats*, and despite subsequent involvement of the Parsis in the ritual life and education of Iranian priests, in diaspora neither would accept the priestly authority of the other. On each coast of America – in California and in New York – this led to the formation of two Zoroastrian Associations: one Parsi, one Iranian. In New York, the division was exacerbated by debate over who controlled the first purpose-built Zoroastrian prayer hall (*Dar-i Mihr*) in the USA. The two New York communities have worked out some of their differences through proportional representation on the Board of Trustees and in membership dues, and now often arrange joint events together. This *modus operandi* seems to work in many of the communities where there are Zoroastrians from both Indian and Iranian backgrounds.

In London, where there have historically been close ties to the Parsi communities in India since the time of Dadhabhai Naoroji, the assumption of familiarity with Gujarati terms and Parsi rituals and celebrations has been moderated to acknowledge festivals belonging to the Iranian calendar, such as *Jashne Sadeh, Tirgan* and *Mihragan*. Events are usually sponsored by Parsis and Iranian Zoroastrians respectively, but both groups will join together to celebrate *(Jamshedi) Nav Ruz* at the time of the spring equinox, and most of the other festivals. Both commemorate *Zartosht no Diso* (the death of Zarathushtra) according to their separate calendars.[6] The move from the original Zoroastrian House in north-western London to a new premises in a converted cinema in Harrow was initially intended to incorporate a consecrated *Atash Dadgah*, but that plan was shelved for logistical reasons. The new Zoroastrian Centre often opens its doors to all, including the prayer room (*setayash gah*), but is closed to non-Zoroastrians during *Muktad* and for some individual and community religious events. The ZTFE Constitution of 1979, in its Articles of Association, states that members include 'Parsees of Zarathushtrian faith'. The original constitution was in Gujarati, and this particular phrase 'Parsee Zarathushtrian' was not translated intentionally, in order to be synonymous with Justice Davar's definition of Parsi Zoroastrians. This would signify that, although the founding members of the Trust were both 'traditionalists' and 'reformers', they considered the use of the *anjuman* to be for the benefit of Zoroastrians who were not converts.

While birth is regarded by many Parsis as a prerequisite to being a Zoroastrian, the concept of patrilineality that was included in the summation of Justice Davar has not been so readily exported to diaspora, even though Parsis – particularly in London and Hong Kong – still consider this important.[7] For example, the 'Autonomy Clause' of the FEZANA Constitution of 1987 states that nothing in its rubric is to be construed to impair the religious and administrative autonomy of individual Associations or individual Zoroastrians. In other words, decisions regarding such matters as conversion, or the acceptance of non-Zoroastrian spouses of either gender, are in the hands of local Zoroastrian Associations.

FEZANA forms an overarching organization that acts largely as a point for the gathering and dissemination of material relating to the study, understanding, perpetuation and practice of the Zoroastrian religion 'as set forth in the teachings of the Prophet Zarathushtra and the Zoroastrian faith'. It is also concerned to foster the welfare of Zoroastrian communities and 'to encourage Zoroastrian fellowship in the North American continent', including supporting 'activities that nurture and support the Zoroastrian faith and Zoroastrian communities'. The establishment of FEZANA has done much to facilitate dialog and encounter among Zoroastrians in North America. FEZANA sponsors an annual North American Youth Congress, through its sub-committee ZYNA (Zarathushti Youth of North America), and co-ordinates regional seminars for 15–40-year-olds with local Zoroastrian Associations. The FEZANA Journal functions as both a global community newsletter and an educational tool.

Further internal discourse has been promoted among the dispersed Zoroastrian communities through a series of World Congresses, the first of which was held in Tehran in 1962. The next few Congresses were held in Bombay, until Tehran hosted the 1996 Congress. The first World Congress to take place outside the traditional homelands was the 1999/2000 millennial event in Houston, Texas. This was possibly the largest gathering to date of Zoroastrians from around the world, and marked a new chapter in the transnational development of the religion. World Congresses are planned every four to five years, at a different location in the world: London was the 2005 location, and Dubai in 2009. One of the outcomes of the 2005 London conference was the creation of a Coming Together Roundtable (CTR) that provides an informal, unstructured forum in which Zoroastrians in leadership positions from around the world can discuss and act on matters of import to the global collective. The notion of Zoroastrians as 'a community without borders' forms the core of a new model that reflects a movement away from ethnicity as the main determinant of religious affiliation.

Many associations organizing global gatherings of Zoroastrians exercise restrictions as to who can attend, including 'outsider' speakers. The regulations at the 2007/8 World Youth Congress in Ballarat, Australia, caused some contention, however, by including an affirmation by attendees that they were 'Zoroastrian youth born and bred', and practicing the faith in line with 'current established practices'. This rubric represents what some refer to as the 'traditionalist' stance, but which most Parsis would call the 'orthodox' position. It reminds us that Zoroastrians continue to be defined not only by the labels they choose for themselves, but often by labels chosen for them by sociologists or anthropologists.

The plurality of labels used to identify the spectrum of Zoroastrian belief and practice indicate that contention exists regarding the definition of 'authentic' or 'true' Zoroastrianism. The 'Traditionalists' are augmented by 'Neo-Traditionalists' – that is, those Parsis who apply a Western academic interpretation to the religious texts while seeking to revive and to reaffirm religious praxis, rather than to reform. In the late 1970s, the Mumbai-based Zoroastrian Studies was founded by an Oxford-educated Parsi as an educational program for children and adults, intended to promote cultural awareness of the religion and its history as a means of shoring up the faith against the detrimental threat of intermarriage and iconoclasm. English-language materials and lectures provided through this organization continue to have an impact on the spiritual lives of Parsis from diverse groups.[8]

The Neo-Traditionalists present a systematic theology and doctrine of Zoroastrianism from a 'dualistic' perspective, which sits uncomfortably with some.[9] In 2005, a group of 'orthodox' Parsis in Mumbai (comprising both Traditionalists and Neo-Traditionalists) formed the World Alliance of Parsi and Irani Zarthosthi (WAPIZ) to act as an anti-assimilationist counterbalance to the World Zoroastrian Organization (WZO), which allows individual membership including that of non-Zoroastrian spouses.

WZO was established in 1980 to work with governmental agencies around the world in providing assistance to several hundred Iranian Zoroastrian refugees. WAPIZ seeks to keep up the *dakhmenashini* system (disposal of the dead in the *dakhma*) as the authentic funeral rite, and promotes the concept of *Parsipanu* – Parsi culture and identity – that emphasizes the continuity of the faith as an ethnically-linked tradition, preserved over the centuries in direct descent from Zarathushtra to the present day. Today, Zoroastrian refugees to India desiring support from the Bombay Parsi Punchayat must produce an identity card issued by their local *anjuman* in Iran and a *sudreh* and *kusti*, and be able to recite certain prayers in Avestan, such as the *Ahuna Vairya* and the *Ashem Vohu*.[10] These are considered aspects of the faith, which distinguish *bona fide* Zoroastrians from Iranians seeking asylum under false pretences.

Debate between the 'orthodox' and the 'reformists' in Mumbai plays out in print in sectarian publications such as *Parsiana*, a bimonthly magazine now available internationally, the more local *Jam-e Jamshed* and *Deen Parast*, which is firmly 'orthodox'. These magazines are also partially or wholly available online, and the Internet has thus become a powerful resource for both consolidation and division. In fact, cyberspace has become the preferred forum for Zoroastrian organizations and individuals throughout the world to air their positions on controversial matters, such as conversion or adherence to the ancient purity regulations of the *Videvdad*, particularly with regard to disposal of the dead. Even though social attitudes have changed considerably in the last century, and many of the purity laws advocated in the later Zoroastrian texts are no longer rigidly adhered to, many woman in menses do not enter a fire temple, and take particular care to maintain a respectful distance from the fire at community celebrations or in the home. Others have jettisoned such constraints as being incompatible with a modern rationalist approach to religion, and seem to feel no ensuing sense of guilt.[11]

This shift indicates a change in perception of the source and nature of evil as emotional or mental, rather than physical or metaphysical.[12] Some priests also lean towards this refutation of actual 'forces of evil', while maintaining through their prayers and rituals the stark opposition of good and evil.[13] Debate also centers on the emblem of fire itself – that most enduring index of the religion. The two communities in California that have a prayer area with fire use gas to light it, although will 'feed' the fire with dry sandalwood. The *setayash gah* in London is lit only with wood and allowed to 'grow cold'. Such subtle changes in both praxis and belief challenge the ancient concept of the resonances between the *menog* and *getig* worlds. Increasingly, religious lives of Zoroastrians are pragmatically shaped to an urban environment and to personal needs, rather than rigid adherence to tradition. Public religious discourse concerning such sensitive matters of 'orthopraxy' and 'orthodoxy' is generally conducted by the laity, without significant input from the priesthood, although there are exceptions.

In the Winter 2004 *FEZANA Journal*, which dealt with the demographics of global Zoroastrianism, Firdosh Mehta asked: 'How should the North American community respond to Neo-Zarathushtis?' This is a question that is particularly pertinent for Zoroastrian groups in Europe, as well as North America. 'Neo-Zoroastrians' are those with no immediate Zoroastrian roots, but who have chosen to adopt the religion. The most numerous groups of Neo-Zoroastrians, however, are those who do come from an ethnically-Iranian background, who have either migrated from Iran or are Tajiks living in Central Asia or abroad, and who regard the espousal of the religion as a return to their ancestral 'birth faith'.[14]

These converts from Islam largely adopt a monotheistic approach along the lines of the Abrahamic religions, and accept the *Gathas* as the sole teaching attributable to Zarathushtra, and therefore the only source of knowledge about the religion, alongside individual reason. They perform the *sedreh-pushi* (initiation) of both children and adults, and celebrate Iranian festivals such as *Nav Ruz*. A similar ethnic legacy among Kurdish peoples, especially the Yezidis, has led some to express nominal ties with Zoroastrianism. Zoroastrians from India and North America have made contact with such Neo-Zoroastrians, particularly those from Tajikistan, in order to find out more about them.[15]

The wider term, 'Para-Zoroastrianism', has been coined to encompass those forms of the religion not recognized as 'legitimate offshoots of institutional Zoroastrianism by established Zoroastrian organizations'.[16] Such 'Para-Zoroastrian' groups emphasize belief and commitment rather than birth, although the registered Zoroastrian Community of St. Petersburg was founded by a TV personality named Pavel Globa, the great grandson of an Iranian Zoroastrian, whose interest lies in the more esoteric aspects of the religion. This Russian network has transliterated the Avesta into Cyrillic script, and its members are initiated and wear the *sudreh* and *kusti*, but they place particular emphasis on the astrology and mysticism of the Middle Persian texts, such as the *Bundahishn*, rather than the *Gathas*.[17]

Since the dismantling of the Soviet Union, and the discovery of fire temples in Azerbaijan, Uzbekistan and Turkmenistan, an interest in the earlier Zoroastrianism of these regions has become widespread. There is now an Avesta Museum in the old city of Khiva, where the displays and dioramas include somewhat fanciful recreations of 'Zoroastrian' festivals, rituals and practices in Karakalpakstan (Fig. 28). This fascination with the Zoroastrian religion in Uzbekistan, Turkmenistan and the Caucasus nations is expressed largely through an exploration of cultural and historical roots, rather than an ideological adherence.

While many Zoroastrians, particularly the self-proclaimed 'orthodox', recognize that the different religious factions are irreconcilable, and that Zoroastrianism must split into diverse (and divorced) groups, others are optimistic that a new paradigm will arise that will encompass the range of understandings. The latter approach considers that all forms of the religion are equally valid, whereas the former construes its own form to be more authentic than others. The claim to embody the 'true and original form' of Zoroastrianism is also taken up by other groups, such as the Zarathushtrian Assembly of California, which interprets the religion in part according to Dastur Dhalla's reformist, *Gathas*-only approach.[18]

The Assembly was initially conceived as a non-denominational movement, and chose not to identify itself with Zoroastrianism as an 'ethnic entity'.[19] In its dissemination of 'the Divine Message of Zarathushtra' and promotion of 'Zarathushtrian fellowship', the Assembly has accepted many non-Iranians as Zarathushti – including some in Venezuela and Brazil – but its majority appeal remains among Iranians. While many 'born Zoroastrians' either publicly or privately approve the Assembly's presentation of the religion as progressive and modern, some of the older supporters express concern at the use of the vernacular, rather than the ancient Avestan prayers which they had learnt as children and continued to recite in their daily devotions.

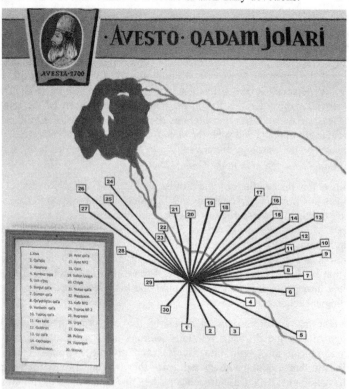

Fig. 28. Map showing the 'spread of the Avesta' from Khiva. Avesta Museum, Khiva.

In a paper presented at the North American Mobed Council's (NAMC) conference of 30 July 2005, Khushroo Mirza wrote: 'The Zarathushti religion is not rooted in buildings and neighborhoods, otherwise it would have ended in Iran. It lives within us and survives. The doctrine is not enshrined in books but in how we keep it in our hearts and in our lives.' Such expressions remind us that Zoroastrian moral philosophy remains a constant, as does belief in Ahura Mazda as the good Creator and in Zarathushtra as the conveyor of the Creator's wisdom. The maxim of the trifold ethic – 'good thoughts, good words, good deeds' – is still the heart of the Zoroastrian 'creed'.

Each group of Zoroastrians around the world, however it defines itself or is defined by others, manifests a strong sense of community and religious affiliation. Such cohesion is demonstrated by the ability of Zoroastrians to reshape their circumstances and yet preserve their identity. The *Yasna*, which has been the kernel of priestly praxis for centuries, as an act that reaffirms the divine order and beneficence inherent in the cosmos, has been replaced in diaspora by the *jashan* and *gahanbar*, both of which incorporate the *afrinagan*, a ceremony of blessing. The *jashan* is an 'outer' ritual that can be celebrated in the home, a public place or a fire temple, and can be adapted for almost any occasion: honoring a dead person; blessing a new home; welcoming the installation of a new *dastur* or *mobed*; giving thanks for victory in war; or praying for rains to relieve a drought.

The dispersal of Zoroastrians across the globe has led to the recognition that such community festivals and rituals, which always involve the preparation and sharing of food, bring not only ontological benefit, but also social cohesion. From this perspective, although the majority of Zoroastrians now live in urban rather than rural settings, the celebration of a community festivity remains an important expression of collective religious practice. Since there is no single day of worship each week, the celebration of a seasonal *gahanbar*, or of a designated *jashan*, has become the most prevalent means of bringing adherents – who may be scattered across a wide area – together.

Parsi communities in diaspora gather to observe *Muktad* at the end of the year, just as Iranians observe *Farvardigan*. The honoring of the *fravashis* at this time functions on both a vertical and horizontal plane, connecting those who participate with both physical and metaphysical antecedents, as well as with their co-religionists. This dimension is reiterated at all *hambandagi* gatherings. The food that is prepared for these occasions – such as the *sirok* and the *ash* (bean and vegetable soup) by Iranian Zoroastrians, and the *dhansak* (a lamb or chicken curry) and sweet dishes of *ravo* (semolina) and *sev* (vermicelli) by Parsis – contain their own ritual significance, and act as a mnemonic to the immediate and more ancient past.

Such gatherings, whether at a community *Dar-i Mihr* or in a private home, help to sustain both individuals and families in the religion, and to encourage them to participate in the long tradition of the oral transmission of Avestan prayers. They also provide an opportunity for youngsters to socialize together as a supportive group, and thus to propel the religion into the next generation. The World Youth Congresses, which take place every three and a half to four years, are intended not only to bring young Zoroastrians together to discuss their faith, and other topical issues, but also to function as 'mixers' for eligible single young men and women. Such educational and social events are also arranged by local Zoroastrian Associations, who organize youth seminars, summer camps, picnics, ski trips and cruises.

Traditionally, a *jashan*, like the inner ritual of the *Yasna*, needs two priests, which is not always practicable in this time of a decreasing priesthood, so the ritual is often modified for just one priest or *mobedyar* to perform. Let us revisit young Burzin, whom we first encountered at the beginning of this book. His story provides one optimistic model for the future of the religion.

Burzin's father, Poras, graduated from an engineering school in India, and came to the USA for his doctoral studies. Poras, thinking that he would not have the time or the opportunity to perform rituals in his new situation, decided to leave his priest's outfit and ritual implements back home. Soon after arriving in Pennsylvania, however, Poras discovered a thriving Zoroastrian community nearby, which needed a priest. So, on his next trip back to India, he retrieved his priestly accoutrements. He began to serve as a volunteer priest to Zoroastrians in Pennsylvania, and also to participate in interfaith activities. Burzin was impressed to see his dad performing *jashans* and other rituals. One day Burzin asked if he, too, could become a priest, and was told that he could, if he really wanted to, and was prepared to study hard to learn the prayers and the rituals. After his *navjote*, Burzin's training started with his dad: 'I spent a couple of hours almost every day for over two years to learn all the prayers. Every now and then when I heard my friends playing, I felt like playing too.... So I would take a short break and then go back to my training because it is important for us to have Zoroastrian priests here in the USA to perform ceremonies and also for me to carry on my father's tradition' (Fig. 29).

At the California Zoroastrian Center (CZC) in Westminster, Dr Mobed Vahidi initiated a *herbad* and *mobedyar* training program in April 2008. This is a new venture in diaspora, and there are six participants in the program, including one female. Some are from priestly families, others from a lay background. The students are engaged in a program of study similar to that of priestly *nowzut* candidates. This includes knowledge of sufficient Avestan and Middle Persian to recite prayers, and a familiarity with rituals. They are studying the *Gathas*, learning about the history of Zoroastrianism in Iran and

India, and discussing the religious issues facing Zoroastrians today. The course also includes inquiry into the major world religions. Assessment will include a written analysis of a related topic; an oral test in the recitation of Avestan prayers; and an interview by a committee of learned *mobeds*. Successful candidates will be initiated as *mobedyars* in the *nowzut* ceremony by members of the Council of Iranian Mobeds of North America (CIMNA). This Council consists mostly of non-practicing Iranian *mobeds*.[20] Parsi laity may also train as *mobedyars*, and as of 2010 at least one Parsi woman in the USA was a *mobedyar*-in-training.[21]

In early 2009, I was copied on a posting from the zrenovators@yahoo.com website. It addressed the audience using a range of 'insider' self-definitions that included 'intellectual Zarathushtrian', 'comfort Zarathushtrian' and 'ethnic Zarathushtrian'. After this acknowledgement of the range of perspectives among its readers, the message called upon all Zoroastrians to become *saoshyants* – to choose 'to live a life in dedication to the vision of a world governed by righteousness, truth and benevolent thinking, which is the essence of the Manthran's divine message'. This call to participate in the realization of *frashegird* will resonate with all self-defined Zoroastrians, but how they choose to respond will differ from one individual to another. The varying 'isms' that exist within the Zoroastrian religion may be said to reflect a diversity that has always existed historically – both horizontally (consider, for instance, 'Zurvanism;' the reception of certain Babylonian astrological themes and Near Eastern divinities in the Achaemenid period, and elements of Greek philosophy in the Sasanian; or the syncretistic expression of the religion among the Sogdians) and vertically (the development of the religion from the Old to the Young Avesta and then to Middle Persian texts). This fluidity, with periods of expansion/inclusivity and contraction/ exclusivity, is common to many religious traditions, but throughout its long history the Zoroastrian religion has interacted closely with more examples of the religiously 'Other' than any other faith, which is a measure of its adaptability and longevity.

Fig. 29. Three generations of priests: Burzin, after his navar ceremony, with his father and grandfather. At initiation, Burzin received the bull-headed 'mace of Mithra', recalling the club that the yazata *wields against the forces of evil (Yt 10.96).*

It remains to be seen which (if any) current manifestations of the religion will survive into the next century. Many of the issues that face the Zoroastrian religion are similar to those facing other faiths, but the paucity of numbers of Zoroastrians lends urgency to their search for resolution and concentrates the minds of adherents, most of whom are reluctant to watch passively as the fire dies out. How – and who – keeps the flame alight, and whether it is gas-fired or wood-burning and whether the accompanying prayers are in Avestan or the vernacular, are concerns symptomatic of wider and more diverse issues being addressed differently, depending on the predisposition. Current trends indicate that any universally-applicable resolution is likely to occur in diaspora, and to involve a 'both...and' approach, rather than an 'either...or'.

Chapter IX

Zarathushtra Present and Past

'Prophets are revolutionaries, and Zarathushtra was the earliest one... He was the messenger of Ahura Mazda, the refuge of the weak, the solace of the suffering, the hope of humanity, and the regenerator of the world.'

Dastur M.N. Dhalla[1]

Zarathushtra Now

It is time now to speak of Zarathushtra. Some readers will have been concerned that the key figure in the *dramatis personae* of the *Gathas* has not been particularly prominent in this brief history of the evolution of the religion. This omission was not intended to be disrespectful of the centrality of Asho Zarathushtra for adherents. It was an intentional reflection of the fact that, for much of the history of what we now refer to as 'Zoroastrianism' – the 'religion of Zarathushtra' – emphasis has not been on the eponymous recipient of the *manthras*, but on the one who generated the *manthras* – Ahura Mazda – and transmitted them to Zarathushtra, who was the human mouthpiece for the wisdom of the ages (*Gathas* 1.29.10–11). There is no mention of Zarathushtra in Old Persian or Middle Persian official inscriptions – the focus is entirely on Ahura Mazda. My attempt to present a chronological approach to the religion made me reluctant to include the emphases of later texts, or of motifs that are not evidenced in the western Iranian material until later.

The expression '*Zarathushtri*' is found in an early Avestan text, where it is often translated as 'Zoroastrian', but should more accurately be translated as '[a follower/supporter] of Zarathushtra'. The term occurs in the *Fravarane*, the Avestan 'declaration of faith', which begins with a rejection of the false gods (*daevas*) and the words:

I declare myself a Mazda-worshipper like Zarathushtra, rejecting the *daevas*, accepting Ahura's instruction. (Y 12.1)

Affiliation to the guidance (Av. *tkaesha*) of Ahura Mazda includes acknowledgement that Ahura Mazda is the source of all good, that praise and worship are due to the *amesha spentas*, and particular reverence given to *asha* (Y 12.1–3). The *Fravarane* acknowledges Zarathushtra as the epitome of Mazda worship: he is a paradigm for others who profess the same faith. Emulation of Zarathushtra involves aspiring to attain the close communion with Mazda that he is said to have experienced. Zarathushtra's 'conversations, meetings and discussions' with Mazda both reflected and strengthened his rejection of the *daevas* (Y 12.5). Zarathushtra's choice to follow the path of *Asha* and to reject the *daevas* and the way of the *dregvant* is also the chosen path of the Mazda-worshipper throughout the ages, from Vishtaspa, Frashaoshtra and Jamaspa, through all the *saoshyants:*

As a Mazda worshipper, like Zarathushtra I reject the way of the *daevas*, even as he, Asho Zarathushtra, has rejected them. (Y.12.7)

The phrase 'Asho Zarathushtra' is one used by Zoroastrians today to express their sense of cohesion with the choices made by Zarathushtra. As I was putting this book together, a Parsi friend who lives in the USA gently reminded me that it is common for Zoroastrians to refer to Zarathushtra using the epithet '*Asho*', meaning 'endowed with *asha*' – popularly translated as 'righteous' – since Zarathushtra is considered to be an embodiment of *asha*. My friend compared the use of this honorific title to the use of 'Christ' or 'Buddha', as a respectful reference to inspired leaders in other traditions. Like the founder figures of Christianity and Buddhism, Zarathushtra becomes a cipher through which revelation of a cosmic truth is transmitted to humanity. Unlike Christ, Zarathushtra is not considered to be divine, although he is admitted into the presence of the divine and is endowed with the wisdom of Mazda.

Christian missionary repudiation of the authority of Zarathushtra, as divinely inspired in his teachings and his works, prompted many Zoroastrians in the nineteenth century to evaluate their own status as a revealed religion. In response to John Wilson's castigations, Parsis claimed that the miracles of Zarathushtra were as authenticated as those of Christ, and began to speak of Zarathushtra in terms of the first 'prophetic revolutionary' to reveal the way to paradise, beginning the millennium that ended with the advent of Jesus.[2] From the Achaemenid period through to the Sasanians there is no iconography relating to Zarathushtra, but from the late nineteenth century onwards, an icon based on that of Mithra on a fourth-century CE Sasanian relief at Taq-e Bostan has been used (see Fig. 30).[3] An image on a third-century CE fresco from the Mithraeum at Dura Europos is popularly identified as 'Zoroaster', but this seems to be a representation of 'the Persian', which was one of the seven stages of initiation into Roman Mithraism.[4] Popular current iconography of Zarathushtra resembles Victorian Sunday School portraits of Christ, depicting him with a beard, flowing robe and halo, but in India, he is also often garlanded like a respected Hindu *swami*, or coroneted with a rayed nimbus.

The Zoroastrian conception of Zarathushtra today incorporates multiple identifications, and debate continues as to his person. The question that Nietzsche asks in his philosophical poem, *Also Sprach Zarathustra*, remain relevant to Zoroastrians today: 'Who is Zarathushtra to us? What shall we call him?' To paraphrase Nietzsche, in seeking the answer to those questions one could list the possibilities: A priest? A revolutionary prophet? An enlightened philosopher? A ritualist? A thaumaturge? A historical figure? A figment of faith?

Most Zoroastrians accept as a given that a person named Zarathushtra existed, and that the *Gathas* were the work of a single mind. Many scholars support this attribution, including philologists who have demonstrated the complex, interconnected nature of all Gathic composition. Recently, however, the historicity of Zarathushtra as sole author of the *Gathas* has been questioned by other philologists, who have focused on the lengthy period of oral transmission, and who consider Zarathushtra as the first to 'make heard' the 'poems of praise' (as in 1.29.8 and Y 57.7–8), but not the only one to perform them in public before they were finally written down. Such discussion reminds us that oral transmission relies on interaction and reaction between the person reciting and the receptive audience.

The actions of giving voice to and listening to the Gathic *manthras* are both praised as beneficent acts that promote *asha* (1.29.8 again). As the reciters and audience change, so those *manthras* will be transmitted and received in each time and place in a unique manner, just as each human being applies her or his own interpretation to the recital or reception of any inspirational piece of music. The diversity of approaches to the *Gathas* found among Zoroastrians today does not in any way diminish Zoroastrian allegiance to Zarathushtra as one whose innovative vision for the transformation of the world they choose to follow, and whose teachings and philosophy are ideal in addressing the discontent, restlessness and suffering of today.

Fig. 30. A late nineteenth-century representation of Zarathushtra.

Although the name 'Zarathushtra', within its Old Avestan context, is most readily translatable as 'owner of old camels', debate continues as to the meaning of the name.[5] It is popularly understood as 'He of the Golden Light'. This translation relates to the classical Greek version of the name, 'Zoroastres', which was understood to have a metaphysical meaning. As early as the fourth century BCE, both the Greek historian Dinon, and one of Plato's companions, Hermodorus, explained the name as signifying *astrothutes*, or 'star-diviner'; that is, one who makes offerings to the heavenly luminaries, or who foretells the future from stars.[6] This connection with that which is beyond in terms of time and space, whether an accurate reflection of the name or not, relates closely to the belief that Zarathushtra's cosmic and ethical vision was a turning point in history, which continues to illuminate the way forward for those who follow in his footsteps.

Zarathushtra Then

That there continues to be discussion concerning the translation of Zarathushtra's name reminds us that questions relating to the person of Zarathushtra continue to perplex. When the name 'Zarathushtra' is mentioned, which Zarathushtra is intended? The elusive Zarathushtra of the *Gathas*? The Zardosht of Middle Persian hagiography? Or the Zoroaster of European philosophers and textual exegetics? Can, or should, a reconstruction of the eponymous originator of the religious system be attempted?

This question was another reason for my reluctance to place Zarathushtra at the front and center in my analysis of the development of the religion. Just as the religion evolves, so the person of Zarathushtra can be seen to develop from the emblematic recipient of the Old Avestan *manthras*, until he is accorded the status of 'true Prophet, whose religion is brighter than the Sun', in an English translation of a Gujarati religious hymn in the late nineteenth century.

In both his *Zoroastrian Theology* (1914) and *History of Zoroastrianism* (1938), Dastur Dhalla traced the person of Zarathushtra from the Gathic period down to 'the revival' of the nineteenth century, maintaining that, although Zarathushtra's mission and teaching remained the same, aspects of his life were expanded upon or introduced as time progressed. The *Gathas*, unlike expressions of belief in many other religions, do not present a coherent picture of the one who first vocalized them. Only a few biographical details about Zarathushtra are contained, including several allusions to his family and to certain incidents in his life. Some of the chief characters of the *Gathas* recur in the *yashts*, but these hymns contain little reference to historical events and virtually nothing biographical. The person of Zarathushtra is then taken up and placed in an 'historical' context within the Zoroastrian mythology of space and time, such as is found in Middle Persian texts. In works concerning the life of Zarathushtra – the *Denkard* (particularly Book 7), *Bundahishn*, *Wizidagiha-i Zadspram* and the *Zand-i Wahman Yasn* – the *manthran* of the *Gathas* has been transformed into a mythic figure, and his personality magnified by miracles and heroic legends. These texts, along with the *Pahlavi Rivayat accompanying the Dadestan-i Denig*, celebrate such qualities of

Zarathushtra as 'wisdom', 'compassion' and 'the performance of good deeds'. He is perceived as one who advocated moderation – 'the right measure' (MP *payman*) – in all things, emphasizing justice and morality, rather than extremist revolutionary or ascetic behavior (PRDd 62.18).

The depiction of Zarathushtra in the Iranian national epic, the *Shah Nameh*, was instrumental in establishing his role as messenger of the faith and mentor to Kavi Vistaspa. The section relating the story of Zarathushtra appears to have been composed largely by the poet Daqiqi (d. c. 976), based on an earlier Middle Persian source. In the *Shah Nameh*, Zarathushtra is described as the one 'who killed Ahriman the maleficent' and who advocated wisdom and the religion of goodness, without which kingship is worthless. The thirteenth-century *Zardosht Nameh* (the 'Book of Zarathushtra'), which was also based on an earlier hagiography, has endured as the principal source of information and inspiration for Zoroastrians concerning Zarathushtra's birth, childhood and early promotion of the faith, culminating with the conversion of Vishtaspa. In *Zardosht Nameh*, Zarathushtra's biography is perceived as beginning long before his actual birth, incorporating the concept that Ahura Mazda pre-ordained his birth as a means of releasing the world from the grip of Angra Mainyu. Zarathushtra is said to issue from the 'glorious stock' of the ancient Kayanian king Feridun, and to have inherited the *farr* ('[divine] fortune or glory') through his mother, Dugdow. In this manner, Zarathushtra is portrayed as of equal standing to the heroic rulers of Iranian mythico-history, although his agency is spiritual.

While including much material found in earlier texts, *Zardosht Nameh* incorporates additional legends relating to the birth of Zarathushtra, and places particular emphasis on the miracles he performed as both a child and an adult. The narrative elaborates on the account of Zarathushtra's cure of Vishtaspa's favorite black horse, indicating that this incident was a crucial factor in persuading the king to convert. The fact that *Zardosht Nameh* was written in New Persian meant that it remained accessible to Zoroastrian laity in both Iran and India at a time when the Middle Persian texts were no longer comprehensible. Oral transmission of religious knowledge from generation to generation also continued to keep much of the tradition alive, particularly stories about Zarathushtra as an embodiment of actions and teachings that prescribe beliefs and practices.

The Persian *Rivayats* also provide some insight into the perception of Zarathushtra in both India and Iran between the fifteenth and eighteenth centuries. Zoroastrians in both countries venerated the *fravashi* of Zarathushtra on a daily basis through the *Yasna* liturgy, and each year the whole community commemorated the anniversary of his death.[7] A prevalent belief was that *Yasna* offerings in the name of Zarathushtra or 'other sainted dead persons' could counter the evil plots of enemies; rout demons (*divs*) and fairies (*peris*); oppose tyrannical rulers; withstand famine and disease; prevent the evil consequences of bad dreams; and secure various other advantages.[8]

External Perceptions

Zarathushtra's name and his centrality to the religion of the Ancient Persians probably became known to the Greeks through the *magi* in western Iran. Our earliest reference for the Greek name 'Zoroastres' is Xanthos of Lydia (mid-fifth century BCE), whom Diogenes Laertius later quotes in his *Lives of the Philosophers*. Xanthos places Zoroaster 6,000 years before Xerxes' expedition against the Greeks, and claims that he was succeeded by a large number of *magi*. Theopompus, in his *Philippika*, contained an excursus on *thaumasia*, or 'wondrous happenings', related to religious prophets including Zoroaster. The Greek sources are preoccupied with the connection between Zoroaster and their own ancient philosophers, as well as his association with astrology, 'magic' and mineralogy.

Classical texts, such as Pliny's *Natural History*, Porphyry's *Life of Pythagoras*, Clement of Alexandria's *Stromata* and Apuleius' *Florida*, which speak of Zoroaster as the instructor of the Greeks in philosophy, astrology, alchemy, theurgy and magic, appealed to early Renaissance clerics and scholars in their search for a more rounded picture of the created world and the sequence of historical progress than was provided by the Christian church of the time. During the Renaissance, these texts, studied in the original, became the sources of reference regarding the ancient world. Certain Christian scholars were greatly influenced by the Greek perception of Zoroaster as a figure of authority and wisdom, preceding the great philosopher, such as Pythagoras and Plato. Others perceived Zoroaster as a transforming magician, astronomer and alchemist. For some, the two facets were connected. This reinvented 'Zoroaster' was accorded authority as a humanist voice that addressed the dilemma of the age.

The trend to incorporate Zoroaster into existing schemes found pictorial expression in fifteenth- and sixteenth-century illustrations. When, in 2005, the British Library organized an exhibition on 'The Image of Zoroaster' to run simultaneously with that of the British Museum's 'Forgotten Empire: The World of Ancient Persia', one of the two medieval pictorial depictions of Zoroaster on display was by Cotton Augustus, dated 1475–80. This painting showed Zoroaster as founder of the seven liberal arts. Raphael's well-known 'School of Athens' fresco (c. 1511) in the Vatican is thought to incorporate Zoroaster among the geometrists and astrologers on the right side of the scene. The figure assumed to be Zoroaster faces forward, holding a celestial sphere, while Ptolemy, with his back to the viewer, holds the sphere of the earth.

Europeans often saw in Zoroaster an 'Eastern' alternative to the perceived rigidity of existing tradition. This perspective continued through Mozart's protagonist Sarastro in 'The Magic Flute', to the Zarathustra of Nietzsche's philosophical poem. In the *Oberdeutsche Staatszeitung* of Salzburg on 23 March 1786, an intriguing anecdote describes how a masquerader, dressed in the guise of 'an Eastern philosopher', distributed portions from 'Zoroaster's Fragments', printed for the edification of the revelers. Mozart's letters of the same period reveal that he was the masked figure, and the leaflet a pseudonymous treatise of his own invention. This action on Mozart's part highlights not only the general interest in 'Iranian philosophy' during the late eighteenth century, but also the manipulation of the image of Zoroaster for the purposes of the dissemination of 'wisdom'.

The character of Sarastro exhibits many of the features associated with Zoroaster and the Magi at the time the libretto for 'The Magic Flute' was written. These ancient Iranian sages held particular appeal for European Freemasons, who were engaged in the intellectual exploration and application of universal moral themes. Towards the end of the seventeenth century, the higher degrees introduced into European masonry included a notable amount of Zoroastrian symbolism.

Just before his death, Voltaire (1694–1778), who once wrote 'On parle beaucoup de Zoroastre et on en parlera encore' ('Much is said about Zoroaster, and more will be said in the future'), was introduced to a Masonic lodge in Paris by the American activist, Benjamin Franklin (1706–90). Franklin had already encountered Zoroaster as the source of 'a nice Morality'. In a letter sent from London on 13 January 1772, to Ezra Stiles (President of Yale, 1778–95), Franklin recommended the purchase of the work entitled '*Zend-Avesta*, or the *Writings of Zoroaster*', containing 'the Theological, Philosophical and Moral Ideas of that Legislator and the Ceremonies of Religious Worship that he established'.[9] This was a reference to the recently translated publication by Anquétil Duperron. In a postscript, Franklin added that a Mr Marchant, understanding that Stiles was curious 'on the Subject of Eastern ancient Religions', would send him the book. Franklin went on to become one of the Founding Fathers of the USA.

Such influential literati, from Franklin and Voltaire, through the German and English Romantic poets to Nietzsche, were attracted to Zoroaster as a kind of archetypal *übermensch*. It was Friedrich Nietzsche (1844–1900) who, towards the end of the nineteenth century, brought Zarathushtra once more to the forefront of public attention. Nietzsche's work represents the confluence of early European – that is, classically-based sources with the newly accessible Zoroastrian texts, in particular the *Gathas*. The resulting appropriation of 'Zarathustra' retains some memetic connection with the original, not just in his name, but in connection with his morality. Nietzsche declared that the 'Persian' Zarathushtra's unique contribution to history was that he 'was the first to see in the struggle between good and evil the actual wheel in the working of things; the translation of morality into the realm of metaphysics, as force, cause, end-in-itself, is his work'.[10] For Nietzsche, however, this understanding of value opposition was an error that *his* Zarathushtra had come to correct.

There is sufficient material in the text of *Also Sprach Zarathustra* to indicate that Nietzsche was familiar with Zoroastrian accounts of the life of the prophet, and of Zoroastrian cosmology.[11] Millennial eschatological motifs familiar from Middle Persian Zoroastrian texts are also present in the concepts of 'the thousand-year Zarathushtra kingdom', the use of the word *hazar* (the Persian word for a thousand) and the immanence of 'the great noontide', when Zarathushtra will be with humans 'a third time' to celebrate.

Nietzsche's Zarathustra, as with all 'outsider' appropriations of the image, is not the Zarathushtra that belongs to the Zoroastrians. Zoroastrians are now attempting to reclaim their own source of 'authority' in the person of Zarathushtra. Such reclamation of the image of Zarathushtra can be literal, as in a recent case where Zoroastrians in Melbourne, Australia, garnered support through the Internet from other Zoroastrians around the world, to persuade a local art gallery to modify the title of a massive bronze nude male sculpture from 'Zarathustra' to 'Thus Spake Zarathustra'.[12] In this instance, although many Zoroastrians were affronted by this depiction, others were not offended, and viewed the sculpture as an aesthetic piece or as a work that had little or nothing to do with their own faith position. The range of reactions reminds us that Zoroastrians tend to address those two questions posed by Nietzsche – 'Who is Zarathushtra to us? What shall we call him?' – in individual, rather than global terms. Each carves her or his own understanding of what it means to be *Zarathushtri* – 'like Zoroaster' – and retains thereby a deeply personal approach to the religion that bears Zarathushtra's name.

Appendix 1

Textual Timeline

Old Avestan	**mid to late second millennium BCE**
Gathas	(oral transmission)
Yasna Haptanghaiti	
OAv. Prayers	

Young Avestan	**early to mid-first millennium BCE**
YAv. parts of the *Yasna*	(oral transmission)
Videvdad (*Vendidad*)	
Visperad	
Yashts	
Khordeh Avesta	
Hadokht Nask	
Herbadestan	
Nerangestan	sixth/seventh century CE,

Avestan corpus written down

Old Persian   **late sixth–fourth centuries BCE**

Cuneiform
inscriptions

Middle Persian   **300–1000 CE**

Middle Persian
Inscriptions

Zoroastrian Middle Persian texts, including:

Ayadgar-i Zareran

Arda Wiraz Namag

Bundahishn   Most Zoroastrian texts written down c. ninth century
                                CE after a long oral transmission

*Chidag Andarz-i
Poryotkeshan*

Dadestan-i Denig

Denkard

*Karnamag-i
Ardashir-i Papagan*

*Madayan-i Hazar
Dadestan*

Menog-i Xrad

*Phl. Riv. Dadestan-i
Denig*

*Shkand Gumanig
Wizar*

*Wizidagiha-i
Zadspram*

*Zand-i Wahman
Yasn*

New Persian **1000 CE–present**

Shah Nameh

Zardosht Nameh

Persian Rivayats

Ulama-i Islam

Qesse-ye Sanjan

Appendix 2

The Five *Gathas*

Each of the five *Gathas* is named after its opening words.

1 Ahunavaiti *Gatha*

Haiti 1–7 (Yasna 28–34)

2 Ushtavaiti *Gatha*

Haiti 8–11 (Yasna 43–6)

3 Spentamanyu *Gatha*

Haiti 12–15 (Yasna 47–50)

4 Vohuxshathra *Gatha*

Haiti 16 (Yasna 51)

5 Vahishtoishti *Gatha*

Haiti 17 (Yasna 53)

Throughout the text of this book, any reference to verses from the *Gathas* includes both their current placement within the *Yasna*, the 72-section Zoroastrian liturgy, as well as their numbering according to each of the five consecutive poems.

Most translations do not, however, include the fivefold division, so the second number indicates the more familiar placement of each Gathic *haiti* within the *Yasna*.

Appendix 3

Outline of the *Yasna*

Yasna 1	Invocation to Ahura Mazda, *amesha spentas* and *yazatas*
Yasna 2	*Barsom Yasht*: the litany to *barsom*
Yasna 3–4	*Dron* ritual: consecration of sacred bread
Yasna 5	Prayer (over food)
Yasna 6	Dedications to *Sraosha*, to *fravashi* of Zarathushtra, and to fire
Yasna 7–8	Prayer extolling the *Ahuna Vairya manthra*. Fire fed with sandalwood and frankincense. *Zot* (chief officiating priest) eats *dron* dipped in ghee.

Yasna 9–13   Hom Ritual

Yasna 9–11	*Hom Yasht*: litany to *hom*, ends with drinking of *parahom*
Yasna 12	*Fravarane* ('Confession of Faith')

Yasna 13	Invocations

Yasna 14–59	***Staota Yasnya*; (words of) 'worship and praise'**

Yasna 14–18	Invocations
Yasna 19–21	*Bagan Yasht* ('Praise to the Prayers')
Yasna 22–27.11	Praises to all the elements of the ritual. *Hom*-pounding
Yasna 27.11–34	*Ahuna Vairya, Ashem Vohu* and *Yenghe Hatam manthras*

Yasna 28–34	*Ahunavaiti Gatha*
Yasna 35–41	*Yasna Haptanghaiti*
Yasna 42	Praise for the *amesha spentas* and the elements of creation
Yasna 43–6	*Ushtavaiti Gatha*
Yasna 47–50	*Spenta.Mainyu Gatha*
Yasna 51	*Vohuxshathra Gatha*
Yasna 52	Prayer of blessings to all of creation
Yasna 53	*Vahishtoishti Gatha*
Yasna 54	*A Airyema Ishyo prayer*

Yasna 55	In Praise of the *Gathas*
Yasna 56–7	Litanies to *Sraosha*
Yasna 58	*Fshusho Manthra.* Prayer for protection against evil, and praise of Ahura Mazda, the *amesha spentas*, Fire and the *Staota Yesnya*
Yasna 59	repeats Y 17 and 26
Yasna 60–1	Blessings on the house of the *ashavan*, praise of the three sacred *manthras*
Yasna 62	Praise of Fire (*Atash Niyayish*)
Yasna 63–70	Praise to and consecration of water for *ab zohr* (Y 65 *Aban Nyayish*)
Yasna 70–2	Concluding invocations and prayers; *ab zohr* poured into the well

For detailed descriptions of the *Yasna* ceremony in Parsi and Iranian Zoroastrian contexts respectively, see F.M. Kotwal and J.W. Boyd, *A Persian Offering. The Yasna: A Zoroastrian High Liturgy*, Studia Iranica 8, Paris: Association pour l'avancement des etudes iraniennes, 1991; and M.M.J. Fisher, *Mute Dreams, Blind Owls, and Dispersed Knowledges: Persian Poesis in the Transnational Circuitry*, Durham, NC and London: Duke University Press, 2004: 25–65.

Appendix 4

A Selective Historical Timeline

c. 1500 BCE Iranians in Central Asia/northern Afghanistan

Ninth century BCE Persians and Medes in (north)western Iran

c. 550–330 The Achaemenid Empire

539 Cyrus II (the Great) captures Babylon

522–486 Darius I

515 New Temple dedicated in Jerusalem

472 Aeschylus' play *The Persians* is staged in Athens

486–465 Xerxes

465–424 Artaxerxes I: time of Nehemiah and Ezra

c. 430–425 Herodotus' *Histories*

404–358 Artaxerxes II – Xenophon: *Anabasis, Cyropaedia*

334–330 BCE Alexander overthrows Achaemenids

312 Seleucid Dynasty founded

305–280 Seleucus, king of Persia

c. 270-231 Ashoka, ruler of Buddhist Maurya Empire

c. 247 BCE–224 CE Arsacid (Parthian) Empire

171–139/8 BCE Mithradates I

c. 123–70 BCE Mithradates II

c. 57–38 BCE Orodes II; death of Crassus 53 BCE

c. 63 BCE–24 CE Strabo: *Geography*

c. 40–51 CE Godarz II

c. 37–100 Josephus: *Antiquities*

46–120 CE Plutarch: *Life of Crassus, On Isis and Osiris*

51–78 CE Valakhsh I

c. 78–105 CE Pacorus

105–47 CE Valakhsh III

213–24 CE Ardavan V

216 Mani born

224–651 CE Sasanian Empire

224–c. 240 CE Ardashir I

c. 240–72 Shapur I; Kerdir rises to power

274–6 Bahram I

276–93 Bahram II; Kerdir at the peak of his power

293–302 Narseh

309–79 Shapur II

420–38 Bahram V

438–57 Yazdegird II

531–79 Khosrow I

b. c. 532 Agathias, *Histories*

590–628 Khosrow II

632–51 Yazdegird III

Islamic Rule in Iran

661–750 CE Umayyads

750–1258 Abbasids

892–1005 Samanids rule in northeastern Iran/Sogdiana

934–1055 Buyids rule in Fars

997–1040 Ghaznavids rule in northeastern Iran

1040–1157 Seljuqs rule in Central Asia and Iran

1258–1368 Mongols

1368–1506 Timurid dynasty

1502–24 Safavid dynasty

1736–47 Nader Shah

1750–94 Zand dynasty

1779–1924 Qajar dynasty

1925–79 Pahlavi dynasty

1979 Islamic Republic of Iran

1526–1707 Mughal Rule in India

1556–1605 Akbar

1612–1757 British East India Company active in India

1757–1857 BEIC rule in India

1858–1947 British Raj in India

1947 Indian Independence

Glossary of Names and Terms

aban	the waters
ab zohr	libation to the waters
Adurbad-i Mahraspandan	high priest under the Sasanian king, Shapur II
afarganyu	(PGuj.; also *afrinagan*) 'fire vase'
afrinagan	ceremony; a ceremony of blessing
agiary	(PGuj.) fire temple
Ahura Mazda	the 'Wise Lord'
Airyaman	*yazata* of 'friendship'
Ameretat	'immortality'or 'continuity of life'. One of the *amesha spentas*
amesha spentas	the 'beneficent immortals'
Anahita	female *yazata* of the benevolent waters
Angra Mainyu	(MP *Ahriman*) the 'destructive impulse/spirit'
anjuman	association, 'community'
aramgah	literally 'place of peace'; cemetery

Armaiti	'right-mindedness'. One of the seven *amesha spentas*
Asha	'order', 'right', 'truth'. One of the seven *amesha spentas*
ashavan	one who follows *Asha*
astodan	'bone holder', ossuary
Astvat-ereta	'he who embodies *asha*'. The name of the final *saoshyant*
Atash Adaran	second grade of ritual fire in fire temples
Atash Bahram	highest grade of fire; name of 'cathedral' fire temple
Atash Dadgah	third and lowest grade of fire, can be in a house or minor fire temple
atashkadeh	'house of fire'. Iranian term for fire temple
Avesta	corpus of sacred texts of the Zoroastrians
Azi Dahaka	'snake' or 'dragon Dahaka', of Avestan and later myth
bareshnum	nine-night ritual of ablution and purification
baresman/barsom	the twigs or metal rods held by the priests in ritual
baug	a place where weddings or initiations are celebrated; a Parsi housing estate
behdin	(MP *weh den*) of the 'good religion'
chaharom	the rituals on the fourth day after death
chahartaq	'four arched' edifice within which stood a fire-holder
chinvat peretu	'crossing-place of the account-keeper', the bridge where the soul is judged at death
daena	(MP *den*) [religious] insight; religion

daeva	(OAv.; OP *daiva*) 'false/erroneous god'; (MP *dev*, NP *div*), 'demon'
dakhma	site of exposure of the dead – 'tower of silence'
dakhmenashini	system of exposure in a *dakhma*
Dar-i Mihr	'Gate' or 'Court' of Mithra; a fire temple
dastur	highest rank of priest
dregvant	one who follows *druj*
drigu	(OAv.) 'poor'
dron (*darun*)	flat unleavened wheat bread consecrated by the priest
druj	(OAv.) deceit, chaos, confusion
Farvardin	month name
Ferdowsi	composer of *Shah Nameh*
Feridun	(Av. *Thraetaona*) Iranian mythical hero
frasha	(Av.) 'wonderful', 'perfect'; OP 'excellent'
frasho.kereti	(MP *frashegird*) 'the making wonderful/perfect' of the world; the renovation
Fravardigan	(*Farvardigan*) festival commemorating the *fravashis*
fravashi	the 'pre-soul' that pre-exists and post-exists the individual, and is venerated as efficacious on behalf of the living
gahanbar	one of six seasonal festivals
garo.demana	(YAv. *garo.nmana*, MP *garodman*) 'house of song'

Gathas	The Old Avestan 'songs' of Zarathushtra
Gaya maretan	the primal mortal
getig	(MP) the corporeal world
hambandagi	'bondedness together'; communal prayer
haoma	(MP *hom*) the beneficent plant pressed during the *Yasna*, and offered with milk and water as *ab zohr* at the end of the liturgy
Haurvatat	one of the *amesha spentas*: 'wholeness' or 'health', associated with the waters
herbad	'religious teacher'; now, priest who has completed the first level of training (*navar*)
Ilm-i Khshnoom	'knowledge of spiritual satisfaction'; an esoteric interpretation of Zoroastrian texts and rituals
imamzadeh	shrine to a deceased descendant of a Shi'a *imam*
jashan	ceremony of praise or thanksgiving
jizya	poll tax on non-Muslims
jud den/juddin	a non-Zoroastrian
Kayanian	the second mythological dynasty of Iranian kings
Kerdir	a powerful priest under several early Sasanian monarchs
Keresaspa	ancient Iranian mythical hero
Khordad Sal	sixth day of Farvardin month, birthday of Asho Zarathushtra
Khordeh Avesta	prayer book

kusti	woven cord of wool (usually lamb, but can be camel or goat hair) made of 72 threads; tied around the waist over the *sudreh* after initiation
loban	incense
lork	(NP) the festival food of seven kinds of dried fruits, dates, chickpeas and nuts, which are eaten at the end of the *gahanbar* prayers
magu-	(OP) 'priest'
manthra	powerful word or prayer
menog	(MP) 'conceptual' existence
Mihragan	a seasonal celebration in honor of *Mithra*, held in the autumn
Mithra	(MP *Mihr*) 'bond'; male *yazata* of the contract
mobedyar	lay helper to the priest, functions as priest in Iran
mowbed	(MP: NP *mobed*) priest
Muktad	Parsi celebration before *Nav Ruz* (equivalent to Iranian *Fravardigan*)
najes	Arabic term referring to anything that is impure
nask	'bundle': refers to the 21 collections of Avestan texts
nasu	(Av.) 'dead matter'
navar	first grade of ordination as a Parsi priest
navjote	(PGuj.) 'initiation'
Nav Ruz	'New Day', Zoroastrian New Year
Nerangestan	an Avestan text on priestly ritual, with an MP exegesis

nirang	consecrated bull's urine; a formulaic prayer
Ohrmazd	(MP) Ahura Mazda
padan	(Av. *paitidana*) mouth covering worn by priest before the fire
padyab	washing of hands and face
panthak	(PGuj.) jurisdiction of Parsi priest
Pazand	Middle Persian texts transcribed into Avestan
Pishdadian	the first mythological dynasty of Iranian kings
Rivayats	(Persian) correspondence sent from Iranian Zoroastrians to Parsis between the fifteenth and eighteenth centuries
Rostam	an eastern Iranian heroic figure, whose stories appear in *Shah Nameh*
saoshyant	'one who will be strong'
sedreh-pushi	Iranian Zoroastrian term for initiation
Shah Nameh	Iranian national epic, composed by Ferdowsi, late tenth–early eleventh century CE
Siyavush	a heroic figure in *Shah Nameh*
spenta	(Av.) 'bringing increase'
Spenta Mainyu	'beneficent inspiration/spirit'. One of the *amesha spentas*
Sraosha	(MP *Srosh*) 'readiness to listen'; a *yazata*
sudreh	white cotton shirt invested during initiation
Suren	Parthian noble family; Parthian general who defeated Crassus

Tirgan	festival dedicated to *Tishtrya*, held in midsummer
Tishtrya	male *yazata* of water, fertility
Tosar	priest under the Sasanian king, Ardashir I
varasyo	consecrated white bull
Videvdad/Vendidad	YAv. text
Vohu Manah	'good thought'. One of the *amesha spentas*
weh den (MP)	'good religion'
Xshathra Vairya	'desired rule'. One of the *amesha spentas*
xwarenah	(MP *xwarrah*, NP *farr*) '[divine] fortune or glory'
Yasht	Young Avestan hymns to the *yazatas*
Yasna	(Av.) 'worship/consecration': term used for the liturgy and its Avestan text
yazata	(MP *yazad*) being 'worthy of worship'
Zahak	(Av. *Azi Dahaka*) evil king in ancient Iranian myth and *Shah Nameh*
zand	exegesis, commentary on the Avesta
zandik	interpreter; revisionist
zaothra	(MP *zohr*) libation

Illustration, Map and Picture Credits

Map showing the main places mentioned from different historical eras.
All maps redrawn by Adrian Roots from originals supplied by Jenny Rose

Chorasmian and Sogdian sites, fourth–ninth centuries CE.

. Map showing cities in North America with Zoroastrian groups or associations, and *Dar-i Mihrs*. Based on information from *FEZANA Journal* (Winter 2004), 55–59.

1.*Gahanbar* celebration in the community prayer hall, Mazra-ye Kalantar, Yazd province, Iran.
Copyright © Jenny Rose

2. *Navjote* (initiation) ceremony attended during the author's first visit to Bombay in 1987.
Copyright © Jenny Rose

3. Diagram of the 'two worlds' and the 'two forces'.
Copyright © Jenny Rose

4. Diagram of the 'three times' and the 'turning point'.
Copyright © Jenny Rose

5. King standing before the fire-holder, with the winged figure overhead. Above the tomb of one of the Ancient Persian kings, Naqsh-e Rostam.
Copyright © Jenny Rose

5. One of the two fire plinths at Pasargadae.
Copyright © Jenny Rose

7. Two priests in front of a tomb. Funerary stele, Daskyleion. Istanbul Archaeology Museum.
Copyright © Jenny Rose

8. The Tomb of Cyrus, Pasargadae.
Copyright © Jenny Rose

9. Seleucid-era relief of magus holding *barsom*, Dokhan-e Davoud,

Kermanshah.
Copyright © Jenny Rose

10. Relief of a mounted Parthian king, Godarz II (c. 40–51 CE), offering the ring of power to a local ruler.
Copyright © Jenny Rose

11. Plan of fire temple, Mele Hairam.
Copyright © Barbara Kaim

12. Relief depicting an offering to fire (*atash zohr*), Bisutun.
Copyright © Jenny Rose

13. Investiture of Ardashir I by Ohrmazd, Naqsh-e Rostam.
Copyright © Jenny Rose

14. Silver coin of Ardashir I, inscribed 'Fire of Ardashir'.
Copyright © Keyvan Safdari

15. Kerdir, Naqsh-e Rajab.
Copyright © Jenny Rose

16. Sasanian fire-holder from Bishapur.
Copyright © Jenny Rose

17. Ossuary, Mulla Kurgan.
Copyright © Frantz Grenet

18. Varakhsha fresco, Bukhara Museum, Uzbekistan.
Copyright © Jenny Rose

19. The Sogdian *Ashem Vohu*.
Copyright © The British Library Board Or 8212/84

20. Panel from a Sogdian funerary couch.
Copyright © Miho Museum, 2009

21. Bird-priest, Wirkak's sarcophagus.
Courtesy, Judith A. Lerner

22. Drawing of East Wall of Wirkak's sarcophagus.
Courtesy, Judith A. Lerner

23. *Dakhma* at Cham, Yazd province, Iran.
Copyright © Jenny Rose

24. Pir-e Sabz shrine and sheltered area for pilgrims, Yazd province, Iran.
Copyright © Jenny Rose

25. The upper façade of the Atash Bahram in Yazd.
Copyright © Jenny Rose

26. Shereen Khorshid Boga, the author's grandmother.
Copyright © Jenny Rose

27. Cusrow Baug Agiary, Mumbai.
Copyright © Jenny Rose

28. Map showing the 'spread of the Avesta' from Khiva. Avesta Museum, Khiva.
Copyright © Jenny Rose

29. Three generations of priests.
Copyright © Poras Balsara

30. A late nineteenth-century representation of Zarathushtra.

Notes

Introduction

1   For a recent survey of Zoroastrian scholarship, see M. Stausberg, 'On the State and Prospects of the Study of Zoroastrianism', *Numen* 55 (2008): 561–600.

2   Dk. 6.259.

3   For a discussion of the use of the term 'diaspora' in relation to the Zoroastrians, see J. Hinnells (2005), 18; and M. Stausberg, 'Para-Zoroastrianisms', in Hinnells and Williams (2007), 236.

Chapter 1 Zoroastrians Present and Past

1   For an explanation as to how to read this enumeration of the *Gathas*, see Appendix 2.

2   J.A.L. Lemay (ed.), *Benjamin Franklin: Writings*, New York: Library of America (1987), 675.

3   For the origins, meaning and practical expression of *hambandagih* (also written *humbandagi*), see M. Stausberg, 'Monday Nights at the Banaji, Fridays at the Aslaji', in Stausberg (2004), 700.

4   A 'priest's assistant'; that is, someone from a non-priestly family, who functions as a priest.

5   MX 4.5, 57.13.

6   Dhabhar (1999), 541.

7   Dk 3.263.

8   CK 26–8, also Dk. 5.24. CK is a Middle Persian text that survives in *Pazand*; that is, transcribed into Avestan alphabet. See H. Junker, *Der wissbegierige Sohn. Ein mittelpersischer Text über das Kustik,* Leipzig: Harrassowitz (1959); also M. Stausberg, 'The Significance of the *kusti:* A History of Its Zoroastrian Interpretation', *East and West* 54/1 (2005), 9–30.

9 The impact of this ruling is discussed in Chapter VII.

10 Fischer (2004), 25.

11 For succinct summaries of recent approaches to and analyses of key terms in the *Gathas*, see Shaked, 'The Iranian Canon of Scriptures', in Vahman and Pedersen (2007), 1–24; and P.O. Skjaervø, 'The State of Old Avestan Scholarship', *JAOS 117/1* (1997), 103–14.

12 cf. Yt 13.143–4. The identification of Ragha in *Videvdad* with Rayy, to the south of Tehran, remains disputed.

13 ShE 4; see T. Daryaee, trans. and comm., *Šahrestānīhā-ī Erānšahr: A Middle Persian Text on Late Antique Geography, Epic, and History*, Costa Mesa, CA: Mazda (2002).

14 A. Hintze, 'The Migrations of the Indo-Iranians and the Iranian Sound-Change s>h', in *Sprache und Kultur der Indogermanen*, Innsbrucker Beiträge zur Sprachwissenschaft: Innsbruck (1998), 140–53; 143f. See also J.P. Mallory, 'Archaeological Models', in Sims-Williams (2004), 31.

15 A. Parpola, 'Proto-Indo-Aryan and Proto-Iranian', in Sims-Williams (2004), 43–102; 69.

16 Parpola, 'Proto-Indo-Aryan', 68.

17 See P.O. Skjaervø, 'Iran. vi. Iranian Languages and Scripts', *Encyclopaedia Iranica XIII/3* (2006), 34–77.

18 For a detailed exploration of such complexities, see M. Schwartz, 'How Zarathushtra Generated the Gathic Corpus: Inner-textual and Intertextual Composition', in *Bulletin of the Asia Institute* 16 (December 2006), 53–64; also A. Hintze, 'On the literary structure of the Older Avesta', *Bulletin of the School of Oriental and African Studies* 65 (2002), 31–51; and H-P. Schmidt, with contributions by W. Lentz and S. Insler, *Form and Meaning of Yasna 33*, New Haven: American Oriental Society, 1985.

19 Cognate with OI *asura*, 'lord', an epithet used of both Varuna and Indra in the *Rig Veda*, as well as other divinities.

20 2.46.14, 4.51.16, 5.53.2.

21 RV 1.10.129 speaks of *kavis*, who 'seek in their hearts with wisdom'.

22 For detailed analysis of *Yasna Haptanghaiti*, see Hintze (2007).

23 Another verbal root *zao* can mean 'to call' or 'to invoke', but the noun is *zbatar*. Zarathushtra is referred to as *athaurvan* in a couple of Young Avestan texts (Yt 13.88, 94, Yt 19.53), and the term is used generally elsewhere (cf. Vd 8.19). It was originally thought to incorporate the

Iranian *atar* meaning 'fire', but the function was not linked with fire, and is thought to be a general term for 'priest'; see A. Hintze, 'Disseminating the Mazdayasnian Religion', in W. Sundermann *et al.* (eds), *Exegisti monumenta; Festschrift in Honour of Nicholas Sims-Williams*, Wiesbaden: Harrassowitz (2009), 171–90; 175–79.

24 1.31.12; 1.33.5, 1.34.12; 1.28.1; 1.34.10.

25 1.28.1–2; 2.43.3; 3.48.11; 2.44.18, 2.45.5.

26 2.45.5; YH 37.3.

27 1.34.5; 1.27.13.

28 1.27.13; 5.53.9.

29 Cf. Dk. 6.141–6, 281, 292, 310 (MP *driyos*). In Sogdian Christian, Manichean and Buddhist texts, cognate terms mean 'disciple'. NP *darvish* can refer to both a poor person and a member of a Sufi order.

30 1.30.6; cf. Yt 13.89–90.

31 cf. 2.45.4, 1.31.8.

32 1.30.9, 1.31.4.

33 1.34.4, 2.43.4.

34 2.44.6, 2.46.12.

35 YH 37.2, YH 39.3.

36 Cf. Yt 15.43.

37 2.46.11, 4.51.13.

38 2.43.5.

39 2.43.4, 3.47.6; 4.51.9, 1.32.7.

40 4.51.15; YAv *garo.nmana*. Some scholars prefer to translate this as 'house of welcome'; see, for instance, J. Kellens, *Les noms-racines de l'Avesta*, Wiesbaden: Reichert (1974), 27–9.

41 1.32.15; 3.47.5.

42 Cf. Yt 12.35–6.

43 1.31.19; 2.44.2, 16.

44 3.49.11.

45 4.51.14, 1.31.20.

46 1.30.10; 1.31.18; 5.53.9.

47 1.30.4; 1.31.20.

48 Cf. 3.50.11, 2.44.2.

49 For example, see 1.31.6, 1.34.11, 2.44.17.

50 3.50.7.

51 See 2.45.1 and 1.29.8 respectively.

52 See, for instance, P.O. Skjaervø (2008) 117–133.

53 See, for instance, P.O. Skjaervø (2005), 22.

54 3.48.11–12.

55 3.48.9, 2.45.11, 5.53.2.

56 3.48.12, 1.34.13, 2.46.3.

57 22 if *Srosh yasht* is included.

58 Yt 10.5; 79–80; 28, 30.

59 Yt 10.13, 51, 82.

60 Yt 10.93.

61 For example, Yt 9.30–1; 19.87.

62 Vd 19. 1–10, 43–7.

63 Vd 21.4; 5.19; Yt 12.17.

64 Yt 19.1f.

65 Cf. Vd 6.3–9, 26–41.

66 Unconsecrated bull's urine (*gomez*) appears as a ritual 'cleansing' agent in various Zoroastrian texts. The Hindus also use cow urine in some purification rituals.

67 Vd 3.10, 14.5–6; cf. 1.34.9.

68 Vd 3.15–23.

69 Vd 19.27, HN 2.1, 3, 5. For a translation of the *Hadokht Nask*, see J. Darmesteter, trans., *The Zend Avesta Part II* (Sacred Books of the East 23), Oxford: Oxford University Press, 1882; rep. (1965).

70 HN 2.15.

71 HN 2.11.

72 Vd 13.9.

73 HN 2.33.

74 Yt 19.67.

75 Yt 19.89–96; Y 70.4.

76 Yt 13.142; Yt 19.94.

77 Yt. 19.35–8.

78 Y.9.3–5. This is how old the hypostatized thoughts, words and deeds of the *ashavan* appears at the Chinvat crossing (HN 2.9).

79 *ashaunam fravashaiio*; Yt. 13.145. See also YH 37.1.

80 D.F. Karaka, *History of the Parsis*, Vol. 1, New Delhi: Cosmo, rep. (1999), 151.

Chapter II The Ancient Persians: Truth-Tellers and Paradise-Builders

1 P.O. Skjaervø, 'The Achaemenids in the Avesta', Curtis and Stewart (2005), 52–84; 63.

2 W.R.M. Lamb (trans.), *Plato, Vol. 8*, Cambridge, MA: Harvard University Press; London, William Heinemann Ltd (1955) [Perseus online]

3 For this, see Briant (2005) and Wiesehöfer (1996).

4 See Skjaervø, 'The Achaemenids'; De Jong (1997); and A.S. Shahbazi, 'Persepolis and the Avesta', *Archaeologische Mitteilungen aus Iran* 27 (1994), 85–90.

5 See, for instance, D. Stronach and M. Roaf, *Tepe Nush-i Jan 1: The Major Buildings of the Median settlement*, London: BIPS and Leuven: Peeters, 2007.

6 See Yt 17.16; Y 70.1.

7 Cf. 2.46.17; 4.51.18; Yt. 5.68.

8 Xenophon, *Cyropaedia* 8.4

9 Plutarch, *Life of Artaxerxes*, 11.

10 Diogenes Laertius, *Lives of the Philosophers*, 3.25.

11 J. Tavernier, 'Iranica in the Achaemenid Period', *Orientalia Lovaniensia Analecta 158* (2007), 334, 343.

12 Eumanes lived in Hieracome, later known as Hierocaesarea, a site mentioned by Pausanias as the location of a temple to the 'Persian Artemis' (Pausanias, 7.6.6).

13 Cf. Yt 13.53.

14 Herodotus, *Histories* 3.90; Diodorus Siculus, *Library of History*, 17.77.5.

15 Yt 8.8.

16 Xenophon, *Anabasis* 4.5.24, 35.

17 Skjaervø, 'The Achaemenids', 53.

18 See A. Hintze, 'The Greek and Hebrew versions of the Book of Esther and Its Iranian Background', in S. Shaked and A. Netzer (eds), *Irano-Judaica III*, Jerusalem: Ben-Zvi Institute (1994), 34–9.

19 The connection of Jamshid with *Nav Ruz* may provide a clue as to the later designation of the title 'Takht-e Jamshid' (*Throne of Jamshid*) for Persepolis.

20 B. Lincoln, 'A la recherche du paradis perdu', *History of Religions 43/2* (2003), 139–54, 145.

21 Skjaervø (1999), 38.

22 Diogenes Laertius, *Lives of the Philosophers*, 1.8.

23 Ibid.

24 See, for instance, M.L. West, *Early Greek Philosophy and the Orient*, Oxford: Clarendon Press, rep. (2002), 111–202.

25 *Natural History*, 30.3.

26 Plutarch, *On Isis and Osiris*, 47.

27 See P. Kreyenbroek, 'Millennialism and eschatology in the Zoroastrian tradition', in A. Amanat and M. Bernhardsson (eds), *Imagining the End*, London, New York: I.B.Tauris (2002), 33–55; 50.

28 See, for instance, A. de Jong, 'The Contributions of the Magi', in Curtis and Stewart (2005), 85–95; 94.

29 Bd. 1.28: 'three thousand years will pass according to the will of Ohrmazd; three thousand years in the mingled state, according to the will of [both] Ohrmazd and Ahriman; and, in the final contest the Evil Spirit [will be rendered] useless.' See Chapter IV for a more detailed outline of this scheme.

30 *Anabasis* 9.11, 13, 16.

31 An article in *Der Spiegel* of 15 July 2008, entitled 'Falling for Ancient Propaganda: UN Treasure Honors Persian Despot', prompted many Iranians to rush to the defence of Cyrus. As early as the second millennium BCE, the law code inscribed on the basalt stele of the Old

Babylonian king, Hammurabi, provided a system of legal recourse for rich and poor, free and enslaved Babylonian subjects.

32 For a recent translation of the whole cylinder, see http://www.british-museum.org/explore/highlights/article_index/c/cyrus_cylinder_translation.

33 Nabonidus had pledged to restore the temple of Sin at Harran, and Esarhaddon to rebuild Babylon; E.J. Bickerman, *Studies in Jewish and Christian History* 1, Leiden: Brill (1976), 76.

34 The Book of Ezra is usually ascribed to the time of Artaxerxes I (465–424 BCE), which would place Ezra's return in 458 BCE; if it is Artaxerxes II, then the events are about 60 years later. Ezra contains an edict similar to that of the Cyrus cylinder (*Ezra* 1.1–4, 6.1–5), indicating that such propaganda may have been disseminated in many languages.

35 See B.A. Strawn, 'A World Under Control: Isaiah 60 and the Apadana Reliefs from Persepolis', in J.L. Berquist (ed.), *Approaching Yehud: New Approaches to the Study of the Persian Period*, Atlanta: Society of Biblical Literature (2007), 85–116.

36 DNb 40–5, 6–8.

37 E. Voegelin, *Order and History Volume III: Plato and Aristotle*, ed. D. Germino, Columbia and London: University of Missouri Press (2000), 339, 343.

38 Herodotus also specifies that the water was 'bitter and salty', both qualities which, in excess, are later associated with killing, rather than nurturing, life; Bd. 7.13.16.

39 For instance, Boyce (1982), 189–90. Nehemiah was a cupbearer to Artaxerxes, and came from the Persian court in 455 BCE with the king's authority to become governor of Judah (Neh. 2.1). He returned to court in 433/2 BCE, and later went back to Jerusalem with the leave of the king (Neh. 13.6–7).

40 C. Clemen, *Fontes historiae religionis persicae*, Bonn (1920), 30–1.

41 Cyrus pitches his tent facing the east and chants a hymn at daybreak (*Cyropaedia* 8.5.3, 8.1.23), and sacrifices to Hestia, the hearth fire (7.5.57).

42 Stronach and Roaf, *Tepe Nush-i Jan*, 82–5 (see above, n.5); also D. Stronach, *Pasargadae*, Oxford: Clarendon Press (1978), 141.

43 Clement of Alexandria, *Protreptikos* 5.65.3.

44 Vd. 8.81ff.

45 For more detailed discussion, see D. Stronach, 'On the Evolution of the Early Iranian Fire Temple', *Acta Iranica Vol XI* (1985), 605–27.

46 This term could be etymologically equated with Old Persian *apadana*, which could then be a toponym for a sanctuary dedicated to the waters. See Henkelman (2008), 396–7 and n.911.

47 Clement of Alexander informs about Berossus; *Protrepticus*, 5.65.3.

48 That included Susa, Ekbatana, Persepolis, Bactra, Damascus and Sardis.

49 For a detailed analysis of the cult of Anahita, see De Jong (1997), 268–84.

50 The phrase *ashat haca* – 'according to *asha*' - is also found in Yt 8.15.

51 *Cyropaedia* 8.3.11, 8.1.23. For discussion of the term *magi*, see De Jong (2005), 387–413.

52 An unprovenanced seal provisionally dated to the late fourth century BCE contains a representation of *magi* making an offering to the fire in a three-stepped fire holder; see P. Bordreuil, *Catalogues des sceaux ouestsemitiques*, Paris: Bibliotheque Nationale, 1986, 104 (seal no. 136). Above is the winged figure, and an Aramaic inscription *zrtshtrsh*, which has been read as 'of Zarathushtra', echoing the Avestan term; see R. Schmitt, 'Onomastica iranica symmicta', in R. Ambrosini *et al.* (eds), *Scri'bthair a ainm n-ogaim 2* (1997), 921–7; 922–3. This is the only attested use of the ritual or the name in a document ascribed to the Achaemenid era.

53 M. Dandamayev, *Iranians in Achaemenid Babylonia*, Costa Mesa, CA: Mazda (1992), 166–7.

54 Hintze (2004), 308.

55 See K. Tsantsanoglou, 'The First Columns of the Derveni Papyrus and their Religious Significance', in G.W. Most and A. Laks (eds), *Studies on the Derveni Papyrus*, Oxford: Clarendon (1997), 93–128; 95–6.

56 Cf. Yt 5.21.

57 K. Tsantsanoglou, 'The Derveni Papyrus', 95–6.

58 See Kreyenbroek, 'Millennialism', 41.

59 See Skjaervø (2005/6) for discussion of the oral transmission of text.

60 For instance, Pseudo-Platonic *Alcibiades* I.121; Pliny *Natural History* 30.

61 See P. Kingsley, 'The Greek origin of the sixth-century dating of Zoroaster', *BSOAS 53/2* (1990), 245–65; 253.

62 Kingsley argues that Heraclides work is fictitious; 'The Greek origin', 263f.

63 See A.S. Shahbazi, 'Astodan', in *Encyclopaedia Iranica Online*.

64 See, for instance, J.R. Russell, 'Ezekiel and Iran', in S. Shaked and A. Netzer (eds), *Irano-Judaica V*, Jerusalem: Ben Zvi Institute (2003), 1–15.

65 For an analysis of this passage, and a wider discussion of the Achaemenid *paradeisos*, see the article by Lincoln, above, n.20.

66 Stronach, *Pasargadae*, 107–10.

67 Stronach, *Pasargadae*, 36.

68 DNa 52, 57, Xph 57, A2Sa 5.

69 See P. Kingsley, 'Meetings with Magi: Iranian Themes Among the Greeks from Xanthus of Lydia to Plato's Academy', *RAS 5* (1999), 173–209; 187–8.

70 J. Russell, 'The Platonic Myth of Er, Armenian Ara, and Iranian Ardāy Wīrāz', *REArm NS 18* (1984), 477–85.

71 Cf. Voegelin, *Plato and Aristotle*, 338–46.

72 An Akkadian cuneiform inscription on brick discovered in Ur contains a claim that 'the great gods' have delivered all the countries into Cyrus' hands, and that in return he has brought 'a peaceful habitation' to those lands: Dandamayev (1992), 95.

73 For a nuanced discussion as to the Sasanian memory of the Achaemenids, see T. Daryaee, 'The Construction of the Past in Late Antique Persia', *Historia 55/4* (2006), 493–503.

Chapter III A Zoroastrian Presence from Seleucia to Sistan: The Parthian Period

1 Adapted from F.C. Babbitt, (trans.), Plutarch's *Moralia*, Vol. 5, London: Heinemann, 1936: [online: penelope.uchicago.edu]

2 Arrian, *Anabasis* 4.18.4–19.6.

3 D.T. Potts, 'Foundation Houses, Fire Altars, and the Frataraka: interpreting the iconography of some post-Achaemenid Persian coins', *Iranica Antiqua 42* (2007), 271–300; 272.

4 Cf. Daryaee (2008), 4–6.

5 A. Sachs, 'Achaemenid Royal Names in Babylonian Astronomical Texts', *American Journal of Ancient History 4* (1979), 129–47; 131–9.

6   V.A. Livshits, 'Three New Ostraca Documents from Old Nisa', *Webschrift Marshak   2003,   Ērān   ud   Anērān*: http://www.transoxiana.org/Eran/Articles/livshits.html

7   De Jong (1997), 150–5.

8   Particularly the *Shih-chi* ('Historical Records') and *Han Shu* ('Book of [early] Han').

9   See N. Sims-Williams, 'The Bactrian Inscription of Rabatak: A New Reading', *Bulletin of the Asia Institute 18* (2004), 53–68.

10 N. Sims-Williams, 'Four Bactrian Economic Documents', *Bulletin of the Asia Institute 11* (1997), 3–15. See also N. Sims Williams, 'The Bactrian Inscriptions of Rabatak: A New Reading', *Bulletin of the Asia Institute 18* (2004), 53–68. This inscription elevates the female divinity, Nana, whose role in Central Asian Zoroastrianism is discussed further in Chapter V.

11 N. Sims-Williams (2004: BAI 18), 56. For discussion of the religious affiliation of the Kushans, see J. Cribb, 'Das Pantheon der Kushana-Könige', in C. Luczanits (ed.), *Gandhara: das Buddhistische Erbe Pakistans – Legenden, Kloster und Paradiese:* Mainz, Bonn: Zabern (2008), 122–5.

12 S. Shaked, 'Iranian Functions in the Book of Esther', in S. Shaked (ed.), *Irano-Judaica 1*, Jerusalem: Ben-Zvi Institute (1982), 292–303; 292.

13 Skjaervø (1999), 9.

14 J.R. Russell, 'Aristotle and the *Ashem Vohu*', *Ushta Newsletter* 7/2 (August 1986), 3–4.

15 Cf. R. Beck, 'The Mysteries of Mithras: A New Account of their Genesis', *Journal of Roman Studies 88* (1998), 115–28.

16 See above, n.10.

17 Cf. Yt 13.2. The conception of the world as an egg is also a motif in the Rig Veda (RV 10.121.1).

18 Cf. De Jong (1997), 403.

19 These are known as *gosans.*

20 A Greek statue of a reclining Herakles dated by inscription to 148–47 BCE – at around the time the Parthians were entering the region – is still in situ at Bisutun.

21 The Parthians held Dura Europos from about 113–65 CE, when it was occupied and fortified as a Roman garrison. No inscriptions from Dura

name a Parthian king, but documentation from the Parthian period mentions Iranian personal names; P. Huyse, 'Zum iranischen Namengut in Dura-Europos', *Anz. Öst. Akad. Wiss 125* (1988), 19–32.

22 Cf. J. Russell, 'Zoroastrian Elements in the Book of Esther', *Irano-Judaica II*, S. Shaked and A. Netzer (eds), Jerusalem: Ben Zvi Institute (1990), 33–40.

23 See Boyce and Grenet (1991), 137.

24 Boyce and Grenet (1991), 130.

25 D.A. Scott, 'The Iranian Face of Buddhism', *East and West 40* (December 1990), 43–77; 67–8, 71.

26 Khotanese Buddhist texts also refer to the goddess of abundance as *śśandrāmatā* rather than the Indian form, *Sri-Mahadevi*: this is the Avestan *Spenta Armaiti*; see P.O. Skjaervø, 'Hunting the Hapax', in Sims-Williams (2004), 1–17; 8–9.

27 From the time of the Sasanian Hormizd II (302) onwards, coins show the monarch – identified by his crown – rising from the fire.

28 Scott, 'The Iranian Face of Buddhism', 45, 60.

29 V. Curtis, 'Investiture during the Parthian period', *Encyclopaedia Iranica Online*.

30 V. Curtis, 'The Iranian Revival in the Parthian period', in Curtis and Stewart (2007), 7–25; 21.

31 Av. *xvaetvadatha*; Vd 8.12-13, Visp. 3.1–4.

32 M. Boyce, *Letter of Tansar*, Rome: IsMEO, 1968, 47.

33 Stronach, 'On the evolution of the early Iranian fire temple', 612.

34 Russell (1987), 262–5.

35 De Jong (1997), 272.

36 Curtis, 'The Iranian Revival', 16, 22.

37 Dhabhar (1999), 328, 418.

38 See Chapter II, n.51.

39 De Jong (1997), 130–2. This is replaced with clarified butter in the *Yasna*.

40 The possibility of married women leaving home for a certain period to pursue the activity of an *athaurvan* in instructing others in the religion, and to perform religious services, is raised in *Herbadestan*; see A. Hintze,

'Disseminating the Mazdayasnian Religion', in W. Sundermann *et al.* (eds), *Exegisti monumenta*, Wiesbaden: Harrassowitz (2009), 171–90.

41 See B. Lincoln, ' "The Earth Becomes Flat" – A Study of Apocalyptic Imagery', *Comparative Studies in Society and History 25/1* (Jan. 1983), 136–53.

42 Aeneas of Gaza also attributes Theopompus with knowledge of such Iranian ideas concerning the resurrection; De Jong (1997), 224.

43 M. Stausberg, 'Para-Zoroastrianisms: memetic transmission and appropriations', in Hinnells and Williams (2007), 236–54.

44 These connections are discussed in Hinnells (2000), 87–92.

45 See A. Hintze, 'The Saviour and the Dragon in Iranian and Jewish/Christian Eschatology', in S. Shaked and A. Netzer (eds), *Irano-Judaica IV*, Jerusalem: Ben-Zvi Institute (1999), 72–90.

46 Asmodaios slays the seven husbands of a Persian Jewish woman living in Hamadan; *Tobit* 3.7–9; 6.14–19; 8.2–3.

47 J.R. Russell, 'God is Good: On Tobit and Iran', *Armenian and Iranian Studies*, Cambridge, MA: NELC, Harvard University and Armenian Heritage Press (2004), 1129–34; 1132.

48 J.J. Collins, *Apocalypticism in the Dead Sea Scrolls*, London: Routledge (1997), 43.

49 G. Riley, *River of God: A New History of Christian Origins*, New York: Harper Collins (2001), 30.

50 For more detailed discussion of this coherence of Zoroastrian thought, see Shaked (1987), 59–107 and 227–34.

51 *Isaiah* 44.28–45.1.

52 The revolt was partly spurred by Hadrian's incorporation of the Temple Mount into his reconstruction of Jerusalem as Aelia Capitolina. Coins struck by Bar Kochba show the Temple in Jerusalem with a star on the roof, indicating his identification with Balaam's prophecy that 'a star will come out of Jacob and a scepter will rise out of Israel' and defeat all enemies (*Numbers* 24.17–19).

53 See Hinnells (2000). 32–4.

54 *Antiquities* 18.2.4, 16–17; *Mark* 12.18.

55 For further discussion of this, see Hinnells (2000), 61–5.

56 An outline of arguments supporting this is provided in Cereti (1995), 18–

21.

57 The world ages are also found in the *Mahabharata* (3.186–9).

58 The description of the successive world ages as the body parts of a great image have also been compared with the ancient Indian 'world man' (*Purusha*) of RV 10.7.90.1–16. Purusha represents the totality of creation, however, including the fourfold social division, rather than four successive ages within a cosmic cycle.

59 For instance, Hesiod has a myth of five succeeding races (*genos*) of human beings; *Works and Days*, 109–201.

60 Again, for discussion of these views, see Cereti (1995), 23–4.

61 See Hintze, 'The Saviour and the Dragon', 83.

62 Y 9.8, Yt 5.34, Yt 17.34, Yt 19.92f. See also C. Watkins, *How to Kill a Dragon: Aspects of Indo-European Poetics*, Oxford: Oxford University Press (1995), 316, 464, *inter al.*

63 See T.C. Mitchell, 'Achaemenid History and the Book of Daniel', in J. Curtis (ed.), *Mesopotamia and Iran in the Persian Period*, London: British Museum Press (1997), 68–78.

64 Shaked (1995), 193, 206–13; Dk. 6.214, 7.1.40, 9.28.2, Bd. 33.28.

65 See Shaked (1987), 238.

66 Riley, *River of God*, 215. The Gnostic Demiurge has also been compared with Zurvan.

67 4.51.16.

68 Dk.7.4.84–6 and PRDd 47.15–30.

69 For a detailed analysis of this text, and discussion as to its possible influence on the Book of Revelation, see D. Flusser, 'Hystaspes and John of Patmos', in S. Shaked (ed.), *Irano-Judaica I*, Jerusalem: Ben-Zvi Institute (1982), 12–75.

70 Flusser, 'Hystaspes', 34–5.

71 See A. Hultgard, 'Persian Apocalypticism', in J.J. Collins (ed.), *The Encyclopaedia of Apocalypticism Vol. I*, New York: Continuum (1998), 39–83; 74–6, 81–3.

72 *Adversus gentes*, 1.52.

73 *Opus Imperfectum in Matthaeum*, reproduced in J. Bidez and F. Cumont, *Les Mages Hellénisés*, Paris: Société d'Éditions Les Belles Lettres (1938),

118–19.

Chapter IV Eranshahr: The Sasanian Center of the World

1   *Mazdesn bay ardashir shahan shah eran ke chihr az yazdan.* The MP
    word *bay* from OP *baga,* 'god', is usually translated as 'majesty' in this
    context.

2   Basil uses the term 'Magusaean', which seems in this context to refer to
    an expatriate Zoroastrian community; cf. De Jong (1997), 404–13.

3   D.M. Lang (trans.), *Lives and Legends of the Georgian Saints,* London
    and New York: Allen and Unwin (1956), 22–3.

4   S. Kurtsikidze, 'The Survivals of Zoroastrianism in the Traditional Life
    and Culture of the East-Georgian Mountaineers', Dissertation, Tbilisi,
    1993 (in Georgian, summary in English).

5   MP *herbad* derives from a YAv. *aethrapati,* which seems to describe one
    who instructs priests; M. Boyce, *History of Zoroastrianism I,* Leiden: Brill
    (1975), 12. It is now the title given to a priest who has completed the first
    initiation into the priesthood.

6   See Shaked (1994), 99–103.

7   For further discussion of this connection, see P.O. Skjaervø, 'Kirdir's
    Vision: Translation and Analysis', *Arch. Mitt. Aus Iran 16* (1983), 265–
    305.

8   There are controversies surrounding the origins of the name 'Sasan'. For a
    detailed discussion of this, and further references, see Daryaee (2008), 8–
    9.

9   See T. Daryaee, 'A Review of the *Encyclopaedia Iranica*', *Iranian
    Studies, 31: 3/4* (1998), 431–61; 433–4.

10 KAP notes that Ardashir had become a skilled chess player at the Parthian
    court. This early textual reference, alongside archeological evidence from
    ancient Samarkand, tells us that chess was a significant element of upper-
    class life. It is as much a game of psychological warfare as of strategy.

11 P.O. Skjaervø, *The Sasanian Inscription of Paikuli: Part 3 Commentary,*
    Wiesbaden (1983), 21f., 29.

12 M. Boyce (trans.), *Letter of Tansar,* Rome: IsMEO (1968), 33–4.

13 J. Stevenson (ed.), *Creeds, Councils and Controversies,* London: SPCK
    (1966), 348–9.

14 There is an inconsistency in texts as to exactly when.

15 De Jong (1997), 233–4.

16 Cf. *Shayest ne Shayest* 6.7.

17 D. MacKenzie, 'Mani's *Šābuhragān*', *BSOAS 42/3* (1979), 500–34, 510–11.

18 *Dastgerd* could also mean *protégé*.

19 The word '*but*' – Buddha – comes to mean idol in New Persian, as in *botkhaneh* – 'idol temple'. Another MP word translated as 'idol' is *uzdes*, but again it is unclear whether these are indigenous or 'foreign' images. Cf. Dk. 6.93, 275, Bd. 18.13, 33.28.

20 A. de Jong, 'The Contribution of the Magi', in Curtis and Stewart (2005), 85–99; 92.

21 Boyce (1968), 62.

22 Adapted from S. Shaked (trans.), *The Wisdom of the Sasanian Sages (Denkard VI)*, Costa Mesa, CA: Mazda (1979), 15, 17, 171.

23 MX 2.17, 33–6; 4.3–7; 6.6–9. MX is a Sasanian precursor to the NP *Saddars* – handbooks concerning the transmission of religion to the laity, which were compiled in the medieval period.

24 De Jong (1997), 234.

25 My thanks to Oktor Skjaervø for alerting me to this etymology, and for his online translation of MX.

26 My thanks to David Stronach for this information.

27 See D. Stronach, 'The Kūh-i-Shahrak Fire Altar', *Journal of Near Eastern Studies 25/4* (Oct., 1966), 217–27.

28 J.R. Russell (2004), 154.

29 *De Antro Nympharum* 6. Nymphs personified the regeneration of nature, and were associated with springs. Porphyry compares this cavern to the Platonic world-cave, but an Iranian prototype may be found in Yima's *var*, the underground enclosure with its own water supply and light source, which contains everything needed to repopulate the world after the winter of Ahriman. For a connection with Mithraism, see R. Beck, *The Religion of the Mithras Cult in the Roman Empire*, Oxford: Oxford University Press, 2006.

30 In the tenth century, Mas'udi describes the ruins of an ancient fire temple at Istakhr, considered by his time to be the mosque of Solomon.

31 See J. Russell, 'Ezekiel and Iran', 13.

32 Russell (1987), 380, 393, n.27.

33 The Iranian Zoroastrian name for this bread is *sirok*.

34 Russell (1987), 216.

35 R. Ehrlich, 'The celebration and gifts of the Persian New Year (Naw Ruz) according to an Arabic source', *J.J. Modi Memorial Volume*, Bombay (1930), 95–101.

36 A.S. Shahbazi, 'Mazdean Echoes in Shi'ite Iran', in Godrej and Mistree (2002), 247–57; 253.

37 Russell (1987), 251f., 378–80.

38 M. Boyce, 'Iranian Festivals', in E. Yarshater (ed.), *Cambridge History of Iran 3.2*, London: Cambridge University Press (1983), 801.

39 Stronach, *Pasargadae*, Oxford: Clarendon Press (1978), 163–5.

40 The noxious miscreations (*xrafstra*) of Ahriman. For a translation of the entire text, see Skjaervø, 'Kirdir's Vision'.

41 ZWN 3.1–18; Cereti (1995), 150–1.

42 *Mang* seems to have been an intoxicant of some kind, perhaps hemp.

43 Paintings from a seventeenth-century manuscript can be seen in J. Choksy, *Evil, Good and Gender: Facets of the Feminine in Zoroastrian Religious History*, New York: Peter Lang (2002), 65–70.

44 Choksy (2002), 14.

45 '*humihrih-i frazami*'; this 'friendship of Mithra' is alluded to in PRDd 10.l.1.

46 For more details concerning this mural, see F. Grenet, 'Bamiyan and the Mihr Yasht', *BAI 7* (1993), 87–94.

47 *Kinnaras* are Buddhist half-bird, half-human celestial musicians.

48 See Chapter V. The motif of the sun god on his chariot recurs in the 'thousand Buddha' caves along the Central Asian trading routes, including Kirish-Simsin, near Kucha; the Kizil caves, where both the solar deity in his chariot and the scarf-holding wind deity are depicted in the centre of the ceiling; and Cave 285 at Dunhuang (c. 538 CE). Such typology of Mithra is also found in the later eighth-century Sogdian frescoes at Shahrestan and Panjikent.

49 D.A. Scott, 'The Iranian Face of Buddhism', *From East and West*, IsMEO Vol. 40, Nos. 1–4 (Dec. 1990), 43–75, 57.

50 Adapted from Shaked (1979), 173.

51 Shaked (1994), 101–2.

52 Shaked (1994), 113–14.

53 Kingsley, 'The Greek Origin', 255.

54 Cf. S. Adhami, 'On the Contrarieties in Denkard IV', *Studien zur Indologie und Iranistik 23* (2002), 1–25.

55 See Shaked (1995), 217–27.

56 A 1425 *Shah Nameh* manuscript records that the Iranian heroic narratives were put into chronological order under Yazdegird I and collected in several editions, including one in the time of Khosrow I.

57 Shaked (1994), 112.

58 T. Nöldeke, trans., *Geschichte der Perser und Araber zur Zeit der Sasaniden aus der arabischen Chronik des Tabari* (Leyden, 1879), 391.

Chapter V The Zoroastrians of Central Asia

1   N. Sims-Williams, 'Some Reflections on Zoroastrianism in Sogdiana and Bactria', in D. Christian and C. Benjamin (eds), *Realms of the Silk Roads: Ancient and Modern* (*Silk Road Studies 4*), Turnhout: Brepols (2000), 1–12; 6.

2   Sims-Williams, 'Some Reflections', 4.

3   Cf. N. Sims-Williams, 'The Sogdian Merchants in China and India', in A. Cadonna and L. Lanciotti (eds), *Cina e Iran da Alessandro Magno alla dinastia Tang*, Florence: Olschki (1996), 45–67; 50–2.

4   T. Daryaee, trans. and comm., *Šahrestānīhā-ī Ērānšahr: A Middle Persian Text on Late Antique Geography, Epic, and History*, Costa Mesa, CA: Mazda (2002), 32. Then, the story goes, Alexander – the accursed – burnt it and threw it into the water.

5   In some places it is described like a raised tomb (Vd 3.9, 13); one passage describes it as a place of corruption (Vd 7.56–8); elsewhere the word is used to refer to an open place of exposure (Vd 8.2, 5.14).

6   Dhabhar (1999), 104–5.

7   S.N. Lieu, *Manichaeism in the Later Roman Empire and Medieval China*, Manchester University Press (1985), 182–3.

8   Cf. I. Yakubovich, 'Mugh 1.1. Revisited', *Studia Iranica 31* (2002), 249.

9   G.A. Pugachenkova, 'The Form and Style of Sogdian Ossuaries', *BAI 8*

(1994 [1996]), 227–43; 227.

10 J. Lerner, 'Central Asians in Sixth-Century China: A Zoroastrian Funerary Rite', *Iranica Antiqua XXX* (1995), 179–90; 183.

11 J.J. Modi, *Religious Customs and Ceremonies of the Parsees*, Bombay: Parsee Vegetarian and Temperance Society, rep. (1986), 53.

12 See Choksy (1997), 5.

13 N. Sims-Williams, *Sogdian and Other Iranian Inscriptions of the Upper Indus, Part 1: Inscriptions of the Seleucid and Parthian Periods of Eastern Iran and Central Asia,* London: Corpus Inscriptionum Iranicarum and SOAS (1989), 84.

14 R.N. Frye (trans.), *The History of Bukhara*, Princeton: Marcus Wiener, revised edn (2007), 10, 60–2.

15 See B.I. Marshak, 'The Sogdians in Their Homeland', in Juliano and Lerner (2001), 230–7; 233; and Boyce and Grenet (1991), 168. The fire- or incense-holders are similar to the *thymiateria*, which are found in Achaemenid depiction. For further discussion of the censer, see P.O. Harper, 'From Earth to Heaven: Speculations on the Significance of the Form of the Achaemenid Censer', *BAI 19* (2005), 47–56.

16 Lerner, 'Central Asians', 182; and V.G. Shkoda, 'The Sogdian Temple: Structure and Rituals', *BAI 10* (1996 [1998]), 195–206; 197.

17 ShE 4–5.

18 Frye, *History of Bukhara*, 29–30.

19 J.R. Russell, 'Zoroastrianism and the Northern Qi Panels', in *Armenian and Iranian Studies*, Cambridge, MA: Harvard University and Armenian Heritage Press (2004), 1449.

20 Frye, *History of Bukhara*, 190; A. Dien 'A Possible Occurrence of Altaic Idughan', *Central Asiatic Journal 2* (1956), 12–20; Lerner (1995), 184.

21 *Hsi-fan Chi*, cited in Lieu (1985), 182.

22 See F. Grenet and B Marshak, 'Le mythe de Nana dans l'art de la Sogdiane', *Arts Asiatiques 53* (1998), 5–18, especially 8–9. Nana had been illustrated earlier on the coins of the Kushan king Kanishka, sometimes with Mithra: see J. Cribb, 'Das Pantheon der Kushana-Könige', in C. Luczanits (ed.), *Gandhara: das Buddhistische Erbe Pakistans – Legenden, Kloster und Paradiese*, Mainz, Bonn: Zabern (2008), 122–5; 123.

23 Cf. B. Stavisky, 'Bactria and Gandhara: The Old Problem Reconsidered in

the Light of Archaeological Data from Old Termez', in Allchin (1997).

24 G. Azarpay, 'Nana, the Sumero-Akkadian Goddess of Transoxiana', *Journal of the American Oriental Society 96/4* (Oct.–Dec. 1976), 536–42; 541; G. Azarpay, *Sogdian Painting: The Pictorial Epic in Oriental Art,* Berkeley: University of California Press (1981), 30. See also above, Chapter III, n.26.

25 Sims-Williams, 'Some Reflections', 5.

26 See F. Grenet, 'Religious Diversity among Sogdian Merchants in Sixth-Century China: Zoroastrianism, Buddhism, Manichaeism and Hinduism', *Comparative Studies of South Asia, Africa and the Middle East 27/2* (2007), 463–78; 473.

27 B.I. Marshak, 'Pre-Islamic Painting of the Iranian Peoples and its Sources in Sculpture and the Decorative Arts', trans. B.I. Groudinko, in E. Sims (ed.), *Peerless Images: Persian Painting and Its Sources,* New Haven, CT, and London: Yale (2002), 7–19; 18.

28 This may be the same ethnic group referred to as 'Hun' in Sogdian inscriptions and documents: *xwn* is a name found in the Indus graffiti, and in Mugh documents.

29 Tang Chinese tombs contain many examples of tomb figures (*mingqi*) of painted pottery horses attended by their foreign handlers.

30 B.I. Marshak, 'The Sogdians in Their Homeland', 234.

31 For further references and discussion concerning the interpretation of the murals at Afrasiyab, see M. Compareti and E. de la Vaissière (eds), *Royal Naurūz in Samarkand: Proceedings of the conference held in Venice on the pre-Islamic paintings at Afrasiab* (Supplement 1, *Rivista degli Studi Orientali* 78), Pisa/Rome: Instituto Editoriali e Poligrafici Internazionali (2006).

32 R.N. Frye, 'Bukhara and Zanandaniji', in *Central Asian Textiles and Their Contexts in the Early Middle Ages,* Riggisberg: Abegg-Stiftung (2006), 75–80; 75, 77.

33 De la Vaissière (2005), 132f.

34 E.H. Schafer, *Golden Peaches of Samarkand: A Study of Tang Exotics,* Berkeley: University of California Press, rep. (1985), 10.

35 See Chapter IV, n.XX.

36 Marshak, 'Pre-Islamic Painting', 17.

37 S. Whitfield and U. Sims-Williams (eds.), *The Silk Road: Trade, Travel,*

War, Faith, Chicago, IL: Serindia (2004), 249.

38 For the translation of *xian* as 'Zoroastrian', see A.E. Dien, 'A Note on Hsien "Zoroastrianism"', *Oriens 10/2* (December, 1957), 284–8.

39 De la Vaissière (2005), 128 and n.39.

40 Grenet and Guangda choose the gloss '*bao*' for '*sai*' to translate the term as 'thanksgiving': F. Grenet and Z. Guangda, 'The Last Refuge of the Sogdian Religion: Dunhuang in the Ninth and Tenth Centuries', *Bulletin of the Asia Institute 10* (1996), 175–86; 182f. Supplies at Dunhuang comprised 30 sheets of paper 'to paint the *xian* deities', and at Turfan, cereals are mentioned for the 'cult to the heavenly god', perhaps designating Ohrmazd.

41 Sims-Williams, 'Some Reflections', 5.

42 The Sogdian form would be *rtu* or *reshtyak*; P.O. Skjaervø, personal communication 9/10/08.

43 See Sims-Williams, 'Some Reflections', 6–7, for detailed discussion of these terms.

44 Cf. P.O. Skjaervø considers the story of Siyavush to be part of this eastern Iranian epic tradition, which interacted with Buddhist Ashoka legends preserved in Khotanese; 'Eastern Iranian Epic Traditions I: Siyavash and Kunala', in J.H. Jasanoff *et al.* (eds), *Mir Curad: Studies in Honor of Calvert Watkins*, Innsbruck: Institut fur Sprachwissenschaft der Universität Innsbruck (1998), 645–58.

45 E.H. Schafer, 'Iranian Merchants in T'ang Dunasty Tales', in W.J. Fischel (ed.), *Semitic and Oriental Studies*, Berkeley and Los Angeles: University of California Press (1951), 403–22; 408.

46 Schafer, 'Iranian Merchants', 10.

47 Sims-Williams, 'The Sogdian Merchants', 51.

48 De la Vaissiere (2005), 151.

49 See Russell, 'Zoroastrianism', 1447–9 and Lerner, 'Central Asians', 180–1, for further details of this scene.

50 Grenet, 'Religious Diversity', 472.

51 P.O. Skjaervø was the first to make this connection; see F. Grenet, P. Riboud and Y. Junkai, 'Zoroastrian Scenes on a newly discovered Sogdian tomb in Xi'an, northern China', *Studia Iranica 33* (2004), 273–84; 278–9.

52 Grenet *et al.*, 'Zoroastrian Scenes', 283.

53 Grenet *et al.*, identify this woman as the *daena*; 'Zoroastrian Scenes', 282.

54 Grenet *et al.*, 'Zoroastrian Scenes', 281.

55 Lerner (2001), 226.

56 Choksy (2006), 138.

57 Choksy (1997), 84. Many had 'converted' under Umayyad pressure in the late 720s, with the promise that they would be exempt from the *jizya*. When the *jizya* was demanded from them, they 'apostatized' and rebeled; Madelung, 'Religious Trends in Early Islamic Iran', Albany, NY: Bibliotheca Persica (1988), 16–17.

58 Choksy (1997), 104–5.

59 J. Choksy, 'Zoroastrians in Muslim Iran', *Iranian Studies 20/1* (1987), 17–30; 27.

Chapter VI Gabr-Mahalle: Zoroastrians in Islamic Iran

1 J. de Menasce (ed.), *Škand-gumanik Vizār: la solution décisive des doubtes,* 1945, trans. J.P. Kunst, http://www.avesta.org/mp/shkand.html

2 For a recent analysis, see Parvaneh Pourshariati's *Decline and Fall of the Sasanian Empire: The Sasanian-Parthian Confederacy and the Arab Conquest of Iran*, London: I.B.Tauris, 2008.

3 A Middle Persian apocalyptic poem entitled, *Abar Madan-i Wahram-i Warzawand* ('On the advent of the miraculous Wahram'), describes Wahram in terms of the *saoshyant* of Zoroastrian expectation; see Daryaee (2008), 102–3.

4 J. Choksy, 'Zoroastrians in Muslim Iran: Selected Problems of Coexistence and Interaction during the Early Medieval Period', *Iranian Studies 20/1* (1987), 17–30; 26. *Mawali* translates as 'clients', that is converts.

5 Choksy (1997), 97.

6 See T. Darayee, 'A Historical Episode in the Zoroastrian Apocalyptic Tradition: The Romans, the Abbasids and the Khorramdens', in T. Daryaee and M. Omidsalalar (eds), *The Spirit of Wisdom*, Costa Mesa, CA: Mazda (2004), 72–3.

7 Cf. Frye (1988), 129ff.; W. Madelung, *Religious Trends in Early Islamic Iran*, New York: Bibliotheca Persica (1988), 6f.

8 E.G. Browne, *A Literary History of Persia from the Earliest Times until*

Firdawsi, London, Fisher Unwin (1902), 335–6. Afshin died in prison.

9   Khanbaghi (2006), 25.

10 Choksy (1997), 143.

11 M.G. Morony, *Iraq after the Muslim Conquest*, Princeton, NJ, Princeton University Press (1984), 110.

12 J. Choksy, 'Zoroastrians in Muslim Iran', *Iranian Studies 20/1* (1987), 22.

13 The Seljuk vizier, Nizam-ul Mulk, equated those of *dhimmi* status with heretics, implying that all other faiths were inimical to Islam; Choksy (1997), 121.

14 Choksy (1997), 97.

15 R. Bulliet, *Conversion to Islam in the Medieval Period*, Cambridge, MA: Harvard University Press (1979), 43–4.

16 Frye (1988), 101.

17 The record of the collection of the scattered parts of the Avesta was reiterated in Arabic sources as a means of legitimating the authority of the Abbasids; see D. Gutas, *Greek Thought, Arab Culture: The Graeco-Arabic Translation Movement in Baghdad and Early 'Abbasid Society*, London: Routledge (1998), 38–9.

18 This is said to be the prayer Zarathushtra chanted to ward off the incursion of Angra Mainyu and Druj (Vd 19. 2, 10). In the fire temple today, a bell is rung 21 times, symbolic of both the prayer and the Avestan *nasks*.

19 E.W. West (trans.), *Sacred Books of the East Vol. 18*, Oxford: Oxford University Press, 1882; http://www.avesta.org/mp/dd.htm#chap41

20 See M. Stausberg, 'The Significance of the *kusti:* A History of Its Zoroastrian Interpretation', *East and West* 54/1 (2005), 17-20. In the Persian *Rivayats*, the weaving of the *kusti* is referred to as the occupation of the priests; Dhabhar (1999), 25. In Iran, the priests continued with the weaving, until a group of laywomen assumed the work in the 1920s.

21 The *mu'tazili* are referred to by name, SKW 11.280.

22 Cf. A.V. Williams, *The Pahlavi Rivayat Accompanying the Dadestan i Denig Part II*, Copenhage: Munksgaard (1990), 63, 85.

23 Frye (1998), 210.

24 Frye, *The Heritage of Persia*, Costa Mesa, CA: Mazda, rep. (1993), 283.

25 Choksy (1997), 135.

26 Khanbaghi (2006), 89.

27 Dhabhar (1999), 52.

28 Boyce (1989), 100. A Persian term for Zoroastrian women in menses is *'bi namaz'* – literally, 'without prayer'.

29 Cf. PRDd 2.

30 Boyce (1989), 206.

31 See Russell (1987), 376f., 380f.

32 SGW 1.1–6.

33 W. Chittick, *The Sufi Path of Love: The Spiritual Teachings of Rumi*, Albany, NY: SUNY (1983), 54.

34 For a recent example of the diverse approaches within Zoroastrianism, see K.P. Mistree and F.S. Shahzadi, *The Zarathushti Religion: A Basic Text*, FEZANA (1998), 6–11, and Appendix B.

35 For a detailed exposition of both texts, see F. de Blois, 'The two Zoroastrian treatises called *Ulama i Islam*', in Vahman and Pedersen (2007), 199–210.

36 A. Schimmel, *Mystical Dimensions of Islam*, Chapel Hill: University of North Carolina Press (1975), 107.

37 Boyce (1977), 32–4.

38 For many examples of correspondences between Zoroastrian tenets and motifs and Islamic concepts and practices, see E. Yarshater, 'The Persian Presence in the Islamic World', in Hovanissian and Sabagh (1998), 4–125.

39 Schimmel (1975), 261.

40 For a more detailed analysis of the appropriation of pre-Islamic themes in *Shah Nameh*, see Fischer (2004), in particular the chapter entitled '*Shahnameh*: Parable Logic'.

41 Both shrines are first recorded in texts from the seventeenth century; see R. Langer, 'From Private Shrine to Pilgrimage Centre', in Stausberg (2004), 563–92; 571.

42 M. Boyce, 'Bibi Shahrbanu and the Lady of Pars', *BSOAS 30* (1967), 30–44.

43 E. Yarshater, 'Ta'ziyeh and Pre-Islamic Mourning Rituals in Iran', in P. Chelkowski (ed.), *Ta'ziyeh: Ritual and Drama in Iran*, New York: New York University Press (1979), 88–94; 90.

44 M.N. Dhalla, *History of Zoroastrianism*, Bombay: KRCOI, third edn (1994), 444.

45 Dhabhar (1999), 603.

46 Kreyenbroek, 'The Zoroastrian Priesthood after the Fall of the Sasanian Empire', in *Transition Periods in Iranian History*, Paris: Association pour l'Avancement des Etudes Iraniennes (1987), 151–166; 164f.

47 Dhabhar (1999), 433.

48 Dhabhar (1999), 423ff.

49 Khanbaghi (2006), 98.

50 Choksy (2006), 136.

51 Firby (1988), 41.

52 Choksy (2006), 139.

53 Firby (1988), 46.

54 Dhabhar (1999), lix.

55 Firby (1988), 52; Bd. 23.2.

56 Schimmel (1975), 209f.

57 R.W. Ferrier (trans. and ed.), *A Journey to Persia: Jean Chardin's Portrait of a Seventeenth-century Empire*, London, New York: I.B.Tauris (1996), 162, 23.

58 Firby (1988), 60.

59 Dhabhar (1999), 356, 362–93; Vd 9.

60 Choksy (2006), 140–1; Khanbaghi (2004), 156–7.

61 Article XIX, 'Extract from a letter addressed by Professor Westergaard to the Rev. Dr. Wilson in the year 1843 relative to the Gabrs in Persia', *Journal Asiatique of Great Britain and Ireland 7* (1846), 349–55, 350. The Rev. Dr John Wilson was a seminal figure in Parsi life in the mid-nineteenth century.

62 P. Jamzadeh, 'Some Zoroastrian architectural features', *Studia Iranica 30* (2001), 17–29; 18.

63 Choksy (2006), 136.

64 For a more detailed account of this mission, see M. Ringer, 'Reform Transplanted: Parsi Agents of Change among Zoroastrians in Nineteenth-Century Iran', *Iranian Studies 42/4* (2009), 549–60; 550f.

65 For an introduction to and translated excerpts from Maneckji's report, see M. Giara, R.P. Karanjia and M. Stausberg, 'Maneckji on the Religious/Ritual Practices of the Iranian Zoroastrians', in Stausberg (2004), 481–515; see also Ringer, 'Reform Transplanted', 556f.

66 Stausberg (2002:1), 365–72.

67 N. Malcolm, *Five Years in a Persian Town*, Bibliolife (2009), 45–6.

68 For more details about Maneckji's personal and ideological impact on the promotion of Zoroastrianism, see A. Marashi, *Nationalizing Pre-Islamic Iran: Culture, Power and the State, 1870–1940*, Seattle and London: University of Washington Press (2008), 61–3.

69 Such charitable activities are detailed at length in J.R. Hinnells, M. Boyce and S. Shahrokh, 'Charitable Foundations ii. Among Zoroastrians in Islamic Times', *Encyclopaedia Iranica* V (1992), 382–5.

70 Marashi (2008), 83–4.

71 See S. Bekhradnia, 'The Decline of the Zoroastrian Priesthood and its effect on the Iranian Zoroastrian Community in the Twentieth Century', *JASO 23/1* (1992), 37–47; 39–40.

72 Stausberg (2002:2), 239–141.

73 See particularly, Mary Boyce's *Persian Stronghold of Zoroastrianism*, Lanham, MD: University Press of America (1989), which was written following her year-long stay in Sharifabad (1963–64); and Michael M.J. Fischer's doctoral dissertation *Zoroastrian Iran Between Myth and Praxis*, unpublished: Chicago University (1973), which incorporated his experiences of Zoroastrianism in Yazd from 1969–71.

74 Bekhradnia, 'The Iranian Zoroastrian Community', 45.

75 Choksy (2006), 153–4.

76 Choksy (2006), 161.

77 See E. Sanasarian, *Religious Minorities in Iran*, Cambridge: Cambridge University Press (2000), 154. Sanasarian discusses the various articles of the Constitution relating to religious minorities at length on pages 64–72.

78 *FEZANA Journal* 23/2 (Summer 2009), citing the Amordad News blog. The school was founded by Parsis and, until recently, run by the Zoroastrian *anjuman*.

79 Stausberg (2002), 2:218f.

80 Choksy (2006), 164–70.

264   Zoroastrianism: An Introduction

81 *FEZANA Journal 17/4* (2004), 22–4, 26–30.

82 Choksy (2006), 172–3; Bekhradnia 'The Iranian Zoroastrian Community', 42.

Chapter VII Parsipanu: Zoroastrianism in India

1   S. Bean, *Yankee India*, Mumbai: Mapin (2006), 164.

2   For a new analysis and translation of this text, see A. Williams, *The Zoroastrian Myth of Migration from Iran and Settlement in the Indian Diaspora*, Leiden and Boston: Brill (2009).

3   C. Cereti, 'Some Primary Sources on the Early History of the Parsis in India', in Vahman and Pedersen (2007), 211–21; 211.

4   F.M. Kotwal, 'Some observations on the history of the Parsi *dar-i mihrs*', *BSOAS 37/3* (1974), 664–9; 664.

5   J.K. Choksy, 'Iranians and Indians on the shores of Serendib (Sri Lanka)', in Hinnells and Williams (2007), 181–2; Maneck (1997), 15.

6   Cereti, 'Some Primary Sources', 212.

7   Palsetia (2001), 8–9.

8   See W. Braun, 'Dakhmenashini: The Current Legal, Ethical, and Theological Conflict over the Zoroastrian Community's Disposal of the Dead in Mumbai', in *International Journal of Medicine and Law 29/4* (December 2010), forthcoming.

9   Jordanus, *Mirabilia Descripta: The Wonders of the East*, trans. H. Yule, London: Elibron Classics, Adamant Media, 2001.

10 Maneck (1997), 33.

11 Kreyenbroek, 'The Zoroastrian Prietshood', 163.

12 Cereti, 'Some Primary Sources', 214–16.

13 Bean (2006), 164.

14 Palsetia (2001), 22.

15 Khanbaghi (2006), 153.

16 In the nineteenth century, Parsi priests' wives took over the weaving of the *kusti* from their husbands.

17 Maneck (1997), 20–1.

18 D.A. Scott, 'Zoroastrian Responses to Hinduism, Past to Present – The Interaction of Religion and Politics', *Temenos 24* (1988), 89–119; 109.

19 S. Stewart, 'Parsi Prayer and Song in India', in Hinnells and Williams (2007), 59–77. For a detailed description of Parsi engagement and marriage rituals, see Kreyenbroek and Munshi (2001), 29–34.

20 K. Dalal, *Delicious Encounters*, Mumbai: Vakils, Feffer and Simons (2000), 6.

21 Scott (1988), 108.

22 Palsetia (2001), 17. The hair from the bull's tail is used to make the sieve for the *hom*.

23 Dhabhar (1999), 275–6.

24 Palsetia (2001), 8.

25 Subsequent court rulings, however, returned minor children to their parents or guardians. I am grateful to Jesse Palsetia for informing me of this.

26 Wilson, *The Parsi Religion*, 170–1.

27 Wilson, *The Parsi Religion*, 397.

28 Wilson, *The Parsi Religion*, 175.

29 Wilson, *The Parsi Religion*, 41.

30 Wilson, *The Parsi Religion*, 37.

31 M.N. Dhalla, *History of Zoroastrianism*, Bombay: K.R. Cama Oriental Institute, third edn (1994), 463ff. The most illustrious of these sages was said to be a *dastur* named Azar Kaivan, who had come from Iran to Patna at the age of 28 with several Zoroastrian disciples, and whom a number of *mobeds*, as well as Muslims and Hindus, followed.

32 Dhalla, *History*, 446.

33 Wilson, *The Parsi Religion*, 40.

34 M. Haug, *Essays on the Language, Writings and Religion of the Parsis*, New Delhi: Cosmo, rep. (1978), 300.

35 Hinnells (2000), 183.

36 M.N. Dhalla, *Zoroastrian Theology from Earliest Times to the Present Day*, New York: A.M.S. Press, rep. (1972), 77.

37 J.J. Modi described the rituals relating to *Muktad/Fravardigan*, and to many other aspects of Parsi religious life in his 1922 book, *The Religious Ceremonies and Customs of the Parsees*, Bombay: Parsee Vegetarian and Temperance Society, second edn rep. (1986), 435–49.

38 Kreyenbroek and Munshi (2001), 258ff.

39 M. Stausberg, 'Monday Nights at the Banaji, Fridays at the Aslaji: Ritual Efficacy and Transformation in Bombay City', in Stausberg (2004), 653–717.

40 Hinnells (2000), 159.

41 Palsetia (2001), 45.

42 See, in particular, J. Hinnells, *Zoroastrians in Britain*, Oxford: Clarendon Press, 1996.

43 *Iran Shah* was moved to the *Atash Bahram* in Udvada in 1742. It was moved to a nearby agiary while the temple was renovated, and re-enthroned in March 2009 with ceremonies conducted by nine ritually pure priests, followed by a *jashan*.

Chapter VIII Zoroastrians Present: Revisited

1   Hinnells (2005), 124–26.

2   *Parsiana*, 7 June (2009), 16.

3   Hinnells (2005), 398.

4   A.V.W. Jackson, *An Avestan Grammar*, Stuttgart: Kohlhammer (1892), v.

5   For in-depth discussion and analyses of living and lived Zoroastrianism, see in particular the work of Hinnells, Kreyenbroek and Munshi, and Stausberg, in the General Bibliography.

6   This event is not mentioned in the Avesta, but MP texts record that Zarathushtra was killed by a Turanian (Dk 5.3.2; ZWY 2.3).

7   Although the Hong Kong community is numerically small, its philanthropic work is substantial, and influential in Mumbai.

8   See T. Luhrmann, 'Evil in the Sands of Time: Theology and Identity Politics among the Zoroastrian Parsis', *Journal of Asian Studies 61/3* (August 2002), 861–89; 876–82.

9   Kreyenbroek and Munshi (2001), 47, 307.

10 Choksy (2006), 176.

11 Kreyenbroek and Munshi (2001), 300.

12 Maneck (1997), 254.

13 See M. Stausberg, 'Zoroastrianism', in P. Berger and P.B. Clarke (eds), *The World's Religions: Continuities and Transformations*, London:

Routledge (2009), 721–36; 732.

14 Palsetia (2001), 332–3.

15 See, for instance, the account by Dolly Dastoor (FEZANA president, 1994–8) of meeting with such groups in Sweden and Russia, in *FEZANA Journal* (Winter 2002), 21–2, 68; also, the report on the Tajik-Indo conference, Bombay (1992), as reported in *Parsiana* (May 1992); and the section on the 'Upliftment Work in Tajikistan' of the Zoroastrian College of Sanjan at http://www.indiayellowpages.com/zoroastrian/

16 See M. Stausberg, 'Para-Zoroastrianisms', in Hinnells and Williams (2007), 236–54; 236.

17 Stausberg, 'Para-Zoroastrianisms', 250.

18 Kreyenbroek and Munshi (2001), 305; Stausberg, 'Para-Zoroastrianisms', 246–8.

19 http://www.zoroastrian.org/info/index.htm

20 S. Bekhradnia, 'The Decline of the Zoroastrian Priesthood and its effect on the Iranian Zoroastrian Community in the Twentieth Century', *JASO* 23/1 (1992), 43.

21 See *FEZANA Journal 24/1* (Spring/March 2010), 98.

Chapter IX Zarathushtra Present and Past

1 M.N. Dhalla, *History of Zoroastrianism*, Bombay: KRCOI, third edn (1994), 26.

2 See Dhalla, *History of Zoroastrianism*, 25, 150, 166.

3 See A.V.W. Jackson, *Zoroaster*, New York: Columbia University Press, fourth printing (1938), 289.

4 This 'Persian' figure is dressed in similar Parthian clothes to Xerxes in the Dura synagogue murals, and is wearing a short sword and carrying a staff.

5 See, for instance, R. Schmitt, '*Zoroaster* i. The Name', *Encyclopaedia Iranica Online*, 20 July 2002, available at www.iranicaonline.org.

6 P. Kingsley, 'The Greek Origin of the Sixth-Century Date of Zoroaster', *BSOAS 53/2* (1990), 245–65; 254.

7 Dhabhar (1932), 423.

8 See M.N. Dhalla, *Zoroastrian Theology: From the Early Times to the Present Day*, New York: A.M.S. Press, rep. (1972), 308.

9 J.A.L. Lemay (ed.), *Benjamin Franklin: Writings*, New York: Library of

America (1987), 675.

10 F. Nietsche, *Ecce Homo*, R.J. Hollingdale (trans.), Harmondsworth: Penguin (1979), 127f.

11 Rose (2000), 175–82.

12 M. Stausberg, 'Para-Zoroastrianisms', in Hinnells and Williams (2007), 236–54; 241.

Select Resources

Online Resources

Encyclopaedia Iranica: www.iranica.com

www.achemenet.com/ (in French)

www.humanities.uci.edu/sasanika

www.avesta.org/

P.O. Skjaervø (2005), *Introduction to Zoroastrianism*; www.fas.harvard.edu/~iranian/Zoroastrianism/zorocomplete.pdf

www.heritageinstitute.com/zoroastrianism/index.htm

General Bibliography

R. Allchin *et al.* (eds), *Gandhara Art in Context: East–West Exchanges at the Crossroads of Asia*, New Delhi: Regency, 1997.

M. Boyce, *A History of Zoroastrianism, Vol. II: Under the Achaemenians*, Leiden/Köln: E.J. Brill, 1982.

M. Boyce, *A Persian Stronghold of Zoroastrianism*, Lanham, MD: University Press of America, 1989.

M. Boyce and F. Grenet, *History of Zoroastrianism III: Zoroastrianism under Macedonian and Roman Rule*, Leiden: E.J. Brill, 1991.

P. Briant, *From Cyrus to Alexander: A History of the Persian Empire*, trans. P. Daniels, Winona Lake, Ind.: Eisenbrauns, 2002.

C.G. Cereti, *The Zand ī Wahman Yasn: A Zoroastrian Apocalyse*, Rome: IsMEO, 1995.

J.K. Choksy, *Conflict and Cooperation: Zoroastrian Subalterns and Muslim Elites in Medieval Iranian Society*, New York: Columbia University Press, 1997.

J.K. Choksy, 'Despite Shāhs and Mollās: minority sociopolitics in premodern and modern Iran,' *Journal of Asian History 40* (2006), 129–84.

J. Curtis and N. Tallis (eds), *The Forgotten Empire: The World of Ancient Persia*, London: British Museum Press, 2005.

V. Curtis and S. Stewart (eds), *Birth of the Persian Empire*, London: I.B.Tauris, 2005.

V. Curtis and S. Stewart (eds), *The Age of the Parthians*, London: I.B.Tauris, 2007.

V. Curtis and S. Stewart (eds), *The Sasanian Era*, London: I.B. Tauris, 2008.

T. Daryaee, *Sasanian Iran: Portrait of a Late Antique Empire*, Costa Mesa, CA: Mazda, 2008.

B.N. Dhabhar, The *Persian Rivayats of Hormazyar Framarz and Others*, Bombay: K.R. Cama Oriental Institute, reprint 1999.

B. Dignas and E. Winter, *Rome and Persia in Late Antiquity: Neighbours and Rivals*, Cambridge: Cambridge University Press, 2007.

N.K. Firby, *European Travellers and Their Perceptions of Zoroastrians in the 17th and 18th Centuries*, Berlin: Dietrich Reimer Verlag, 1988.

M.M.J. Fischer, *Mute Dreams, Blind Owls and Dispersed Knowledges: Persian Poesis in the Transnational Circuitry*, Durham, NC, and London: Duke University Press, 2004.

R.N. Frye, *The Golden Age of Persia: Arabs in the East*, London: Weidenfeld and Nicholson, 1988.

R. Frye, *The Heritage of Central Asia*, Princeton: Markus Wiener, 1996.

P.J. Godrej and F.P. Mistree (eds), *A Zoroastrian Tapestry: Art, Religion, Culture*, Ahmadebad, India: Mapin, 2002.

L. Grabbe, *A History of the Jews and Judaism in the Second Temple Period: Vol.1: Yehud: A History of the Persian Province of Judah*, London & New York: Continuum International, 2004.

W. Henkelman, *The Other Gods Who Are: Studies in Elamite-Iranian acculturation based on the Persepolis fortification texts (Achaemenid History, Vol. XIV)*, Leiden: Nederlands Instituut voor het Nabije Oosten, 2008.

J.R. Hinnells, *Zoroastrian and Parsi Studies*, Aldershot: Ashgate, 2000.

J.R. Hinnells, *The Zoroastrian Diaspora*, Oxford: Oxford University Press, 2005.

J.R. Hinnells and A. Williams (eds), *Parsis in India and the Diaspora*, London: Routledge, 2007.

R.G. Hovanissian and G. Sabagh (eds), *The Persian Presence in the Islamic World*, Cambridge: Cambridge University Press, 1998.

A. de Jong, *Traditions of the Magi: Zoroastrianism in Greek and Latin Literature (Religions in the Graeco-Roman World 133)*, Leiden: Brill, 1997.

A. Juliano and J. Lerner (eds), *Monks and Merchants. Silk Road Treasures from Northwest China. Gansu and Ningxia, 4th–7th Century*, New York: Abrams and Asia Society, 2001.

A. Khanbaghi, *The Fire, the Star, and the Cross: Minority religions in medieval and early modern Iran*, London and New York: I.B. Tauris, 2006.

P. Kreyenbroek and S.N. Munshi, *Living Zoroastrianism: Urban Parsis Speak about their Religion*, Richmond: Curzon, 2001.

B. Lincoln, *Religion, Empire, Torture: The Case of Achaemenian Persia, with a Postscript on Abu Ghraib*, Chicago: University of Chicago Press, 2007.

W. Malandra, *An Introduction to Ancient Iranian Religion: Readings from the Avesta and the Achaemenid Inscriptions*, Minneapolis: University of Minnesota Press, 1983.

S.S. Maneck, *The Death of Ahriman: Culture, Identity and Theological Change Among the Parsis of India*, Bombay: KRCOI, 1997.

F. Mehr, *The Zoroastrian Tradition: An Introduction to the Ancient Wisdom of Zarathushtra*, second edn, Costa Mesa, CA: Mazda, 2003.

J.S. Palsetia, *The Parsis of India: Preservation of Identity in Bombay City*, Leiden: E.J. Brill, 2001.

J. Rose, *The Image of Zoroaster: The Persian Mage Through European Eyes*, New York: Bibliotheca Persica Press, 2000.

J.R. Russell, *Zoroastrianism in Armenia*, Cambridge, MA: Harvard University Press, 1987.

S. Shaked, *Dualism in Transformation*, London: SOAS, 1994.

S. Shaked, *From Zoroastrian Iran to Islam*, Aldershot: Variorum, 1995.

N. Sims-Williams (ed.), *Indo-Iranian Languages and Peoples*, Oxford: Oxford University Press, reprint 2004.

P.O. Skjaervø, 'Avestan Quotations in Old Persian? Literary Sources of the Old Persian Inscriptions', in S. Shaked and A. Netzer (eds), *Irano-Judaica*

IV, Ben-Zvi Institute: Jerusalem (1999), 1–64.

P.O. Skjaervø, 'The Importance of Orality for the Study of Old Iranian Literature and Myth,' *Name-ye Iran-e Bastan* 5/1&2 (2005/6), 9–31.

P.O. Skjaervø, 'Poetic Weaving in the Old Avesta: The Gathas and the kusti', in M. Jaafari-Dehaghi (ed.), *One for the Earth: Prof. Dr Y. Mahyar Nawabi Memorial Volume*, Tehran: Centre for the Great Islamic Encyclopaedia (2008), 117–33.

M. Stausberg, *Faszination Zarathushtra: Zoroaster und die Europäische Religionsgeschichte der Frühen Neuzeit* (*Religionsgeschichtliche Versuche und Vorarbeiten 42*), 2 vols, Berlin and New York: Walter de Gruyter, 1998.

M. Stausberg, *Die Religion Zarathushtras. Geschichte-Gegenwart-Rituale*, Vols 1 and 2, Stuttgart: Kohlhammer, 2002; Vol. 3, Stuttgart: Kohlhammer, 2004.

M. Stausberg (ed.), *Zoroastrian Rituals in Context*, Leiden: Brill, 2004.

F. Vahman and C.V. Pedersen (eds), *Religious Texts in Iranian Languages*, Copenhagen: The Royal Danish Academy of Sciences and Letters, 2007.

É. de la Vaissière, *Sogdian Traders: A History*, Leiden: E.J. Brill, 2005.

P. Vasunia, *Zarathushtra and the Religion of Ancient Iran: The Greek and Latin Sources in Translation*, Mumbai: KRCOI, 2007.

M.L. West, *The Hymns of Zoroaster: A New Translation of the Most Ancient Sacred Texts of Iran*, London: I.B. Tauris, 2010.

J. Wiesehöfer, *Ancient Persia: from 550 BC to 650 AD*, London and New York: I.B.Tauris, 1996.

J. Wiesehöfer (ed.), *Das Partherreich und seine Zeugnisse: The Arsacid-Empire: Sources and Documentation*, Wiesbaden: Franz Steiner Verlag, 1998.

Fiction

Rohinton Mistry, *Such a Long Journey*, Vintage, reprint 1992.

—— *Tales from Firozsha Baag*, New York: Penguin, reprint 1998.

—— *A Fine Balance*, Vintage, reprint 2001.

—— *Family Matters*, Vintage, 2003.

Ashok Mathur, *A Little Distillery in Nowgong*, Arsenal Pulp Press, 2009.

Bapsi Sidhwa, *The Crow Eaters*, Minneapolis, Milkweed, reprint 2006.

—— *Cracking India*, Minneapolis: Milkweed, reprint 2006.

—— *An American Brat*, Minneapolis: Milkweed, reprint 2006.

Thrity Umrigar, *Bombay Time*, Picador, 2002.

—— *The Space Between Us*, Harper Perennial, 2007.

Films

Earth (1998).

Little Zizou (2008).

Such a Long Journey (1998).

I.B.TAURIS INTRODUCTIONS TO RELIGION

Daoism: An Introduction – Ronnie L Littlejohn

HB 9781845116385

PB 9781845116392

Jainism: An Introduction – Jeffery D Long

HB 9781845116255

PB 9781845116262

Judaism: An Introduction – Oliver Leaman

HB 9781848853942

PB 9781848853959

Zoroastrianism: An Introduction – Jenny Rose

HB 9781848850873

PB 9781848850880

Confucianism: An Introduction – Ronnie L Littlejohn

HB 9781848851733

PB 9781848851740

Sikhism: An Introduction – Nikky-Guninder Kaur Singh

HB 9781848853201

PB 9781848853218

Islam: An Introduction – Catharina Raudvere

HB 9781848850835

PB 9781848850842

Christianity: An Introduction – Philip Kennedy

HB 9781848853829

PB 9781848853836

Hinduism: An Introduction – Will Sweetman

HB 9781848853270

PB 9781848853287

Buddhism: An Introduction – Alexander Wynne

HB 9781848853966

PB 9781848853973